Mix Masters:

Platinum Engineers Reveal Their Secrets for Success

Maureen Droney

berklee
press

Berklee Media

Associate Vice President: Dave Kusek
Director of Content: Debbie Cavalier
Marketing Manager: Jennifer Rassler
Senior Designer: David Ehlers

Berklee Press

Senior Writer/Editor: Jonathan Feist
Writer/Editor: Susan Gedutis
Production Manager: Shawn Girsberger

ISBN 0-87639-019-X

1140 Boylston Street
Boston, MA 02215-3693 USA
(617) 747-2146

Visit Berklee Press Online at
www.berkleemusic.com

DISTRIBUTED BY

HAL•LEONARD®
CORPORATION
7777 W. BLUEMOUND RD. P.O. BOX 13819
MILWAUKEE, WISCONSIN 53213

Visit Hal Leonard Online at
www.halleonard.com

Printed in the United States of America by Graphic Services Inc.

10 09 08 07 06 05 04 03 02   5 4 3 2 1

Contents

Foreword

Over the years, we have all read articles written about various music recording and mixing engineers. However, in this book, the author has captured a distinctive insight into the psyche of her subjects. I have often wondered why interviewers don't delve deeper into the subjects that lie beneath the surface of engineering. Revealing such details can be, not only enlightening, but also challenging to the reader. Of course, as any good interviewer knows, high-quality reading is truly dependent upon the questions asked. Ms. Droney not only knows the right questions to ask, but also how to extrapolate the true meaning of her subjects' answers. Her innate curiosity and knowledge of the studio allows her to get to the point while avoiding the usual "puff" pieces. You will find out how these engineers use many of the same tools, and yet create mixes that are quite different from each other's. I have personal knowledge of many of the engineers interviewed in this book, and I am happy to say that anyone who reads it will both enjoy, and learn from, this collection.

Technology is constantly changing; equipment is constantly evolving, and every new generation must either follow or break the rules of the past.

Engineers like Al Schmitt, Leslie Ann Jones, and Chuck Ainlay all learned in different kinds of formal settings, and yet they carry forward a certain tradition. In listening to their work, one understands that the great engineers know how to make technology work for them. No matter how many tracks are recorded, at some point an engineer must use his or her skill to marry a combination of elements, from great live recordings to sampled drum sounds, while still ensuring that the record grooves. And of course, lest we forget who is the star of the music, they must also ensure that the vocal sound is superb!

When I began my own career, I was trained by veterans and influenced by the likes of greats such as Tom Dowd, Bill Putnam, Bruce Swedien, Quincy Jones, Hank Mancini, and George Martin: a technically and artistically diverse group, to say the least. But what they all had in common was a work ethic that revealed their utmost respect for the art.

The engineers interviewed here also have that work ethic in common. Read this book while remembering that you must take this valuable information and apply it in your own way, always allowing yourself to be guided by your own sense of art and taste.

Phil Ramone
SEPTEMBER 17, 2002

Preface

I began writing these interviews because I wanted to learn more about the technical skills of the people who were making great-sounding records. I wanted to know how the best in the field did what they did, in the hopes that I could do it too. It wasn't long before I found myself fascinated, not only by the techniques themselves, but by the thought processes behind the techniques.

To me, the people interviewed in this book are a very special breed. Although many have been amply rewarded for their work, no one becomes an audio engineer for the money. They don't do it for the glamour either. One week of sessions will suffice to weed out anyone who thinks recording music is a glamorous business.

Most engineers, for much of their careers, work long hours, listening to the same song over and over again, in rooms without windows. Their schedules are unpredictable, and that's hard on them and on their families. Within those long hours, they may endure side effects from an artist's sometimes painful creative process, along with large doses of frustration. All this is tempered by occasional transcendent moments, and also, it's true, a whole lot of fun. The real rewards for this job are the music, and the people who make the music. They'll drive you crazy, but it's worth it.

The people interviewed in this book all have different styles and different opinions on what great sound is, and how to get it. Some are

classicists, some are groundbreakers, some are a combination of the two. They work with different kinds of music, on different kinds of equipment. What they all have in common is a love of music and a passion for their job.

Today's rapid pace of technological change began, for recording, as it did in many industries, in the mid '80s. This series of interviews, which began in 1992, extends over a ten-year period in which that change accelerated even more. The equipment choices of those interviewed here reflect that.

On re-reading the older interviews, it became apparent to me that, while what equipment someone chooses to use is, of course, an important creative decision, what's more important is the ability to know what you want that equipment to do for you. That way, you can choose intelligently from among what's available at any given time. The best engineers know what they're going for; the tools that they choose to get it change all the time.

This book is dedicated to all those who labor in the recording studio trenches, and who know both the exhilaration, and the heartbreak, of trying to forge a career capturing the magic of music for others to hear. It is also dedicated to the memory of the great Tom Dowd, the "ideal recording man," who passed away a few days before this book was completed.

May his legacy continue to inspire us all.

Maureen Droney

Acknowledgments

I would like to thank my friend Dan Levitin who encouraged me to go back to my English major roots and become a writer, David Rubinson who gave me my first job in the recording business, Michelle Zarin and Rose Mann, who know everything about recording studios, Tom Kenny, George Petersen, Blair Jackson, Barbara Schultz, John Pledger, and everyone else at *Mix* magazine for their constant efforts to uphold the standards of editorial excellence.

Also, Ron Nevison, David Kahne, Paul Kantner, Patrick Cowley, Gary Belz, T Bone Burnett, Andy Johns, Jim Gaines, Carlos Santana, Don Miley, Chris Stone, Ed Cherney, Randy Jackson, Ken Kessie, Narada Michael Walden, and all the others with whom I've had the pleasure of sharing the agony and the ecstasy of making records.

At Berklee Press, Debbie Cavalier for her enthusiasm, Dave Kusek, Linda Chase, Shawn Girsberger, Ann Woody, and my intrepid editor Jonathan Feist.

Thanks to Karen Ciccone, Nicole Cochran, Edward Colver, Jill Dell'Abate, Gary Gunton, Keith Hatschek, Jac Colman, John Koenig, Howard Massey, Frank McDonough, Natalie Stocker, and everyone who helped me gather photographs and details.

Most of all, of course, my thanks to all of the engineers and producers who so generously shared their time, techniques, and thoughts with me for these interviews. Y'all definitely rock!

Maureen Droney

OCTOBER 31, 2002

Don Murray

JUNE, 1992 ## The Ears Have It: An Engineer's Engineer

It's a typical Grammy listening party for the Best Engineered Album Award. CD after CD and, yes, cassette after cassette, are given a ten-second listen and a quick yank. (Sad but true, some record companies actually send cassettes to be judged for sound quality!). Thumbs down circle the room. Engineers are a notoriously picky bunch when it comes to analyzing other engineers' work. And the well-known and well-respected engineers who sit on the Grammy selection committees are even pickier. So when someone receives seven nominations for Best Engineered Album, it's time to sit up and take notice.

He may not be as well known as Bob Clearmountain and Tom Lord-Alge, but he should be. He's repeatedly praised by his peers, the people with the golden ears, and he owns a contented client list a mile long. His name is Don Murray.

Murray got his start in Philadelphia where he worked with legendary r&b producer Thom Bell on records of such greats as the Spinners and the Stylistics, and that influence is apparent in his current work. Although Murray currently specializes in jazz, he's not into the overly reverent jazz of some, recorded exclusively with 30-year-old mics and no EQ. Using modern production techniques and exquisite taste, jazz recorded by Murray grooves as hard as any new jack swing track. He's a master of live recording, as evidenced by the GRP Records disc called *Fourplay*, currently breaking records with twenty-five weeks in the Number 1 slot on the *Billboard* Contemporary Jazz Chart. I booked Murray for an interview at Andora Studios, a new Los Angeles facility where he's been spending a lot of time.

How did you learn engineering?

I was in music school in Philadelphia, and I had a friend who was a second engineer at Sigma Sound. Things got busy and they needed another second. They asked me, and that was it for music school. The first day I worked a double shift. One of them was a rhythm section for Gamble and Huff, the Delphonics, or somebody. It was the early '70s and Philadelphia was just taking off. It became like a

Selected Credits

Patti Austin
Love is Gonna Getcha,
For Ella

Phil Collins
A Hot Night In Paris

Will Downing
Sensual Journey

Fourplay
Fourplay, Between the Sheets, 4,
Yes Please, Heartfelt

GRP Records
GRP Live in Session;
GRP Superlive;
Happy Anniversary,
Charlie Brown

Dave Grusin
Cinemagic,
The Collection, Migration,
Havana soundtrack

Dave Grusin & Lee Ritenour
Harlequin

Hiroshima
Go, East/West,
Between Black and White

Lee Ritenour
Twenty-one releases including:
Captain Fingers,
Feel The Night, Rit, Festival,
Stolen Moments (direct to disc)

The Spinners
Seven releases including:
The Spinners, Mighty Love,
New and Improved,
Best of the Spinners

The Stylistics
Rock and Roll Baby

factory of producing r&b records. I worked with Joe Tarsia, a great engineer with great ears. My first big client as an engineer was Thom Bell, who was just becoming very hot. The first session I did for him was the Spinners' "One of a Kind Love Affair," which became a Number 1 record. From then on, I worked with him on all of his stuff. I was still playing then, so I played some guitar on those records. I'd hear a part, and at night after he'd gone home, I'd lay it down. Often, he'd like it and keep it. And, if the piano player wasn't available, I'd sit in with the rhythm section and play piano. But after a while, I got too busy as an engineer, and with no time to practice, I stopped playing, pretty much.

Although you've had seven Grammy nominations for Best Engineered Album, the Grammy award that you actually won was for production ....

It was a live recording done in Japan—another GRP Records extravaganza! As far as I'm concerned, there wasn't a whole lot of production involved. It was basically "get the best sound you can" on one show, with a very limited sound check. It was great to win an award for that, but it would be nice to win the engineering award eventually. Really, though, it's a committee of engineers who make those nominations, so it's an honor to be nominated by my peers. Just to have all those nominations means a lot to me.

I think there are a lot of engineers out there who would like to hear real specifics of how you track a record.

I have a process of doing things, and use certain mics that, over the years, I've decided I like and will start off with, but I'm very open to change and to trying things. I'm not one of these people with a notebook full of exactly the way to EQ every microphone. I just sort of take the moment as it comes. I like being spontaneous, and not thinking about it too much beforehand. I go with what the musicians in the room are doing and what the song is like. I also do a lot of listening in the room before I record something. I have an idea of mics I like on certain instruments, but before I listen to the mics, I go out and listen in the room, I listen to the bass drum, the snare, and how the drums feel. If it's not sounding right, then we'll change them or try to find another part of the room that feels better, that projects more.

I start with a Sennheiser 421 on the bass drum. It has a nice attack to it, and it doesn't have such a big bottom that it comes off too puffy sounding. I usually end up putting bottom on the kick drum and taking low mids out, because the low mids are the part of the sound that will distort a speaker.

Photo: Maureen Droney

Like 300 Hz?

Yes, 300, 400 cycles. And then I'll add low end, 50, 100 cycles, and then maybe put a boost at 7 to 10,000 cycles to add even more attack, depending, of course, on what kind of song it is. You have to go by instinct, on how the bass will interact with the bass drum. But generally, I find with the 421 that you have to notch out some low midrange, and then stretch the high end and low end around it.

You get fat, punchy, bass drum sounds. Do you usually use compression to get that?

Yeah, I compress bass drums to begin with during recording, and I'll gate them also. I like to use dbx 165 series compressors. They're my favorite for bass drum.

They have attack and release controls.

Yeah, but they have an auto function also, which I usually use. It sounds fatter to me, for some reason. It just comes from experimenting, but that's one thing I've found about the 165s: with the auto attack and release in, I like the sound better. I've been using Aphex gates lately on the kick. I find that they are very smooth and transparent. You have a lot of room to tweak them, and the VCAs sound better than some other gates. I'll either use GML EQ or an API 560 graphic. The API 560 graphics are great for bass, kick drum, and snare, and I like to use them when I'm recording.

On snare drums, I usually use a dynamic mic on the top, like a Shure SM57, and I'm a fan of AKG 451s or 452s. I'll use one those on top also, and I'll blend the sound of the two. You get more crack out of the 451, but it doesn't have as much punch as a Shure 57, so I'll blend the two together. I'll usually put a bottom mic on. Sometimes I use it, and sometimes I don't. It'll usually be a Shure SM57. Depending on whether I want to hear more snares or not for that particular song, I'll blend in a little of that. I gate the snare also, probably fairly loosely, because often the drummer will play rolls or a cross stick, and you don't want to lose that. I might gate it again in the mix, and fine-tune it then, so that I don't lose anything. Again, I like the API 560 on the snare.

I'll bus all the mics that I'm using to one track, and I'll run the group output through the API 560. I really like their sound. They are not at all masked-sounding. They have a nice presence, and a nice hype, a very musical high end, and a good sounding low end. They are graphics so you can really tweak things in and see what you're doing. And you can notch out at certain frequencies, so you can really make musical adjustments to the sound of those instruments.

On the hi-hat, I usually go for the Neumann KM84. It's not as bright as some of the other condenser mics, but it has a meatier quality to it that I like. I don't like it when the drummer hits the hi-hat cymbal and it screams at you. I like more of the midrange quality of the hi-hat, and then I'll brighten it up if I need to, or I'll take out low end, because sometimes you get a bass buildup around the hi-hat that is a little annoying. I'll use a high pass filter to rid of some of that.

I'll usually use two overheads that are fairly close to the cymbals, and they'll be AKG 414 EBs without any rolloffs or anything. I typically spread them out about three or four feet and angle them down over the cymbals, and I don't have them too high off the cymbals—maybe three feet.

You get a lot of stereo spread in your drums.

Yeah, I like it so that when the drummer hits the cymbals on the left, you really hear them on the left. I do that with the toms, too. I like stereo.

Do you use both top and bottom mics on toms?

No, I just use AKG 451s or 452s, which have a nice attack, and I usually wind up putting low end on.

You get a lot of powerful low end on toms, but they never sound muddy. How do you do that?

Well, I basically stretch out the sound of the tom, adding low end and high end. I'll also put up a directional dynamic mic next to the 451 on each tom, and I use those mics as trigger mics for gates.

I use gates on the toms, and if I used the sound coming through the 451 to trigger the gate, then what would happen, since I'm EQing a lot, is that each time the drummer would hit a cymbal next to the tom, it would open the gates, and I hate the sound of cymbals going through EQ'd tom mics. So, I just use the dynamic mic, and I drastically EQ it, rolling off the high and low end and boosting midrange, so I'm just using the attack for a click that will trigger the mic through the external trigger input of the gate. It doesn't open when he hits the snare or the cymbals, and it gives me a lot of control over the sound of the toms. It helps a lot to give me a nice tight sound on the drums. It also helps in being able to use the overheads as your total overhead sound on the drums. Of course, you can't do this if it's a ballad with brushes on the drums!

If I need a room sound, I'll usually use Telefunken 251s. I'll go for a nice vintage tube sound, but I don't back up my overheads, because I still want that presence on the cymbals. If I need room sound, I'll just add other mics and record them on separate tracks. Then I have control later. Of course, if they want a gated room sound, I'll create it then, trigger the room mics to open from the kick, toms, and snare.

Are most basses that you record taken direct?

Yes, I like the sound of the direct bass, and I have a couple of direct boxes that I use on the bass that I like the combination of.

Your own direct boxes?

Well, one I've used for years. It's called a Fat Box, an active direct box that's been around forever, but I wind up still using because I like the clarity of the sound. I compare it to others, and to me it still beats them all. And I use that in tandem with a big transformer that was built for me, a direct box using a hunky UTC transformer that sounds great. It really has a nice punch to it, and I'll wind up using both the Fat Box and the transformer, two separate inputs into the console. I'll combine them to one track, and depending on what I need, I'll vary the amounts in the combination. On the *Fourplay* album, with Nathan East, we just use the transformer.

It sounds as if you set yourself up to be really flexible.

Well, I have to be. What works in one studio sometimes doesn't work at all in another one.

Do have a favorite bass limiter?

The dbx 165 when I'm recording. The Inovonics 201 is also very good. I don't like Neve compressors as well for bass or kick. They seem to take too much of the attack away. The same thing with tube compressors. I wouldn't normally use them on a bass or a kick. They're too spongy on those instruments, although I use tube compressors and Neve compressors on a lot of other things.

You've worked with pianist Dave Grusin a lot. What mic setups for piano have you developed?

In general, I go for AKG C12 tube mics—two of them, not too close to the strings, and I don't put them together in the old stereo fashion. I like to open up the piano. I like for the piano to be in its own room, because if you have a piano sitting in the middle of a big sound stage, the piano goes out, and it dissipates, and it sounds deader and smaller. If the instrument is placed in an iso booth, or a room where the sound can go out, and then come back at you, the sound builds up in the room and the room resonates. It sounds louder and more present.

Of course, it has to be a good-sounding room. The same thing with acoustic guitar. The sound of it so depends on what room you're playing it in, and you really want the room to resonate with the guitar. It comes alive then. It projects much better.

Do you prefer to record the tracks on albums that you will be mixing?

I do. It's more difficult for me to be happy with the way things turn out if I don't also record the tracks. There are exceptions, but so much of my sound is in how I record something, so if I happen to take a mix session, and someone wants my sound, it's difficult. I don't like being just a mix engineer. People expect something from me that's hard to give them because I wasn't there from the beginning of the process.

Do you have a favorite console?

I prefer mixing on older Neve consoles, specifically the 8078. I like the sound of the 4-band EQ. The Neves have both the warmth and the presence, more than any other console that I've worked on. Sunset Sound Studio 1 has custom console that I like a lot. I mixed the *Fourplay* album and the Gershwin album on that. It's basically their own design, with API 550 EQ in that console and GML [automation]. It's a simple signal path in that console, and that's why it sounds good. Very clear sounding. I definitely go for the simple consoles. The more processing you get in a console, the more I don't like it.

So you're not a big SSL fan.

I'm not, although if it were the right project, I might be. I like the control and the compression on every channel. The quad compressor is probably the best part of the console, in my opinion. You can make it sound so punchy. I've done a lot of records on SSLs. I end up bypassing everything I need to when I'm recording. The same thing with the V-Series Neve. I have a way of setting it up where I'm going through as little processing as possible, and it sounds fine to me. Some of the more complex consoles are good for tracking because you have options like more headphone mixes and loads of inputs, so you can stretch out, and have gates and compressors on each channel, if you want them. It's great if you have a big session. When I'm mixing, though, I like the personality of the old consoles.

Do you usually record to digital?

Well, I used to, but in the last couple of years, I've gotten away from it. I mean, you have to wind up there eventually, but I don't record to it. I really like working with Dolby SR, and the new tapes that are out, like Scotch 996, really got me away from digital. I did comparisons, and the high end is much more three-dimensional with 996 compared to digital. You can hear air and depth around instruments. With digital, it becomes flat and grainy, two-dimensional. Even with low end. The digital has more perfectly reproduced low end, I suppose, but with analog, the tape compression that goes on is more pleasing to the ear. So that combination, much nicer high end, tape compression on the low end, Dolby SR so you don't have to worry about tape hiss, and I'm sold on analog.

Do you mix to analog?

I sure do: half-inch, Studer 820. Scotch 996 and SR sound great on the Studer. ATRs have a low midrange bump, which a lot of people like, but for me, I like the machine to be transparent. Then I make a transfer to 44.1 kHz and I do my EQing through analog EQ at the same time so that my master only has to be transferred once, with no more format conversions. Then we work with that 44.1 EQ'd master to assemble. It saves steps and transferring.

You have a lot of long-term clients. What's your secret?

I like to be open to trying new things and realizing that it's a whole new day, a whole new project starting, and maybe there's something new we can get out of it. It makes it more fun, to be open to new ideas. And I'm lucky that I work with people who have the attitude that they are there to make music and to have a good time.

How far into the future are you booked? Is it true that if Sting called you'd be too busy to work with him?

Well, I have a lot coming up, but things always change, and I'd love to do a project with Sting!

Obviously, much has changed since this initial interview, but in a chat with Murray in 2002, while he was working on an album for Diane Schuur, I found him still experimenting, and still definitely his own man about his choice of equipment. These days, he records to Pro Tools HD and analog two-inch, depending on the project, and he mixes to all sorts of formats, from analog half-inch to Pro Tools HD 24/96 to Alesis Masterlink. As always, his choice of equipment is determined by what he thinks will work best for each project. Technology is changing fast, but using that kind of thoughtful approach, Murray continues to harness it to work for his goals.

Recording the GRP All-Star Big Band Album

For you engineers tired of overdubbing one instrument at a time, here's a recipe guaranteed to alleviate boredom: Take twenty top-flight musicians set up in big band formation; change players, arrangers, and instrumentation for each song; have the horn section and percussionist change instruments during each song; add one video crew, miles of extra A/C cable, and lighting snakes in both the control room and the studio, then mix it all together to get what engineer Don Murray laughingly calls "a recording nightmare."

GRP Records did just that when it decided to celebrate its tenth anniversary by making a big band record containing performances by as many GRP artists as possible. Compiled from two shows recorded live to video and to 24-track in one day, the result sounds great.

Just in case you find yourself in a situation like this, here's a diagram of how Murray set up the session at Los Angeles' Ocean Way Studios for the GRP All-Star Big Band.

DON MURRAY: "I did a rather historic live performance album for GRP in January, an all-star big band record. It includes a lot of tremendous artists, and we cut it live by recording two shows, which were also being taped for a video. It was recorded at Ocean Way, and the band was set up very tight, in a traditional big band setup with no baffles or anything, because the cameras had to be able to get everyone in the shots. I had very little room to set up in with twenty-some guys.

It was an experiment in leakage. The best players in the world: Dave Grusin, Kenny Kirkland, Russ Ferrante, David Benoit, different players for different tunes. Dave Weckl on drums, John Pattitucci on upright bass, Alex Acuna on percussion, Gary Burton on vibes, Lee Ritenour on guitar, Eddie Daniels on clarinet. The horn section was Tom Scott, Bob Mitzer, Eric Marienthal, Ernie Watts, Arturo Sandoval, Randy Brecker, Sal Marques. Sax players on the front riser, trumpets right behind them. I had to put all the horns on separate tracks, because they were changing instruments during almost every song! The reeds played sax, flute, and oboe, and there were English horns and muted trumpets. The leakage really worked, but that way, I had enough control in the mix."

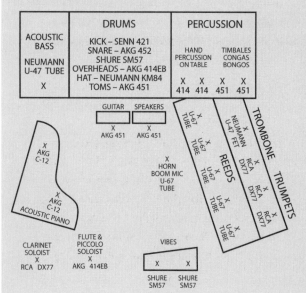

BILL BOTTRELL

Selected Credits

Alisha's Attic
The House That We Built

Tex Beaumont
Restless Heart

Sheryl Crow
Tuesday Night Music Club

Thomas Dolby
Aliens Ate My Buick

Elton John
Songs From The West Coast

Shelby Lynne
I am Shelby Lynne

Madonna
Like A Prayer, "Dick Tracy,"
Truth or Dare soundtrack

Michael Jackson
Dangerous

**Tom Petty And The Heart
Breakers**
"Surrender," *Full Moon Fever*

Kim Richey
Rise

Rusted Root
*When I Woke,
Welcome To My Party*

Toy Matinee
Toy Matinee

Outside the Box

JULY, 1992

Sometimes, it feels as if we're drowning in dance pop records awash with homogeneous reverbs, endlessly sampled drums, and vocals processed beyond recognition. But drop Madonna's "Like a Prayer" or Michael Jackson's "Black or White" on your CD player, and notice the difference. Instead of copycat sounds and cheap tones, you hear real engineering. The difference is Bill Bottrell, one of the few engineer/producers around who's not afraid to put real sounds, expertly recorded, up front, dry, and in your face. His success proves that it's possible to achieve Grammy-nominated quality and top-of-the-charts impact.

I caught up with Bottrell at Toad Hall, his Pasadena, CA studio, where he was working on his roll-around Neve 8058 console, producing the new David Baerwald album. All of Toad Hall's equipment, including the console, is on wheels and can be used in either of two rooms. On the day we were there, he was working in the larger room, which boasts a high, peaked ceiling topped with a skylight, and a back wall lined like a library with hardbacked books. (Bottrell assured me they're are just acoustic treatment.) We adjourned to an upstairs lounge overlooking the studio, where Bottrell could talk and also keep an eye on the session.

This studio feels very comfortable, like a living room.

People really like it here. We keep a very loose atmosphere. Sometimes things get done and sometimes they don't. I like it that way. I don't run a tight ship, on purpose. Technical considerations never take precedence over creative freedom considerations. The basic thing I try to do is just capture moments, put them on tape, and put them out, unadulterated. Of course, for years earlier that wasn't the philosophy. The philosophy was to "engineer" things.

You mean your philosophy?

My philosophy, and a lot of people's philosophy. To put their creativity out and to impose it on the record as an engineer, or even as a producer. I'm trying to get away from that. I'm trying to get

Photo: Maureen Droney

away from "engineering" in general. I'm trying to just avoid it. Avoid doing it, avoid having the engineer do it. The engineer is still here, understand, but he or she should be a ghost, creatively.

Being transparent, you mean, between the music and the tape machine?

Yes. They're a presence personally, and they add to the mix of people in the room, and that's very important, but they don't attempt "engineering." They don't "tweak" things; they don't "get a sound." There's no such thing. You use good gear, the best gear. We use gear from the early '70s and late '60s—tubes or transistors, and you just put a mic up and record it. You don't bother any more than that.

My last album, we didn't mix. Everybody knows you can never beat the rough mixes, right? Well, we actually acted on that and insisted on not mixing, because, yet again, we found we couldn't beat the roughs. We had them all on DATs, so we just used those.

That was the Wiretrain album, *No Soul, No Strain?*

Yes. And there they are. There were a couple of songs where the rough didn't have the right vocal on it or something, so we had to mix them. And we tried to get to the mental space where you're doing a rough mix, so we spent maybe forty-five minutes doing the mixes. Because the tweaking, all the tweaking that's going on, I don't feel like it's valid. It's not honest. I think the tweaking has to come from the song, the music, the player, and the performance.

So you believe a lot of the tweaking that's going on is coming from the ego of the engineer and not from the song?

Yeah. It all started to go wrong in the late '70s when engineers and producers started being allowed to impose their frustrations as musicians on the records. And that never should have happened. Because the artists know what to do, if they are really an artist, and the producer should just set up a situation where the artist feels free to do what they do. The engineer should record it and get out of the way. I've seen way too many examples of engineers hijacking a project and imposing their small-minded technical feelings on a thing. Artists have been brainwashed to think that this is how it is. Because it's been this way for fifteen years now. There's a whole generation of artists who think that's how records are made, and they don't question it.

But there are so many engineers who are working with artists, or maybe we shouldn't call them artists, who don't know what they want.

Well, that's the phenomenon. Once you have this system set up where the artistry is spread thinner amongst more people, the producers and engineers, then the artist and the vision of the thing can be smaller and less significant. And that's what we've been having for a long time, with, of course, notable exceptions. And those exceptions are the only records where an artist truly has a vision, and a reason for being in the studio, and knows it, and refuses to be fooled by the system, and keeps the technology out of their way, consciously—much to the dismay of the engineer, I'm sure. Those records usually turn out to be true statements. They have something to say. Whether you like that kind of music or not, it doesn't matter. You can hear it in a minute. Some records are honest, and some are manufactured bullshit.

I'm as guilty as anyone else, but I have at least spent the last fifteen years learning these things. To me, the sound of an honest recording can be a thousand times more impressive than the one that's heavily tweaked out with the lame ideas of an engineer using twenty or thirty $400 boxes lined up in a rack. The challenge now comes from capturing something pure and simple and honest, and having it sound spectacular—bigger than life. And when you capture some moment of people, or one person, or machines doing something great, and it's good, you try to avoid the layering that tends to happen. You just leave it. If it's good enough, it will make the album. If we get enough better things, then we'll leave it off.

It's not nostalgia, it's not a retro thing, or a roots thing. It's just honesty. And I think that's where things should go...and, hopefully, will go.

Tell me a little about your background. Did you start out as a musician?

I was a guitar player in high school and I gave it up, probably for similar reasons as most engineers. I was insecure and not up to the challenge of being a brilliant guitar player, so I went into engineering. In '85, I started producing with Thomas Dolby on *Aliens Ate My Buick*, and as a producer I got my confidence back for being a musician. Once I got away from the knobs and buttons and started judging musical value, I realized, "I can do that." So I picked up the guitar and other instruments and started playing.

That's moving from engineer to musician, but how did you originally move from musician to engineer?

I was in bands in high school, and we had worked in an 8-track studio. I was the amp guy in the band, and I could fix things. When I decided to get a job as an engineer, I went back to this studio in Hollywood. And the owner remembered me and gave me a job doing the lousy work—commercials, kids' albums, training films. I was never an assistant; I did get to jump right into engineering. But it was all old gear that didn't make much sense. Half the time, I couldn't get the signal to come out of the outputs.

While the client's sitting there looking at the clock?

Yeah, but everyone goes through that.

You did two records with ELO. How did that come about?

My first professional gig was working at Soundcastle Studios. It was just getting started, and I was the all-around engineer and maintenance and whatever. Jeff Lynne came to town and was searching for a studio with a Harrison console and UREI monitors, and we had that combination. And he wanted to use the house engineer to cut the demo! This was just a dream! I had been a huge fan of his, and I knew all of ELO's albums. So I got everything set up for him with all the sounds the way I thought Jeff would like them. And he did; he loved it! I got to mix one song on that album, and then on the next album I mixed the whole thing. Then I engineered and mixed the next couple of albums. I learned a lot from Jeff Lynne.

I know an engineer who uses "Pulp Culture" from [Thomas Dolby's] *Aliens Ate My Buick* to check his monitors.

I'm really proud of that record. Thomas actually got a Grammy nomination for Producer of the Year, and I'm not sure why I didn't, since I was co-producer. It was some kind of technicality.

How do you get so much silence on records?

Self control—that's all it is. You leave the silence and don't try to cover it up. You have to have confidence in the silence.

Actually, I meant sonically. You get a very wide dynamic range. Do you use noise reduction?

No, I never use noise reduction.

Do you mix to digital?

I usually mix to analog 2-track. I'm trying out right now a Studer from the late '50s—a one-inch tube. It's stunning! The problem is mastering. We'll have to carry it with us!

What did you mix to before you had this?

Ampex ATR, quarter-inch, 30ips.

Why don't you use half-inch?

I've never been happy with half-inch because it has this awful head-bump, and fringing....

What's your basic drum tracking setup?

Every song is different, but I have always used as few mics as possible. I would never mic every drum. I've always used the room mics, or near room mics, even when it wasn't fashionable. I've always miked the drum kits as if it's one instrument, pretty much starting out with an overhead pair, a snare and a bass drum mic. I like my Schoeps tube mics for overheads, or one mono overhead U47 is a great sound.

Your records have great bass sounds.

Thanks. I have a bass pre-amp that I designed myself, years ago. It's an extremely high impedance pre-amp, with great big capacitors on the output that allow it to go down to, I think, 4 Hz.

You mean you told someone what you wanted and they built it?

No, I built it myself. I used to have more time. It's a good thing it doesn't break, because I don't know what I'd do without it. It's just standard chips of the day, 5534s, but I found a circuit in one of the old applications manuals that was for a high-input impedance modification to the chip. Other people were designing with FET chips, bi-FETs or whatever they were, which give you a high-input impedance, but those chips never sounded very good. It's probably a known circuit to raise the input impedance of these things, but I raised it to 10 MHz or something, so the bass pickup can plug in there and just bridge into it and there's absolutely no loading on the pickup, and it just blows in and out of the thing. Then it's got a full-on +24 output, and a little gain pot. It's like a buffer. It buffers the bass pickup from all the gear. I usually just plug it right into the machine or into a limiter. By the way, a [Valley People] Dynamite limiter is good for that, too, if you adjust the DC offset wrong so every time it kicks in, it gives a little DC thump on the output.

Those original Dynamites are great limiters.

Limiters are the coolest thing in recording, the strongest tool. You could choose a hundred different limiters for a hundred different jobs, because they all do a different thing. It's much more powerful than tweaking equalization.

You were both engineer and producer on *Toy Matinee*, another record some people use to check their monitors. Kevin Gilbert's vocal sound is a real standout on that album. How it was recorded?

With a tube U-47 (not mine, but a rented one), a Neve Class A mic pre-amp, a Neve limiter, and right into the tape recorder. As a matter of fact, that's the chain for everything I do. [Laughs] No, just kidding.

Your vocal sounds are really dry and really present. What are you using mix-wise to achieve that?

Actually, it's what I'm not using mix-wise. Like reverb. Pavarotti can have reverb, but I'm just a rock 'n' roller, and somehow, a concert hall doesn't have anything to do with it. I use a U-47 and a good amount of compression and avoid the temptation to boost the top end too much, and then just leave it alone.

There's nothing else. People aren't used to hearing a raw vocal shoved right up in their face and turned up loud. Listen to *Highway 61 Revisited*. That's my vocal sound. Try it. But you have to have a U-47, and you can't be afraid to compress the living daylights out of it. If you're an audiophile

guy, then you'd better not compress it, but then your records are like audiophile records, and that would be unfortunate.

What about drums? Are there any samples used to enhance Brian McCloud's drum sounds on *Toy Matinee*?

No, that's just raw drums. Brian is fabulous.

Your mic of choice for acoustic guitars?

Telefunken 251s and KM 54s, the tube version of KM 84s. Tube mics any chance you get, except for percussive things.

You knew Michael Jackson from the *Victory* album. How did you get together for the *Dangerous* album?

I had worked a lot with Michael in between, but nothing that came to fruition. He was producing this time and when he called me to work with him, I said, "Well, now I'm a producer, Michael," and so I produced. The great part about it was Michael asked me to do things I'd never done. I'd never been a songwriter, and he asked me to write songs. So now I'm a songwriter.

And you're a rapper now, too! [on "Black or White"]

Yeah, I'm the rapper. I just kind of filled in things that weren't getting done. That song was sitting there with this big gaping hole for way too long, and it was my production and my responsibility. I was afraid it would get left off the album if it always had this big hole in it when people heard it. So I put the rap in, and it was meant to be a demo for somebody else to do the words. Michael loved it… and he said, "I'm gonna leave it."

Why is it credited "Rap performance: L.T.B." on the liner notes?

[Laughs] That's a reference to my suburban upbringing. It was going to be "MC Leave it to Beaver!"

How long did you work on "Black or White?"

Stretched out, more than two years. This is totally opposite to how I told you I work, right?

What's one essential Bill Bottrell recording effect?

Brutal honesty.

At this point screams from the studio below interrupted us, and Bottrell departed to investigate. The interview was over.

Bottrell went on to produce, write for, engineer, and play on Sheryl Crow's *Tuesday Night Music Club*, which was released in 1993, went 7X Platinum and earned three Grammy awards, including Record of the Year. He also produced Shelby Lynne's 2000 breakthrough *I Am Shelby Lynne*, for which Bottrell was Grammy-nominated for Producer of the Year and Lynne won Best New Artist. He currently lives in rural Northern Calfornia, where he has, of course, a studio. He continues to produce, engineer, and play on projects for artists such as Rusted Root, Elton John, and Kim Richey, as well as performing as a solo act and with his cabaret band, the StokeMen.

SHAWN MURPHY

FEBRUARY, 1994 ## Mixing Under Pressure

Selected Credits

Braveheart

Clear and Present Danger

Dances with Wolves

E.T. the Extra-Terrestrial

Ghost

Jurassic Park

Men in Black

Pretty Woman

Saving Private Ryan

The Sixth Sense

*Star Wars: Episode I —
The Phantom Menace,
Episode II — Attack of the Clones*

Titanic

Need the soundtrack for a $60 million movie recorded tomorrow? Got eighty union musicians on a scoring stage, along with the producer, composer, arranger, music editor, and their various assistants? Got picture projection, clock control, streamer generation, sixteen headphone feeds, and union breaks?

No problem, if the guy in the hot seat is mixer Shawn Murphy. If any of you record engineers out there are still inclined to spend all afternoon on a guitar solo, well, don't even bother applying for this job. The name of the game here is guaranteed results. Great sounds, on schedule, with no problems. And with Murphy, people know that's what they're going to get. You've heard his work — from *Dances With Wolves, Jurassic Park, Batman,* and *Ghost,* to *Patriot Games, Dick Tracy,* and Tim Burton's *The Nightmare Before Christmas.* From *Schindler's List, Swing Kids, and Dracula,* to *Cape Fear, Pretty Woman,* and *Field of Dreams.* He's recorded more than two hundred scores over the past thirteen years, following more than thirty of them to the mix stage for re-recording. He was nominated for an Academy Award for recording *Indiana Jones and the Last Crusade.*

One of the most in-demand sound engineers in the film world, Murphy brings a wealth of experience to his craft. After receiving his M.F.A. in technical theater production from Stanford University in 1972, he worked in production for radio, television, and film, including stints with Filmways/Wally Heider, CBS Television, and Disneyland. Murphy is currently supervising for Todd-AO Studios in Studio City, CA, where he was responsible for renovating the former Evergreen stage, which some call the most technologically advanced in the world.

I visited Murphy at Todd-AO where he was recording with composer James Horner for the Julia Roberts film, *Pelican Brief.* The eighty-two-piece orchestra included thirty-two violins, three pianos, and a harp, yet the mic setup seemed deceptively simple. I had a lot of questions, and at lunch in the studio commissary, Murphy had time to answer a few.

Photo: Maureen Droney

How far in advance do you know the composition of an orchestra for a specific session?

Generally, a week or more, but I will say that we often have changes and additions right up until the day of score. Even though you may know that you have twenty-six violins scheduled, it's fairly common to walk in on the day and find a saxophone or a drum set that you did not know about. It can be a bit disconcerting. You walk in, and the cartage fellows are setting up a drum set and saying, "Where do you want this?"

You came in at 7 this morning for a 10 A.M. start. How many people do you have to help you set up?

The crew on this particular session is three: two assigned to the stage and one to the control room. That's normal for a large orchestra. The crew here is familiar with the two or three basic orchestral setups that I like to use, and the variations are whether they are more squared-off or wrapped around in the strings, where the risers are used, where the harps and pianos are located, how close or distant the brass are.

How do you decide what those variations will be?

Sometimes, by the type of score. From talking to the composer, I'll find out if it is mostly strings or if it's very active, with a lot of chases and action cues. That will determine where you place things. Whether you want an antiphonal effect, or whether you would tend to stack the horns behind the woodwinds. Or you might like a more homogeneous sound that you would get by putting the horns in the center behind the woodwinds and rolling the percussion off to the left behind the strings. It depends on the composer and the music.

So you might go for more isolation of the aggressive instruments for an action movie?

Not more isolation: more real stereo. Very stereo in the room versus something more homogeneous that gives you a big orchestral picture without things coming far left and right. A lot of it is working with different composers and knowing what they would like to hear and how they write. Certain composers emphasize a certain orchestral timbre. For Danny Elfman, it's low strings and woodwinds. You know that a lot of bass clef instruments are going to be featured. In Danny's score, you might have a lot of bass clarinet and contra bassoon with bass sax and celli and basses. So, you try to seat them in a way that they will naturally fall left and right, and their parts will complement each other and be easily heard, as opposed to stacking them all up in the middle where it would be harder to differentiate the parts.

Is leakage a concern for you?

It's a concern only if it's bad-sounding—if it sounds bad off-axis, or it's leakage mostly consisting of slap off walls, or reflections that are coming back out-of-phase. In this sort of ambient-miking setup, if you seat the orchestra properly and work on the balance in the room, by and large, you will have lots of isolation—no matter what dynamic people are playing at. You'd be amazed, if you solo up certain mics, in an orchestra that has no baffles in it. Like today, if you solo the woodwinds or the harp, who are sitting in the front where you might think there would be a lot of spill, it's quite clean. That's because there is true dynamic out there; you don't have to force levels, and you don't have to worry about excessive leakage because the instrument is acoustically sitting in a place that is complementary to the part it is playing.

Of course, one way to get rid of bad-sounding leakage is to not use very many mics.

Right. I noticed you close-miked very few instruments.

Almost nothing. The harp, the celeste, the pianos.

Even the piano mics are set three or four feet above the soundboard.

Yeah, about a meter away on the pianos. We actually closed in a bit on the harp today when we noticed in the score a repetitive sixteenth-note figure that we need to hear. Normally we would mic it a bit farther away.

Percussion is primarily overhead mics, not tight. I don't care for tight-miking. It's also hard to mix in. When you are going for some sort of realistic perspective, close mics don't help you. They destroy the perspective. Pretty soon, you've got things poking through the picture in an unnatural way.

So you make a lot of your artistic decisions at the top with your seating of the orchestra.

Right. How tightly you pack them in, how far back you push the percussion or brass from the main mics, and recognizing the radiation pattern of the instruments. Proximity to the main microphones controls the depth.

You use a lot of tube mics in your setup. I'm a bit surprised you find them reliable enough.

Yes, today the setup is about fifty/fifty. Of course, if you're going to embark on a big tube mic session, you have to have spares, and you have to be able to change over quickly. The guys on the stage can do that very fast.

I tend to go with tube mics on the main system and solid-state mics up close a little more. I don't find the noise floor of tube mics excessive. With an NC 25 or 30, the mic is not that noisy. And I like the warmer character and the overload characteristics.

What are your favorite choices for string mics?

Well, I don't use them! My basic system involves five mics: three M-50s and two wide mics. I add a couple of surround mics, then I put a closer picture on the strings and woodwinds that I record, but probably don't listen to, and a closer picture on the first bass, harp, and keyboards, which I will listen to.

Today, there is also a pair of B&Ks on the tree that we're just goofing off with. We goof off on almost every session with something—testing a preamp, a mic, or a cable, printing them, and listening to them later.

I do record a left-center-right for the strings. Generally, I don't use them. Today, those mics are Neumann 140s. They might be B&K 4011s, AKG C-12s, or the VTL C-12 equivalent with the large capsule on violins. On violas, either Schoeps or B&K 4011s. Celli, depending on over or under the [music] stand… like on Danny Elfman, we might tend to go in close, ending up with C-37As or U67s. Over the stands, Schoeps or occasionally Sanken CU41. On basses, under the stand 67 tube, over the stand Schoeps or Sanken CU41. Again, on the basses, it's a choice whether you are going for a lot of tone on the low end or precision on the string, which is determined by the music. You might go half and half: some over the stand and some under. Your choices are determined by whether you need a lot of presence, impact, and detail or do you want it to be sweet sounding.

What is the pair of mics you have in front, up about ten feet high?

Those are the VTL [Vacuum Tube Logic] tube mics —large capsule, multiple-pattern, condenser tube mics. I'm using them for wide left and right. In the format I'm using, they're string boosters, and they pull the sides out wider for the Dolby matrix.

I also like to record a surround track for the dubbing mixer, whether or not they use it. I have a pair of tube mics in the back of the room going to the surround, and they are stereo. They're basically ambient mics. On this session, I'm using Schoeps with the MK-3 capsule, which has the most high-end. Because they're reverberant field microphones, you want to get them flat in the far field. Sometimes, we use Sennheiser MK20s with the top end tipped up, sometimes B&K—omni of course; no benefit to a cardioid mic that far away.

What preamps do you use?

I use the Avalons. I think they're the most tube-like solid-state preamp. I also have a set of Boulders that I use all the time. I have GMLs, and today we're trying the Millennia. I have a set of tube preamps made by Vacuum Tube Logic that are very simple, one-stage, triode preamps, which on some material sound really wonderful. They have a much richer harmonic content than solid-state preamps— maybe less "real," but really kind of a wonderful sound.

Do you bypass the console when recording?

Yes, straight to the machine. We also have a set of cables that run through a trough in the floor so that we don't have to use studio wiring—just dedicated XL cable directly to the preamps and then directly to the machines.

Do you prefer to record to analog?

Yes. Today is digital only because we have to do a lot of passes; we're adding synthesizers and singers. I don't like to make a lot of passes using analog masters. If I know that the score is just orchestral, I like to use analog. I prefer the sound. The alignment that I like is not elevated; 185, Dolby SR, on Ampex 456, which I like because whether I'm here or in London or on any stage, it's the same, and reliable. We run at 15 ips for the low end.

Your tape alignment is at 0 over 185?

Yes. It means we have lots of headroom, and our transients aren't rolled off on percussion or any sparkling material that contains a lot of peak-to-average range. You're not hitting the tape too hard. I think that's a concern because a lot of people look at a VU meter and think it's fine, but of course, the peak ratio can be much too high. You don't hear it for a while, but the tape is saturated and it's rolling off transients, and it doesn't sound as good. The SR takes care of the low-end noise.

I prefer analog. I can't think of a digital recording we've done for John Williams, with the exception of the *Schindler's List* remote in Boston, where we just simply didn't want to drag two analog 24s and all the SRs out. But we did use 20-bit converters so that we got better resolution on the main system.

You don't use compressors?

No, I don't use any dynamic processing at all, and very little EQ. I tend to like to equalize the bus feeds rather than the individual elements. The EQ provided by the microphone and the mic position is what I'm after.

What do those bus feeds consist of?

Today, we're doing a 4-track mix: left, center, right, and surround. I'm using Cello equalizers, which are the best EQ I've heard, in terms of broadband program EQ. If you start to crank a lot of EQ on the individual instruments, you really hear it, and it alters the characteristic of the leakage, so you're fighting the fact that in order to make the direct sound right on a certain mic, you've got badly EQ'd leakage to deal with.

Like hi-hats in your snare drum.

Right. Usually the cure for something not sounding right is to take the EQ off.

Did you always know that, or did it take a long time to learn?

[Laughs] Well, the quicker you realize it, the better off you are. In terms of orchestral recording, the real magic happens out there, and it's up to me to be able to hear that. It's in the writing and the playing and the conducting. But the more mics, the more processing, the more it gets in the way. The fewer the microphones, the better the setup, the better the players can hear each other, the less in the signal path, the better off you are.

Are you usually the re-recording mixer as well as the scoring engineer?

Usually not. Over the course of a year's time, I might work on the score to twenty or twenty-five pictures, and I would only dub two or three of them. For instance, this year *Jurassic Park* and

Nightmare Before Christmas will probably be the only two that I will dub. Scheduling-wise, it just usually doesn't work out.

You are premixing to six tracks of the 48-track as you are recording. Is that mix likely to be used for the final?

Yes, the live mixes are very often used. With certain composers, like John Williams and John Barry or James Newton Howard, the live mixes are used about 95 percent of the time. With James Horner, some live mixes are used, but since we often overdub on his projects, they often get mixed again.

Do you think we will soon see a digital final product and the end of 6-track sprocketed?

No. Despite the use of workstation in production nowadays, and I think most editors would agree, the format that is the most economical and the fastest to make changes in features is still sprocket mag, in terms of the post-production process.

For the release formats, we already have digital; we have DTS and SR-D. To deliver that kind of format to the theater is very good. You can be on 35mm print, you don't have to blow up a 35mm to 70mm in order to fit the 6-track mag on it, you don't have the deterioration of the mag stripes and the limited level you can put on a 100nwb mag stripe. But in terms of production, it's not going to change. It's extraordinarily expensive, and it needs so much storage capacity. Think of the number of tracks you have to store and the amount of time of each. It's just an immense task. People do use Pro Tools and PostPro and that sort of thing and use them in a limited manner … but that's a supplement, not instead of mag.

What's the worst mistake you can make on a scoring session?

Not checking. You noticed [James Horner] didn't ask for a playback of the last thing that we did. Well, I played it back.

How much can you normally get done in a day?

Today we got about eighteen minutes—eight to nine minutes per [three-hour] session. That's good. Some days, you only get five per session, and every now and then, you'll do phenomenally well and get ten or more.

You started out working in theater and radio.

I sort of earned my way through college working at radio stations and in the theater. I worked for KKHI in the San Francisco Bay Area for a time. They used to go out and record the symphony and different ensembles all the time, and I did that. I was the youngest and the engineer most willing to carry around Ampex 350s in the station wagon. I also taught theater technology in college for a while, then worked in sound reinforcement and production, then recording television shows and wound up at CBS mixing television shows. I started mixing film in about 1980.

What skills are different for a film mixer as opposed to a record mixer?

Well, if you're going to be a scoring mixer, and especially a re-recording mixer, you have to have some sort of dramatic sense. You can't just focus on the music even if you're the music mixer, because it's not the whole show, is it? You have to tell the story. Sometimes, you may make a flute that's eighty feet wide.

What's your advice to someone starting out to be a film mixer?

You have to have patience. I think the film business is more conservative and less willing to take risks on unknowns. You have to prove to people over and over again that you are capable of doing good work and managing a session like this every day, no matter what the requirements. And that takes years. Lots and lots of experience, and lots and lots of time. You also have to know when a good opportunity presents itself and be prepared to take it. When someone gives you a chance to do something important, you have to be there and be able because you may not ever get that chance again—to step forward and show your talents and do a good job.

Mick Guzauski

Secrets From the Top of the Charts

MARCH, 1998

He's the master mixer of smooth and soulful pop, with a list of Number 1 singles that's longer than many engineers' entire discography. Hit artists from Mariah Carey, Toni Braxton, and Michael Bolton, to Barbra Streisand, Boyz II Men, All 4 One, and LeAnn Rimes seek him out to help craft the sound that keeps them out front and on top, and he always delivers. Success hasn't gone to his head, though; Mick Guzauski is a genial, unassuming fellow. The polar opposite of jaded, with almost thirty years spent in the music recording business, he still evinces a sincere and almost childlike fascination with the various technical and artistic elements that comprise his chosen field. These days, Guzauski mixes primarily at his own Barking Doctor Studios about an hour out of Manhattan, where recently, he's been locked in with new projects for Eric Clapton, Lionel Richie, and Monica.

Let's take it from the top. How'd you get started in the business?

I was always interested in music and electronics, and although as a kid I had music lessons, I never believed that I'd be a very good player. But I was pretty good with electronics, so ....

Did you build from electronics kits?

Kits, and I built a lot of my own stuff. I started recording as a hobby in the late '60s, so of course, there was no semipro gear—nothing affordable for a kid. Then, when I was 15, I got my first job repairing turntables and tape recorders for a local hi-fi store, and I started buying used and broken equipment and fixing it up. Then I built a mixer and started a studio in my parents' basement; I was recording demos for local bands by the time I was a senior in high school.

You had a studio in your house even back then?

It was tiny, but in Rochester, New York, there were very few studios, and they were mostly in people's basements. I did that for a couple of years after high school, then I went in with some other guys who had a commercial studio, because my parents didn't want bands in

Photo: Edward Colver

the house all the time. I was doing jingles, as well as those band demos, and I'd been doing it on weekends. But it got to the point, when I had a Scully 4-track machine, that we'd do tracking on weekends when my parents weren't home, then do overdubbing and mixing on weeknights.

So you went into business with those other guys....

They did mostly industrial work, and I kept up the music end—more bands and jingles. There really wasn't that much work in Rochester, so I did P.A. work, as well. I did P.A. for Chuck Mangione and ended up recording for him in the studio and also live in the early '70s. Then, in '75, he signed with A&M and was getting ready to do the album that became *Chase The Clouds Away*, with a live rhythm section and a 44-piece orchestra. He asked me, "Do you think you can handle it?" Of course, I'd never been in a real professional studio, and of course, I didn't think I could do it, but I said, "Yeah, sure."

So I went out to L.A. with him and did the album. It came out good, and everybody was happy. After that, I went back and forth to L.A. for three years, in the studio with Chuck and also doing road work. I finally moved to L.A. in 1978. Now, twenty years later, I'm back in New York!

Your client base grew from Chuck's albums—people heard your work and liked it.

One of the last records I did for Chuck was a pretty big hit called *Feels So Good*, so people had heard of me as an engineer, at least in instrumental jazz. I started getting a lot of calls to do that kind of album—you know how you get sort of pigeonholed. Meanwhile, I'd also gotten my first real job in L.A. as a tech at Larrabee. A friend who worked at Westlake called me up one day, and I went over to see the place. I ended up doing a Chuck Mangione project there, and I became close to the staff. One night, a band was in with James Newton Howard producing and Andy Johns engineering. Andy had double-booked himself, so Jim Fitzpatrick, Westlake's head tech, needed an engineer and called me. The label's chief engineer happened to be George Massenburg. I did a rough mix that he liked, and that's how I got into working a lot in L.A., and went on to work for Earth, Wind & Fire. Things happened faster after that. I was working at Conway Studios with Average White Band, and I met Peter Bunetta and Rick Chudakoff. Through them, I started working with Smokey Robinson, Michael Bolton, Kenny G, and Walter Afanasieff. That's really the chain of events. David Foster, who I do a lot of work for now, I actually met back in Rochester where I did a demo for him in '73 or '74 when he was in a band called Skylark, who were managed by someone who lived in Rochester.

You never went the runner/assistant route?

I never assisted. I came more from a technical aspect. I'm not a designer like Massenburg, but I built stuff for my home studio because I wanted to understand how it worked. I had time on my hands in the early years, and at one time or another, I designed and built every part of the analog chain. Not a whole console, but one channel each of record, tape, and play, so I understood how everything worked from the mic pre to the power amp. Analog, of course. I started getting really busy before digital technology became prevalent, so I haven't had time to learn as much as I should about it. I want to, though; I want to get a DSP development kit and see how it all works.

Your records always sound so warm that I was surprised to learn you work mostly with digital.

I do work pretty much all digitally. It just makes sense because we have the digital final product of a CD. While it's true that analog does tend to warm things up somewhat, with tube gear and such, I believe there's no reason digital can't be warm. I never really have much problem with that. I mix to a DA-88 through a Rane Paqrat. The Paqrat takes a 24-bit digital word and splits it onto two 16-bit tracks of an 8-track machine. You can record 24-bit stereo audio using four tracks of a DA-88, and it will reassemble the 24-bit word on playback.

The system I use now is the AT&T digital mixer core for my SSL console, with a Sony 3348 multitrack. I have an analog multitrack for when people send me analog tapes, but I usually transfer them to digital; then we stay in the digital domain all the way through. I also have a lot of digital outboard gear—TC5000, Valley Compressor, Weiss Equalizer, Eventide DSP4000 and H3000, Lexicon 300s, and a Sony V77—a lot of gear that I can go in and out of and keep everything in the digital domain. I do also use analog—a GML EQ and compressor, and I have a couple of old Eventide SP2016s and an EMT140 plate that I use in combination a lot on vocals. I think that's where some of the warmth in my sound comes from. The 2016 has a nice high-frequency sizzle and definition in the reverb, and the plate has that big, warm sound behind it, because, although the EMT is transistor, not tube, it's still a mechanical device.

The vocal ambiences on your records are always very clear. You may have a lot of reverb going on in a ballad, but it doesn't get in the way.

I always try to make sure that the low end of the echo isn't in the way of anything. Often, I'll EQ the reverb to attenuate lows, so that when it rings in the lower register of the voice, it doesn't cloud any instruments. Usually, I'll roll off some low-mids, around 200 or 300 Hz. I'm very careful that I don't lose richness, but most of the main keyboards and pads will be right in that same area, and it can be a balancing act to keep the vocal clear. I also work very hard on the high-end detail in the vocal to make sure that it's very present—not sibilant, but with enough diction so that you can hear the vocal in the track without putting it incredibly up front.

Are there particular compressors you like to use on vocals?

I'm using UREI LA22s a lot; they were only made for a couple of years. I like their flexibility. In addition to variable attack and release time, the detector is variable from peak to average. Also, you can use it as a frequency-selective compressor—not in the way that a sidechain is frequency-selective, but like a dynamic EQ that will dip a certain frequency. If you have a vocal that at certain levels and frequencies jumps out and gets harsh, you can use a channel of it and actually detect the threshold of that jump, then dip that frequency.

In general, do you vary the attack and release times a lot on compressors?

Actually, for vocals I'll usually leave them set pretty much the same. What seems to work is about a 3:1 ratio, with a 20 to 40 millisecond attack time and a 100 to 300 millisecond release. I don't just leave it set that way for every voice, of course, but I find for most applications, that range works. I usually adjust attack and release a lot more for instruments than on vocals. The envelope of the voice in general is usually close enough so that when a compressor is set this way, it will attack pretty well without pumping. With a slower attack time, you'll hear the vocal attack and then you'll hear the compressor grab. It will be audible. If the attack is faster, you sometimes don't get the transient of a word that's being emphasized. So, in general, these settings work. Once in a while, if something is sung very staccato, I'll have to speed up the release.

It sounds like you ride reverbs and delays a lot during the mix.

Yes, usually I have a couple of automated channels on the console that are sends to different delays and reverbs, mainly for lead vocals and lead instruments. Sometimes, it's an effect to really make a word swim, but more often, the reverb that would sound plenty wet in a sparse part of the track will be too dry as the track builds dynamically. So, often, I'll ride the reverb and delay as the track builds.

You've done a lot of group lead vocals like Boyz II Men and All 4 One. How do you deal with so many vocals?

You'll usually find when you place each individual vocal in the track that certain frequencies will pop out in certain areas, while in other areas they won't be loud enough. When they are soloed and unEQ'd, they sound good, but there may be little spikes that stick out in relationship to the track. So, I'll EQ each vocal individually to be smooth, generally with parametric equalizers with the bandwidth set pretty narrow. I'll boost a frequency a lot to tune right to it, then cut it back to be smooth and in context with the rest of the spectrum. Sometimes, I'll split a vocal on two channels and have a different EQ for verse and chorus. And sometimes, frequency-selective compression will help. If you have a vocal EQ'd pretty bright that sounds nice when the vocalist is singing soft but gets a little nasty when they sing harder, that kind of compressor can automatically ride those changes.

If I'm going to cut back a frequency that's sticking out in the mix, I'll tune it narrow and sharp to find the exact center frequency and boost it to find it, then broaden it up and cut it back as much as I need to. Most of the boosting I'd do is very high-shelf, broadband, so you don't hear one note jump out, unless, of course, something is deficient in one small area.

And with backgrounds?

With BGs, I'll EQ for smooth response; I don't compress them that much. Usually, I get them in stereo pairs per part—one part that's a chord, and a counterpart to that. Sometimes, the parts are individual. Then I'll bus them to a pair of channels so that I can work on them as a whole. I'm always listening for the chords. They may sound perfectly balanced soloed, but something may get lost when it's in the track. I have to say, though, most of the vocals I get are very high quality, very well recorded. Well balanced within themselves and also with the track.

Do you use your console EQ primarily?

Yes, mostly the console EQ, except usually on lead vocals I use the GML parametric. My chain for that tends to be out of the converter to the GML EQ, then the compressor, the de-esser and the console EQ. That way, if I need to cut back on something, I use the GML, and the compressor is reacting to a fairly smooth signal. Boosting, I'll do on the console, post-compression. So usually, I have EQ both pre- and post-compression—cut before compression, boost after.

With the AT&T system, the console is switchable per channel between EQ that emulates both SSL E and G Series and Neve VR curves. Usually, I keep it on SSL E, but on acoustic guitars, strings, and some high percussion, I'll go to the Neve VR curve because the characteristic of the high shelf is very airy. It has a little dip before the shelf starts and then sort of comes up a little steeper and gives you air without getting harsh.

I think of you as a bass expert. Your bottom end is present and big but never loose and boomy.

Well, with some projects I work on, the bass is in such a low register that there's no attack with it, but it works musically. That's where I'm very careful setting the attack time on the compressor. I'll listen to the bass in the track and check the attack of each note. Then, if you slow down the attack of the compressor and compress the track a little, the compressor will actually add some attack because the attack transient of the bass is getting through before the compressor reduces the gain on it. That's a trick I use a lot—to use a compressor with a slow attack and then to adjust the amount of compression so that there's enough of the attack of the note that gets through to define where it is in the track. I also EQ it to make the whole register that the bass is playing in, the whole spectrum, sounds smooth with the track. That doesn't always mean that every note is perfectly even, because something else might be covering the bass notes in some areas. You want to tailor it so it sounds even in the track.

The important thing is, I don't listen to individual tracks alone too much. I'll usually listen to a rough mix first if the client sends it, or else I'll put up all the tracks to hear what the song is about. Then I'll go through the tracks and EQ and set them pretty much where I think they're going to go, and then I'll put everything in and fine-tune.

Like mixing a live band

It is probably a carryover from when I used to do live sound work.

What compressors do you like on bass?

Most of the time on bass, I seem to use the Empirical Systems Distressor because it is so adjustable. I'll also sometimes use an older limiter like the LA-2A or the clone made by DeMaria. It's not very variable, but it has a very complementary attack and release time by itself. That's another optical; I use a lot of the optical compressors. Even though they don't have variable attack and release, their normal characteristics can work very well.

Do you have to do a lot of mixes for each song? Vocal up, down, etc.

Not so much. A mix, then a vocal up, a vocal down, so if later a word or a phrase isn't quite the right level, you can cut them in. I'm also mixing in stems a lot now, where I'll turn the bus compressor off, because of course, that compressor in the final bus reacts to everything. And I'll do, on DA-88, a pair for the track, a pair for BGs, a pair for leads, a pair for orchestration—four different stereo elements of the mix with their effects. That can be combined and sent to a bus compressor if we need to change balances without redoing a whole mix.

I'm also using Pro Tools a lot for that. I should mention that's now one of the most important things in my studio. I have Pro Tools 24 with 24-bit resolution, so I can put a whole mix in it without really losing anything. I use it for editing mixes, for flying, and moving stuff around. I also use the plug-ins with automated EQ. If a vocal comp needs different EQ dynamically as the song goes on, I'll put the vocal in Pro Tools and let it run in sync.

There's also an auto-tune—another plug-in that is the greatest thing. You tell it what key the song is in and how fast and critical you want it to be about pitch. I'll just copy the vocal track into Pro Tools. That's another thing I really like about working digitally: You can copy back and forth, and as long as the clocking of the system is stable, you don't really have any loss. That's a point that should be made about digital. Generation loss in digital is nonexistent only as long as the clocking of the system is stable, all the connections and the wiring are good, and you are not getting noise errors into the chain.

Your console is a 56-input SSL G Series.

Yes. The AT&T digital mixer core has a little card that goes on each channel of the SSL, each multiplexer board, and it picks up the recall information there and sends it to a computer and the AT&T DSP, which is actually just modeling what the whole console does. So, the SSL isn't passing any audio at all; the recall section is all that's running. When the AT&T is operating, it forces the recall circuitry on all the time, so that whenever you are turning a knob or pushing a button, it knows what you've done. And then, of course, it reads the automation for the faders and mutes.

You must use your ISDN lines a lot.

Our system is a Dolby Fax through EDnet, and definitely ISDN lines are one of the reasons that I'm able to have a home studio and to do most of my work here. Being this far from the city, producers don't always want to come. Also, I still have a lot of clients in L.A. For the most part, people don't have the time to get on a plane and come here. This way, I can do the mix and then the clients can either listen at home or at a studio, and we just tweak it together for the last couple of hours. Then we're done.

Which other engineers' work do you like?

Off the top of my head? I love a lot of the stuff Bob Clearmountain does; I think he's a master at getting really interesting spatial things happening. I love Elliot Scheiner, the precision and fidelity of his work. There's a naturalness to it, a natural ambience like everybody's right there in the room that's very good. I've always loved his Steely Dan records, and more recently, Fleetwood Mac's *The Dance* is just great. I love Swedien, Massenburg, Al Schmitt—there are too many excellent engineers to mention them all. There are a lot of great people in this business.

How about some thoughts on the philosophy of mixing?

Well, I think it really is a new profession now, because it's only in the last few years that records have been made that are almost totally synthesized. So, being a recording and mixing engineer are almost two different things now. There are still engineers who do both, guys like Al Schmitt and Elliott Scheiner, who are great engineers and great mixers. And there is the type of music that really needs somebody to do both and to follow a project through—those projects with mostly live instruments, where so much of the mix is created in the recording.

But being a mixer, like me or Bob or Jon Gass, and all the guys that people send their tapes to, really is a pretty new profession. We're creating an ambience for a song, sort of like a photographer does for a picture, because a lot of pop music is mostly synthesized and not recorded with its own particular ambience. So, different mixers interpret the music differently. It really is a different set of responsibilities.

One last thing. Tell us your secret for getting all those Number 1 singles.

Honestly, I have no idea how it happened, but I'm sure glad that it did! Seriously, though, as an engineer or mixer, there would be nothing at all to do without great artists and producers. So that's how it happened. I was lucky enough to hook up with great people, and I'm really thankful to all of them.

Guzauski continues to mix the hits. In 2001/2002, his client list included chart-toppers Brian McNight, Macy Gray, Celine Dion, Jennifer Lopez, Marc Anthony, Faith Hill, and many others. He also continues ahead of the curve in his equipment choices. In 2002, the console at his Barking Doctor Studio was Sony's pioneering digital desk, the Oxford.

CHUCK AINLAY

JULY, 1998 ## Looking for the Magic

Glance at the credits on almost any country superstar's CD and you'll see the name of engineer Chuck Ainlay. Trisha Yearwood, George Strait, Wynonna, Vince Gill, Reba McEntire, Nancy Griffith—the list goes on and on. You'll also find Ainlay's name on CDs by Mark Knopfler and Dire Straits, Lyle Lovett, James Taylor, and many others, as well as on numerous 5.1 surround projects.

Photo: Beth Guinn

Selected Credits

Dire Straits
On Every Street

Steve Earle
Guitar Town

Vince Gill
High Lonesome Sound

Nancy Griffith
Little Love Affairs

Waylon Jennings
Will The Wolf Survive

Mark Knopfler
**Also produced
*Golden Heart,
Sailing to Philadelphia*

Patty Loveless
*If My Heart Had Windows,
Honky Tonk Angel*

Lyle Lovett
Lyle Lovett and His Large Band

George Strait
*Ocean Front Property,
Pure Country,
Road Less Traveled*

Marty Stuart
*Hillbilly Rock,
Tempted*

Trisha Yearwood
How Do I Live

Wynonna
Wynonna

He's engineered in excess of two hundred albums, received a Grammy nomination for Best Engineered Recording Non-Classical, has been a two-time winner of the Nashville Music Award for recording engineer, as well as a two-time TEC-Award nominee. Since 1999, he's also been co-owner of Nashville's BackStage Studio.

With twenty years on the Nashville music scene under his belt, Ainlay is well known for his talents at recording and mixing both classic and modern country, as well as other genres. His mixes evince a transparent blend of natural balances and pop edge — somehow, he makes combining all those instruments seem effortless while still managing to keep the all-important lead vocal pleasingly out front and telling the story.

Easygoing and disarmingly frank, with a self-deprecating sense of humor, Ainlay has developed his own style over the years. That style keeps him in demand and on a nonstop working schedule. At the time this interview was done, recent Ainlay projects had included a new Trisha Yearwood album, production chores for Mark Knopfler's second solo album, Shana Petrone's debut album, the film scores for *Wag the Dog* and *Metroland*, and 5.1 surround-sound mixes for artists including Vince Gill, Trisha Yearwood, George Strait, The Mavericks, and Olivia Newton-John. I caught up with Ainlay during a break in mixing Vince Gill's new album at Nashville's Sound Stage Studios.

How's the new record?

It's great — and very country. I think Vince [Gill] has decided to just go for it and that he doesn't have anything to prove anymore.

Did you record the project also?

Most of it. He wanted to do it whenever he came into town and had time off, so I had to rearrange my schedule to accommodate that. For one tracking date, I was mixing Trisha Yearwood and couldn't make the session, but I did all the rest of the tracking.

Do you prefer to record the music that you mix?

Well, it doesn't always work out that way. I end up mixing more than anything, but I do like to work on what I've recorded. I love tracking; I think it's probably the most fun, because you're there with all the players creating music, and you hear it all come together, from nothing to magic. That one moment when it happens is just amazing — the camaraderie of people coming in and digging what you're doing, and you digging what they're doing; there's nothing like it.

Mixing is different. It's more self-indulgent.

That can be great, too, because you get to sit there and fine-tune things that you hear. It takes time; sometimes you feel like there's nothing there, and then suddenly it all comes together and in that one moment it is just shining in your face, and you're going, "Wow!"

Obviously, I love to do both. But to answer your question, I do prefer to mix what I track because when you're tracking, there are always things that you leave to do in the mix, and it's not always obvious what somebody else had intended to leave to mixing.

Is it accurate to say that most of the music in Nashville is recorded live?

Very little here is done using sequencers, except maybe for the Christian market. Country music is pretty much driven by live musicians and session players.

In general, most of the tracking is done live; the amount of overdubbing of course depends on the album. Because there are so many solo artists, the bands are usually comprised of session musicians, and the studios are set up to where you can get isolation on a lot of players at once. For the basic country record, you cut a track, then the acoustic-guitar player doubles, then the electric-guitar player might take a lead, but usually the steel and the fiddle and all those other solos are done live.

Which is why it's so exciting to track in this town. You get to hear it come together, and it happens really fast, in maybe three takes. From an engineering perspective, you have to be on it for that first take, because that really might be the one. You always need to be ready, because they're going to go with the magic of the track rather than with whether it was technically good or not.

And you sure don't want to have to tell all those musicians you're not ready.

[Laughs] Well, you don't tell them. You fix it in the mix. Live music is one of the great things about working in Nashville. I happen to love real drums, and the fact that there is human error. I don't hear that a lot in the records that are on the radio where the timing is just perfect, and they've put everything in a hard disk system and lined everything up and the pitch is just absolutely dead-on. I don't hear that magic in songs that makes you want to listen to the record over and over again. Sometimes, it seems that there's this thing that everybody is going for now, an instant impression of "Wow, that's great — listen to how tight it is," but as far as that depth, that human feeling that makes you really love a song and dig it for the rest of your life, I don't think it's out there that much.

Instant perfection — something that catches your ear immediately but doesn't have staying power.

It's one of the things that drives me crazy about records today, and it's starting to happen in Nashville, too — the process where you cut the vocal, you comp the vocal, you tune the vocal....

There are a lot of great tracking rooms in Nashville.

You'll find here that even the bigger rooms have a lot of isolation booths. You can put the acoustic, the piano, the fiddle, and the vocal all in separate rooms, with the drums in the main part of the room, so you can get everything live. You need that isolation, though. With acoustic instruments like fiddle or upright bass, there isn't a lot of output, And on modern country records, the drums are a real driving thing; they're played loud.

What are your console preferences?

For tracking, I carry a lot of outboard gear of my own that I use. The desk becomes more of a monitoring desk, so it's not really an issue.

For mixing, I really like the J Series SSL 9000. I also like Neve V Series. While I like the sound of the 8078s and the older Neves, sometimes the facilities aren't there. I have to work quickly, and therefore it gets down to ergonomics — the facilities of the desk play an important role.

Do you mix fast?

I wouldn't say I'm a fast mixer, because I don't think I'm a golden ear kind of guy. I think I'm a hard working kind of guy. I just work until it sounds and feels right. I push all the faders up to begin with, and just listen to the song, and get an image in my head of what it should be as an end result. Then I go to work to achieve that. I generally like to tell clients it's going to take a day a song. I don't think that's fast; I think that's about average.

How did you get started in engineering?

I played guitar in bands in high school in Northern Indiana — actually, I started out with drums when I was a child and then the Beatles came around, so I wanted to be a guitar player. I always loved listening to records and would save up money to buy a new tape deck or some new bit of stereo gear. I would always look at record covers to see who engineered them. When it came time to graduate high school, I went to the guidance counselor and said I wanted to be a recording engineer and he said, "Huh?"

So, I went to Indiana University, and there was a studio in town that had a six-week engineering course. I went through that program and realized that it was truly what I wanted to do. Someone recommended that I check out Belmont College in Nashville, which had a recording business program with an 8-track studio. It was one of the first schools to do that. I went to Belmont for about a year-and-a-half and then got a job in a tourist studio.

A what?

That's where we would have busloads of tourists come into the studio, and we'd put on a skit and record it, then play it back over the speakers and get the audience to clap and shout as an overdub, then play it back for them.

A theme park studio.

Yeah. Then at night, we'd do radio interviews and demos.

What next?

My next job after the tourist studio was as head engineer at a studio up in Fort Wayne, Indiana; I went up there for six months till I realized I didn't want to do jingles. There wasn't anything else going on, so I went back to Nashville and got a job assisting at Quad Studios. That lasted for about a month, until somebody said, if you go tear out all the equipment in the studio and get us out of there so we don't have to pay next month's rent, you can have the equipment. So, we had a 16-track studio for nothing; we got a trailer and built a remote truck, and that was my next deal. That kind of worked into a job at Sound Lab.

Were you ever an assistant engineer?

Well, the way it worked at Sound Lab, the chief engineer got all the record business work, and then, for the custom work and demos, rather than hiring an independent engineer like people might today, the client would just come to the studio, and since they were paying less money, they got the assistant. So, rather than assisting on many albums, I was just thrown straight into the fire doing demos and custom albums, and then worked my way up.

Custom albums?

That's where it's not a label deal, just somebody with money who wants to record an artist. There was a lot of that that went on in town. People who wanted to be a star would come to Nashville and pay to have their record made. There were a lot of people who made a lot of money just doing that.

In country music there usually seems to be a lot going on, and a lot that's in the midrange frequencies —piano, guitars, fiddles. How do you cope with all of the parts?

In the studio at Indiana U where I first had my introduction to recording, the instructor said, "It's not so much blending the instruments together as it is making the instruments not mask each other." That was one of the first things I learned and have held true to the art: It's not so much making each instrument sound great as it is making each instrument have a place to live.

That's part of the art of miking and using equalizers and compressors: to allow all these instruments in the same range, which ordinarily would tend to mask each other; to have a place to live and breathe in the mix.

How do you generally record acoustic guitars?

For an acoustic, I'll generally use a Neumann KM84 or the tube version, a KM56 or 54. I'll go out and listen to determine what kind of guitar it is. If it's

a boomy Martin sort of guitar, I'll tend to stay away from the center; with a Gibson that's more mid-rangy, you can use the hole to get warmth. It's a matter of going into the control room and listening, then going out and adjusting. I do try not to mic too closely. That's one of the benefits of using isolation rooms: you don't have to mic right up on the guitar because you're not as concerned about leakage. A lot of times, I'll track an acoustic using Focusrite modules, because I like the airiness about them. If the acoustic is doing more finger-style stuff or if they are taking a lead, I'll use two mics. The second is usually further out or higher up or towards the rear of the guitar.

Would you usually compress the guitar signal?

When I track, I really tend to shy away from compression; I deal with that more during the mix, when yes, I do generally compress the acoustic.

What sort of compressors would you use?

Actually, for an acoustic, I tend to use an onboard SSL compressor on the auto setting. It just works. For a more classic sound, I may use an LA-2A or my Tube-Tech.

What's in that rack of yours that you bring to the session?

I've got a lot of Neve modules: 1081s and 1073s. I've got GML mic pre's, Focusrite and API modules, Tube Tech, UREI 1176, and GML compressors. I also have a rack of effects gear.

What might your mic choices be for piano?

If I have them, I'll put two C-12s on the piano, and either use GML mic pre's or a lot of times I'll go through Focusrites. I'll use 414s if I don't have C-12s. I never mic right over the hammers; I usually use the bracing in the piano as a mark for where I'll mic. For the high end, it's generally about six inches back and up from the hammers near the upper bracing, and at the low end bracing maybe a bit further toward the low strings, about the same distance up and further back into the piano. For country, you usually want that left hand/right hand spread; you're not generally going for that solid middle kind of thing. I've got a Drawmer 1960 that I like to use on piano for compression. It adds a little air to it. Piano is one of the things I may compress a little when I track.

Any tricks for recording pedal steel guitars?

[Laughs] The thing about recording is that it's so much easier when you're working with the best musicians, like I am. Ninety-nine percent of it is the musicians. Steel guitar, you want to know what I do? I put two 421s out there and cut it flat. I mean, Paul Franklin has the most amazing tone in the world. But, okay, if you really want to know, for steel guitar, it's either a 421 or a 57, and I usually mic a bit off the speaker center, so that you don't get the brittleness that can come from the center. Pretty much, that's how I mic any amped instrument. But for steel, it's a fairly simple signal path: through a Neve module straight to tape. I generally don't do much EQ.

Your records don't sound like they have a lot of EQ in general.

I really would like to emphasize that with me it's all about the music and trying not to overhype things so that the warmth and emotion of the music come through.

Do you do a lot of riding faders by hand in the mix?

I do. I use compression to help me and to make things sound powerful and strong, but there's a lot of riding involved, and I think that's why I generally like to work on the J Series desks — because the automation is killer.

Any favorite snare compressors you'll tell us about?

Once again, I usually use the desk compressor, but I'll also bus the drums out to a separate compressor and bring that up in the mix; I like to use a Calrec or an 1176 for that. My 1081 Neve modules generally end up on the bass drum and snare as well.

In a lot of the music that you work on, the vocals are very out front. That makes the ambience on them apparent and important. Do you have any favorite settings for those ambiences?

For vocals, I spend a lot of time choosing the microphone. It usually ends up being a tube microphone—a C-12 , a U47, or a 251—and I'll either use the GML mic pre's, which I like for their warmth and overall transparency, or I'll use the Neve 1073s with the EQ out, just using the mic preamp section. I almost never use EQ when I'm tracking a vocal, but I'll compress it slightly with my Tube Tech compressor. It's one of the original ones that I really like: a CL1A that they don't make anymore.

For the 'verbs you're asking about, I like to have an EMT 250 around; I like a Lexicon 300, usually a plate program. Then, I may use a [Lexicon] 224X with a longer predelay as well. I usually mix a lot of 'verbs together for vocals, using one for warmth, one for decay, and one for brilliance, and I'll usually use a bit of harmonization — dual Harmonizers split up and down — to spread the vocal a bit. Many times I'll also use some sort of delay to add dimension.

Someone commented to me that you somehow get the vocal to sound like the singer hears it inside his or her head.

You were asking about riding things. I'll spend quite a lot of time riding the vocals. I usually compress them in the mix using the GML compressor. I love that compressor for how it rides the vocal but doesn't sound compressed. It doesn't eat into the air of a vocal. Then, I'll spend a lot of time riding the vocal just trying to get the intent.

Do you use overall stereo compression on your mixes?

I try to make it sound like a finished record. When I'm using an SSL, I'll use the quad compressor, or I like the Alan Smart version of the SSL compressor if I'm working on a Neve. I also have the Calrec compressors; they work in a very similar way to the SSL compressors, and I'll use those sometimes on the overall mix. I don't do any of that digital compression, maxing out a DAT kind of thing, like a lot of people do. I'll leave that to mastering.

What format do you mix to?

I always mix to half-inch with AGFA tape on an ATR 100. I also mix through the Pacific Microsonics HDCD converters to the Genex magneto optical recorder, which allows me to record to at 88.2 24-bit.

What level on the half-inch?

Plus 5 over 250; that works pretty good if I'm using 16 dB headroom on the digital as far as maxing out the digital and still hitting the analog hard enough.

When do you choose between the formats?

I'll wait until I get to mastering. Generally, the half-inch wins. There isn't, in my opinion, a better representation of the console bus than the Pacific Microsonics system, but sometimes, you just can't beat the character that the analog adds.

Why both formats then?

Well, for example on this Vince Gill project, I had to get a single done for his next release. We took the tapes to Denny "Platinum Ears" Purcell at Georgetown Masters, where I master all my records; we decided to go with the 24-bit, and we mastered the song completely flat. I find if you get it absolutely right in mixing, there's just nothing that comes closer to the desk than that [Pacific Microsonics] system. And I've auditioned lots of converters.

What are your main monitoring speakers?

Recently, I've been using KRK Expose 8s, which I love; I've been getting great mixes with them, and Keith Klawitter at KRK has been great. I came across them searching for a good monitor for 5.1, and I've been using them ever since. I also use the M&K subwoofer for the .1 when mixing in surround.

You're one of the main engineers in the forefront of mixing for 5.1. Why is that?

Just pure chance, I guess. DTS approached MCA Records and producer Tony Brown about doing Vince Gill's *High Lonesome Sound* in 5.1. I had been the engineer on that album, so I was given the opportunity to do the project. I had a concept of how to do it, and I guess people are digging it; since then, I've been asked to do quite a few other albums. I really believe that if it wasn't for DTS, music releases of 5.1 probably wouldn't be happening at all. Rory Kaplan and Bill Nabors at DTS are very responsible, I think, for the musical integrity of what's going on by getting creative people with high standards involved and moving the whole concept forward.

So, is it a lot more fun to mix in surround?

Back when I was in high school, I would listen to music all the time with a pair of speakers in front and my dad's speakers in the back. That's how I listened, and I loved it. Then you become a professional, and you get into precise stereo positioning and all. When I did the surround mixing for the first time, I thought, "This is how I remember it!" To have sound coming from all around you — it really is fun. The fact that there are no guidelines of what you are supposed to do makes it very creative. I love it.

Would you like to have your own studio?

I'm thinking about it. I see the need for a facility for mixing 5.1. Rooms now are acoustically designed and optimized for stereo, with the sound coming from one direction. Generally, they are live-end/dead-end situations, so with a surround setup, speakers in one end of the room will sound different than the speakers in the other end. Also, with 5.1, you really have to look at all the reflective surfaces. Because the sound is coming from more directions, your first reflections are more complicated to deal with. I think the big consoles we work on are a major factor as far as an imprint on the sound of the room, and that becomes an even bigger factor in surround. It's leading me to the idea that a digital console with a smaller imprint could work better in a surround room. Also, because it's a pure digital medium that's only going to ever be heard off DVD or DTS CD with a decoder, I see how a digital desk could work. So, that's the thought: a room designed acoustically for surround with a digital desk.

What's up next for you?

I'm finishing Vince Gill's album, then I go out to L.A. to mix Trisha's new album at Capitol Studios; they have a Neve VRP console with the film mods so that I can mix it in surround. That will be a lot of fun, because, at the same time Vince Gill will also be out there doing his Christmas album in the next room with Al Schmitt engineering, and they are recording the whole thing in 5.1. Tony Brown is producer on both those projects.

After that, I'm going to stay in L.A. for a while because I'm producing a Los Angeles band called Spaghetti Western for DTS. Meanwhile, we're also in the process of a Mark Knopfler record.... [Laughs] I guess there's a lot going on. Oh, and of course, I also intend to be doing a lot of water skiing!

AL SCHMITT

A Legend's Tips and Tools

Al Schmitt's had quite a career so far: He's been awarded seven Grammies: Best Engineered Album [non-Classical] — the first, for Henry Mancini's Hatari in 1962 and the most recent in 1996 for *Q's Jook Joint*. [Ed. note: By the time this book was published, Schmitt had received four more Grammies: In 1999, Best Engineered Album for *When I Look in Your Eyes*, Diana Krall; in 2000, two Latin Grammies, Best Pop Album and Album of the Year for Luis Miguel's *Amarte Es Un Placer;* and in 2001, Best Engineered Album, *The Look of Love*, Diana Krall.] He's also collected that coveted award for George Benson's *Breezin'*, *Toto IV*, Steely Dan's *Aja* and *FM*, and for Natalie Cole's *Unforgettable*. In addition to accumulating all those statues, he's been nominated for the award eleven more times, and he's recorded and/or mixed close to 200 Gold and Platinum albums.

Those achievements are mirrored in the respect Schmitt is accorded by his peers. Descriptions of him by people he's worked with tend to go like this: "Naturally musical with amazing ears," "Intuitive, and he gets the big picture," "Always goes the extra mile," "The consummate live engineer, nobody can touch him," and finally, "Al is a class act — just simply the best."

The owner of those amazing ears got his first job at age 19 at Apex Studios in New York City, where he worked with his mentor, Tom Dowd. He went on do to work for Atlantic and Prestige Records, then moved to California to work at Radio Recorders. When RCA opened its own studio at Sunset and Vine, Schmitt was the first engineer hired. He worked for that label as both a staff engineer and producer with artists including Jefferson Airplane, Sam Cooke, Eddie Fisher, and the Limelighters, before going independent in 1966.

These days, you'll find Schmitt working projects as diverse as ever. When I spoke with him, he was mixing at The Village with country artist Michael W. Smith. He'd just finished mixing a Lou Rawls album, recording with Paul Anka dueting with some original Sinatra tracks, and recording orchestras for Bette Midler and new artist Niles Rivers. His upcoming sessions include the stereo and 5.1 surround

Selected Credits

Anita Baker
Rhythm of Love

George Benson
*Breezin', In Flight,
Livin' Inside Your Love,
Absolute Benson*

Jackson Browne
*For Everyman,
Late for the Sky*

Natalie Cole
*Unforgettable:
With Love, Stardust,
Magic of Christmas,
Ask a Woman Who Knows*

Quincy Jones
Q's Jook Joint

Diana Krall
*When I Look In Your Eyes
Look of Love, Live in Paris*

Henry Mancini
*Breakfast at Tiffany's
Hatari!, Greatest Hits*

Joe Sample
Old Places Old Faces

Frank Sinatra
Duets, Duets II

Barbra Streisand
*The Way We Were
[Original Soundtrack],
Mirror Has Two Faces*

Toto
Toto IV, Tambu, Mindfields

Robbie Williams
Swing When You're Winning . . .

Lee Ann Womack
Season for Romance

mixes at Capitol for Vince Gill's Christmas album, an orchestra date with producer David Foster for a Van Cliburn theme for Las Vegas's Bellagio Hotel, album mixing for Monica Mancini, and recording and mixing for the Benny Carter Big Band. You'd think at this stage in his career Schmitt could take weekends off! Instead, on the Saturday we met, he took a long lunch break and settled in for some questions.

Can you describe your style of engineering?

I think a big part of it is the way I started and learned. I've been in the recording studio since I was seven. That's the truth. My uncle had a studio, so as a kid, on weekends, I'd go over and hang out. Seven years old on the subway by myself, from Brooklyn to Manhattan, and I'd spend the weekend watching them recording. They did everything with one microphone.

Then, when I finally started to work in the business, the studio I started at had a 6-input console. We could put up six microphones. I worked with Tommy Dowd, and I learned how to mike—how to get the most out of an instrument and how to place people in the room to capture the best sound with as few microphones as possible. So basically, what I do is acoustic. It's microphone technique. I rarely, rarely use EQ. If you go in and look at the board, you'll see. I may use EQ if I'm mixing something someone else recorded, but, if it's something I've done, I hardly use it at all. And I don't use much limiting or compression. If I do use a compressor or limiter, I'll use a tube one, and I'll pull maybe a dB—I'll use it mostly to get the sound of the tube.

Also, I learned to do everything at one time. When I was doing all those Mancini dates and those Ray Charles dates, it was all done in mono and 2-track, so what you got on tape was it. You had to make sure you got a good balance, and the right perspective in bass, drums, guitar, strings, vocal, echo… It all had to be done at the same time. "Fix it in the mix" was unheard of. There was no mix.

Explain a bit more about how you place a mic.

After years and years of experience, I know most microphones, and if something doesn't sound right to me, I'll move the mic a bit and see what that does, or I'll change the microphone. I'll change a Neumann 67 for another Neumann 67—because they don't all sound the same.

Certainly, if you've got a mic on the kick drum, just moving the mic an inch can make a difference. The same with acoustic guitar or pianos. I used to watch guys have a mic up, and they'd want something to be brighter, and so they'd add 8 dB of EQ to it. That

would be so strange to me. Instead, I'll change the microphone to enhance the sound. To me, unless you're trying for an effect, adding 8 dB of anything is really radical.

I hear you kept a notebook when you were starting out.

I had one of those notebooks like kids take to grade school, and when I watched dates, I'd draw a sketch—a diagram of where they had the microphones—note what microphones, and so forth. That really helped me early in my career. When I would have to do something, I'd get my notebook out. When I first had to do a large orchestra with woodwinds and strings, I was nervous, and I went to a guy named Bob Dougherty, who helped me out. I watched a bunch of his dates and drew sketches. I was worried about recording French horns and so forth, but he told me not to worry, that it was easy. And it was easy. I finally learned, after many times of doing it, that the more people you have in the studio, the easier it is to record. Recording 65 pieces is a snap. It's much more difficult to record an 8-piece! I did something recently with David Foster for Quest for Camelot where we had a 95-piece orchestra.

There's nothing that sounds like 95 pieces going off—you open up those microphones with 8 basses and 12 celli, and 32 violins... It's just magnificent, and really, it's basically all captured with the overhead microphones. You know, I don't have any secrets. Anyone who wants to know what I do—I'm glad to tell them exactly how I do it. Then, they go on and perfect it to their own taste.

Is it true that your first real session was with Duke Ellington and that you didn't know about it in advance?

I had no idea, and I probably would've stayed home if I'd known. I was three months at Apex Studios, and I had graduated to the point where I could do what they called demo records. These were little voice and piano things where somebody had written a song, and they'd come in, and play it on piano and sing. We'd give them a disc, and they left.

It was a Saturday, and I had three things to do. The first one, as I recall, was a cantor. The guy came in and just canted, and I got it on record and gave it to him. The next one was voice and piano—happy birthday to Joe or Sam or whatever. And my last thing, called Mercer, was scheduled for two o'clock in the afternoon and looked like it was booked for half an hour. So I'm waiting for Mr. or Mrs. Mercer, and the next thing I know, the elevators open up and these guys are getting out with trumpets and trombones and saxophones saying, "We're here for the record date." So I said, "Wait a minute, there's a mistake! There's no record date here," and they're saying "Oh yeah, Mercer Records, two o'clock."

I tried to call my boss, I tried to call Tom Dowd, and couldn't reach anybody. We didn't have a maintenance guy; it was just me by myself, and I had to do it. So I got my notebook out and saw what the big band setup was, and we set up everything. Duke Ellington couldn't play piano, because it was actually for Mercer records, his son's label, but they were using the Ellington band, and he sat right next to me. I kept saying "I've never done this before, this is a mistake, and I'm not qualified!" And he kept patting me, and saying "We'll get through this."

So you, all alone, set up microphones, used the console, ran the lathe....

Made sure the exhaust was going on and cut the shellac, as they used to call it.

And wore a tie and a jacket.

Definitely. It was great, when it was over. I felt really good that I did it, but if I'd known the night before, I honestly don't know if I would've come to work. I felt so frightened.

It's what you dream about, and it's what you're in the business for, but the fear.... I remember the first big orchestra date I did—about sixty pieces. I was so nervous that when I walked up to the console I kept my hands in my pockets because they were shaking so much. And when I sat down, I took my hands out of my pockets and grabbed onto the big rotary faders, just so people wouldn't see my hands shake.

Isn't it true that the way you work, you're really mixing right from the beginning—changing levels while you're recording if need be.

When I start a date, I'm planning ahead, and as I'm doing the date I'm not only recording and getting it on tape, I'm also getting it ready to mix to 2-track, so I have an idea of how I'm going to place things. I also try to use similar echoes to what I'll use in mixdown. I think that's something young engineers should get into—to think ahead, not just to think, "Let me get this right now, and I'll worry about that later."

What are those echoes and reverbs you like to use?

Well, of course, I learned on live chambers, and I still like live chambers. That's one of the reasons I love Capitol Studios. They also have one at Village that's great.

When I was a staff engineer at RCA, I used to use five large chambers—one each for center, left, and right; one for left-center; and one for right-center. That's how the returns came back. So if I was putting something in the chamber on the left, it came back on the left also. That's where the echo stayed. It wasn't like using it in stereo. It gave you a lot more transparency. And I always made sure the chambers were working well. I used quality microphones in them—tube 47s—and the walls were shellacked to have a glassy surface. So I still use live chambers when I can. I also like to use plates. I love the old EMT 250. I have the TC Electronic M5000—there are some great chambers in there that I use. And I also like the Lexicon 480. I use a lot of different, discrete echoes: one just for the strings, one for the vocals, and another for drums. I never have a lot of things going into the same chamber.

Are you still mainly recording to analog?

Yes. I prefer it. I did just use digital on the Vince Gill record. We used the new Studer, and I was surprised. It sounded really good. I also hear the 24-bit Sony sounds great. But before that project, I was never really thrilled with digital sound. Analog always sounds much better to me. Even in situations where I'm doing a large orchestra—say Johnny Mandel or something, and he'll want to use a lot of tracks, we'll lock up two 24-track analogs and record that way. It's a little slow, but I prefer it to 48-track digital.

You mix to half-inch.

Usually to half-inch BASF 900 +5 or 6, and on some occasions I'll use Dolby SR.

You've worked with some of the greatest singers. How do you make them feel comfortable.

First of all, when you've been around as long as I have, they know what you've done, and they have confidence.

Well, conversely, I would think sometimes they'd almost be afraid of you!

That has happened with a couple of singers. With one artist, she was so nervous because I was there, I seriously thought about having the assistant do it and walking out of the room so she wouldn't be so intimidated. That's a tough thing to say, but it's true, and so funny because for someone who sings as well as she does....

But singers are often like that—very sensitive.

Exactly. So you just make friends. It's almost like you're stroking them into a sense of, "Look, we're going to get this done, and I want you to be as comfortable as you can. We're gonna put the microphone here. If it's uncomfortable here, we'll move it a little bit. We're gonna make sure you hear well. If there's anything you'd like in the phones, let us know." You try to make them feel like it's their environment, and it usually works.

How do you choose mics for the singer? Do you put up several?

Sometimes. I usually have two or three that I particularly like, and if I know the singer and the type of voice, I pretty much know what microphone I want to use. Again, if the kind of song they're singing changes—sometimes with one artist on ten or twelve songs, we'll use two or three different mics. But generally, I'll use either a 251, a 67, a tube 47, or an M149.

Usually, I'll start with one, and I'll have another warming up right there so if I'm not thrilled, I'll quickly change it. You don't want the artist to think that you're experimenting, so it's nice when you're confident about what you are doing. I also have certain preamps that I like. I use the Martec a lot lately, and I use Doug Sax's Mastering Lab preamps. I love those. So on vocals, it's either one of those. My chain is usually the good microphone into one of those preamps, into the Summit limiter for maybe a dB. I use mostly hand limiting. I ride gain on the vocals, but I use the Summit for the sound.

Do you set up the headphone mixes?

Not as much as I used to, I work with certain guys all the time like Bill Smith and Charlie Paakkari who are so good at that, they really have it down, and I don't get involved so much any more. They're tweaking all the time we're recording, making sure that everything is set. Really, they're mixing the earphones. That's why I like to work with certain people at certain studios—my assistants are always completely involved. It used to be, you turned around and you'd see the guy running the tape machine reading a magazine. That never happens on my dates. Everybody is involved, and everybody gets respect for what they do. I think that's important, and I think the guys then give even more.

Do you own any equipment?

I own a lot, microphones mostly, and preamps: a Martec preamp, the Studer valve preamp—we use that as an A-to-D converter also. Summit limiters. I also own Mastering Lab speakers.

I was just going to ask what speakers you use.

I listen on Mastering Lab speakers, the ones that Doug Sax put together. I bring them around with me. I have two sets, but I need to get one more for doing surround.

Since you use so little EQ, how do you get instruments, especially drums, bright enough?

Again, for me it's where you put the microphones and how they sound. You don't want to be adding a lot of high end to violins or even drums. You can do it with microphones. On the snare, I use a [Sennheiser] 451 or 452 on top, and under I have a [Shure SM]57 that's out of phase. So if I need more crispness, more of the snare sound, I can bring the bottom up and get it that way. I use a 451 on the hi-hat, [AKG] 414s on the toms, and I use bright mics on the overheads—[Neumann M]149s or [AKG]C12s—something that gets a nice cymbal sound. I may add a little air around 20,000. If it's in a big enough studio, I'll use [Neumann]M50s in the room, and that's usually the drum sound. It's really where you put things, how you mix them, and how you use the echoes that makes them sound right.

What mic might you use on bass drum?

An AKG D112 mostly. Sometimes, I'll use two: a D112 up close and tight, and maybe a Neumann FET 47 farther away.

The other thing that's very important to the sound is where you place the musicians in the room. The more comfortable they are, the closer together they are, the tighter they are, the better things sound and the better they play. If you can work it out so that the musicians can play without 'phones, that's ideal. If they can run something down and not have to worry about having the 'phones on, they hear better and the level they play at is comfortable.

Years ago, when we were worried about leakage, guys would try spreading the musicians out, moving them farther and farther away from each other. Well, the drummer would then play louder and louder! So I learned that moving guys closer together made them play at a more comfortable level. It worked better for me and for them.

People are concerned that placing the musicians close together causes problems with leakage, but I learned that leakage is your friend back when we'd record everything at once direct to 2-track. A lot of times, what you picked up from the drums was the leakage going into the bass microphone, acoustic pianos, and so forth. On big band dates, you'd have a mic on the drums, but a lot of the sound was from the drums leaking into other instruments' mics—and it's that leakage that actually will make things sound big. Which is why you should always use really good mics, because you are getting leakage into a really good microphone so the leakage sounds good, and that makes a big difference.

Some more mic questions, please. What do you usually use on a horn section?

Neumann 67s on trumpets, saxes, and trombones, and for the trumpets I'll put them in

omnidirectional. You don't have to worry about much leaking into them, because trumpets are the loudest thing in the room.

I do that a lot with strings too: I use 67s and put them in omnidirectional. The mic sounds better, and you get the room also—that sound coming back off the ceiling or whatever.

People sometimes ask me, "If you only had one mic what would it be?" And it would probably be a Neumann 67, or maybe lately, the M149. I really love that mic. It's gorgeous with a lot of power and a lot of gain. But before that, it was a 67. You can use it on vocals, strings, brass, piano; it works well on anything.

You'd use the 67 on baritone sax as well?

Yes. Again, where you place the mic is so important. The sound doesn't come just from the bell. A lot of people make that mistake. The same with a clarinet —a lot of the sound is coming from around the keys. I always tell guys to go out in the room and listen. Listen to what the instrument sounds like. Then go inside and try to duplicate it. That's what your job is. You're trying to capture that sound out there. I always try, if it's an orchestra date, to be out in the room on the first rundown so I can hear what the arrangement's about and what it sounds like. Then the next time they're running it down, I'm inside getting myself together.

How do you mic French horns?

I use M49s lately. They sound really good. Where you place the mic depends on the sound and the arrangement. In some cases, I'll put the mics behind the French horns, so I'm capturing sound right off the bell. Other times, I'll put the mics in front, with a reflector behind the horns so the sound will come off of it. Most studios have gobos that have a hard side, or I put them in a spot in the room where they're going to reflect off a wall. So, it just depends.

But you have to decide before you start.

Not necessarily. I try to figure it out ahead of time, but sometimes I listen to the arrangement during the rundown and say, "Oops, let's get them out front."

Okay, what's that famous basic Al Schmitt string setup? Two mics in the front up high....

M149s or M50s when you can find them. I keep trying to talk Neumann into making the M50s again—no luck, yet. But I just saw a new mic that they came up with. They only had one, and it's handmade—an M147 that will be out some time this year. It's patterned after the old 47, and it's going to be a really nice microphone.

And 67s on the strings....

Usually two mics on the string section, maybe one or two on the violas, and another couple on the celli, depending on the size of the orchestra.

For the basses, I try to use tube 47s. There's a lot of warmth to them, nice fat bottom. They always sound good, and the bass players appreciate it also. They like those mics.

What advice would you give young engineers who want to know how to have a career as long and successful as yours?

Enjoy every day. Enjoy what you're doing. And also, try to learn something new every day.

When I go home at night, I'll think about that: "What did I learn today that I didn't know?" I consciously do that, and usually there's something, some little thing that I learned. You have to keep learning. There's a lot of things that young engineers do that I hear, and I'll ask, "How did you do that, how did you get that sound?"

My son gets in the car with me with his tapes and plays rap music all the time, and once in a while I'll hear something and think, "How the hell did they do this?" And I'll get the tape from him and bring it into the studio with some assistants and try to figure out how they did it. And I may wind up using it myself or using something similar to it.

I also think it's important to work on different kinds of music. I was really fortunate in my years at RCA that I got to do classical music, country, jazz, and pop. And I still work on all different kinds of music.

So you're still glad to be going to work in the morning.

Absolutely. Setting up an orchestra, putting up mics, and seeing the same woodwind players and string players you see all the time, you get to know everybody, and they help you and you help them. It's always nice when I see somebody who says to me, "I'm glad to see it's you working. I know we'll have a good day." Things like that make me feel good.

Really, we are all blessed in this business. Because, in this business, if you don't like what you do, you don't become good at it. Most of the people you're working with love what they do. Every day isn't perfect, but overall, what's not to love? It's fun to hang around in the studio with musicians. We always make sure we eat well, [laughs] and we make good music.

DAVE JERDEN

Taking Care of Fundamentals From Jane's to Chains, The Offspring, and Beyond

DECEMBER, 1998

A quick perusal of his credits shows that Dave Jerden has worked on a lot of really cool records. He blends a bit of the purist with the iconoclast, and he's assembled a discography that cuts a wide swathe through musical styles. Jerden was one of the very first engineers to use samples, being the recording and mixing engineer on Herbie Hancock's groundbreaking 1984 album *Future Shock* and its hit single "Rockit." He was also the guy behind the board for that unforgettable moment when the guitars come slamming in on Alice In Chains' "Rooster" from 1996's *Dirt*. A few other highlights: Jerden was the recording and mixing engineer on Talking Heads' *Remain In Light* and David Byrne and Brian Eno's *My Life in the Bush of Ghosts*, and the producer/mixer of Jane's Addiction's *Nothing's Shocking* and *Ritual de lo Habitual*, Social Distortion's *Social Distortion* and *Somewhere Between Heaven and Hell*, and the Offspring's *Ixnay on the Hombre*. He has also worked with Frank Zappa, Tom Verlaine, Jane Child, Red Hot Chili Peppers, Anthrax, and the Rolling Stones.

A previous interviewer called Jerden a "sonic bricklayer," an apt description that conveys his unique blend of skills—artistic, yet all business. He's a guitar-loving rock engineer who is also totally comfortable with technology. In person, he comes across as intense, highly creative, and quite serious, with a demeanor rescued from severity by frequent flashes of dry humor.

He'd just finished mixing the Offspring's latest release, *Americana* [*Billboard* Number 1 and multi-platinum smash], when we found him at El Dorado, his Los Angeles recording studio of choice. It's an industrial, warehouse-type space, and the control room was equipped with three separate computer rigs, a super-sized road case packed with guitar amp heads, and a second wall-sized road case filled with Summit tube gear. As we talked, Jerden seemed to be in constant motion—opening road cases to display a piece of gear, paging through screens on a computer, pacing out to the studio to point out a detail. Even in repose, he emanates a considerable energy field.

Did you start out as a guitar player?

Guitar and bass. I started playing in bands when I was twelve. My father was a bass player, and he encouraged me. Most kids, when they get their first guitar, it's a piece of crap. But when I took an interest in playing guitar, my father bought me a really nice Gibson. Then, when I had an opportunity to play bass in a band, he bought me a Fender Precision Bass. I played in bands early on, not because I was any good, but because I had good equipment.

Did you take lessons?

For a few years. My dad was always trying to push me toward heavy reading. He had goals for me to be a jazz musician.

Wait a minute. Nobody's parents' goal is for their kid to be a jazz musician!

I was really fortunate. All along the way, I had encouragement from my family. And when I crossed over to engineering, they were also totally supportive.

How did you make that transition?

I wasn't making any real money as a musician. I was in a band with Eddy Schreyer, who has Oasis Mastering now, and he went to engineering school, so I decided to try it. It was called the University of Sound Arts. It wasn't any great shakes, but one thing I learned there was what books to read. I bought this one book, *Modern Recording Techniques*, by Runstein, and I memorized it. I figured if I knew everything in that book, it would give me a good start. I still to this day use a lot of what I learned in that book.

So you went to school and read books and got a job as an assistant?

I got a job at Smoketree Studios as engineer/assistant/whatever. After that, I worked at a studio called Redondo Pacific, and after I left there, El Dorado hired me because they'd just purchased an MCI automated console, which I knew how to run. That was the first El Dorado—it's now torn down—a studio built in the '60s for rock 'n' roll. Of course, this was the late '70s, and it was still in the '60s. I went in there, and the owner gave me $4,000 to redo the whole studio. So I hired an acoustician for one hour for $160 and had him write down on a napkin what he would do if he was going to remodel. Then I hired a foreman, brought in a crew and redid the control room. And that was the room where I did "Rockit" and worked with the Talking Heads.

That's where I really learned, because I was by myself. I did everything that came in the door and all the maintenance, too. Disco, country, or rock 'n' roll, I approached it all the same. If I didn't know how to do something, I'd get the book and read about it, or I'd make phone calls and pick people's brains.

How did "Rockit" come about?

I'd already worked with David Byrne and Brian Eno. Tony Meilandt, who worked for Herbie Hancock, came to the studio and said, "This will sound crazy, but if I put you with Herbie and this production team called Material, I know we'll get a Gold record."

Bill Laswell and Michael Beinhorn were the two Brooklyn guys who were Material. They had recorded the tracks, then they came out here, and we did overdubs in Herbie's garage and mixed it in a couple of days. The record company people came to the studio for the playback, and when it was over, they just sat there … stunned. Because there was this new thing called sampling on it, and scratching. And no singing. They were like,

Photo: Maureen Droney

"We've got to have vocals, let's put some vocals on it!" Bill Laswell was sitting there with a beer in his hand, and he laughed and said, "I've got a plane to catch."

About three months later, I was in Manhattan, and I saw a kid on the street with a beat box dancing to "Rockit." People were throwing money into a jar in front of him, and I thought, "My God, I've just recorded something big."

You met Herbie because you'd worked with Eno and Byrne. How did you meet them?

After we'd redone El Dorado, we were going to run an ad in *Mix* magazine. I looked at our pitiful equipment list. People back then were using nice live chambers and EMT 140s, and our reverb unit was a BX10, a little cheap, dark, spring reverb. I couldn't advertise that, so I made up something. I said we had a new digital thing called a Lexicon 224. My plan was to go to the owner if we got any bites and say we had to go out and buy it. I'd done this before. He always came through when he saw a need for something that we'd actually make money on.

About a week after *Mix* came out, Brian Eno called. He'd read about the 224 and wanted to look at it. In a panic, I called an equipment broker who had one that was going to The Village Recorder. It was the only one in town, and everybody was screaming to get their hands on it, but I begged him to let me borrow it, and he did.

Luckily, it was easy to use.

I learned it literally an hour before Eno got there. He walked in, and I acted like I knew all about it. How he listened to it was by using some cassettes of beats that he was working on. We scrolled through the different sounds, and I said, "These tracks are really cool." Brian said, "You like this stuff?" and we started talking about music, and then he left. A few days later, the studio manager said, "You must have made a great impression on Brian Eno; he just booked nine weeks with David Byrne." And out of that, I went to the Bahamas and did *Remain in Light*.

Somebody told me once, "If you can picture yourself doing something, you can get there." Well, for me, it's the same with equipment. If I imagine myself using the piece of equipment I want, somehow it arrives in my life. The latest thing my engineer Brian Carlstrom and I were imagining was a full digital studio, and now we've got forty-eight tracks of 24-bit Pro Tools.

You've thought about a digital studio for a long time.

I've always been interested in the idea of hard disk recording. The problem was reliability. The Pro Tools sounds great, and I like all the plug-ins. We haven't had any problems—no system crashes, no loss of information. The biggest problem, I think, even for those with experience, is it leads you to a lot of choices. You can get lost in it. We're good at avoiding that problem. Brian [Carlstrom], my assistant Annette Cisneros, and I have done a lot of records together. So we approach our recordings the same as always. We don't get lost in the process, and instead of adapting to the Pro Tools method, we have the Pro Tools method adapt to us.

Do you record directly to Pro Tools?

We do, on overdubs. We start off on the Studer for tracking, and I mix to the Studer half-inch.

I'm surprised that you record guitars directly to Pro Tools.

Some of them we do, some go to analog. There's so much opinion about digital and analog, and through the years, I've been involved—on the sidelines or actively—in all these different arguments about equipment: about VCAs not being any good, Neve versus SSL, blah blah blah. My whole philosophy has always been to use what gets the job done the best.

I've mixed stuff that's been done on really cheap equipment that sounds gorgeous, and I've worked on a lot of stuff that's been done on all the proper high-end gear, and it sounds like crap. It's all in how you record it. Because most people don't know what a good sound is, they just go fishing.

I've always heard that if you replaced a sound, you were quick to get rid of the original.

[Laughs] It's not that I have to erase stuff to keep my psychological center; it's just practicality. Sometimes, I'd do that only because I didn't have the opportunity to save stuff, because I didn't work in studios where I could make slave after slave. But I don't see any point in holding on to something if I know what I'm going with. I don't always erase everything, but I have absolutely no problem making decisions.

When I first started out, I had a 24-track machine and a 28-in board, so all my recording had to be very organized, and I had to print all my effects. When I shoved up my faders for mixing, it was pretty much just balancing and we were done. I still print any important effects. I'm economical, and I don't leave choices for later.

The studio here seems very live. Is that where you like to put the drums?

Actually, I usually put the drums in the smaller iso booth, then I put a P.A. system out in the studio and pump the drums back out through that. It's a way to control the amount of cymbals, because when you set up in a live room, you often get too much of them. I also control how much cymbals I get by how far I open the sliding door between the booth and the room. That way, I can vary the sound and tailor it for each song, instead of having the same drum sound for the whole album.

I also use Ibanez DM1100s on the room sounds. I got turned onto them when I was doing Jane's Addiction; Perry [Farrell] used one onstage for his vocal so he could adjust the delays and effects as he was singing. He lost the box, though, after the *Nothing's Shocking* tour, and we couldn't find another one. Then, just a couple of years ago, I was in Black Market Music and I found two of them. The guy said, "You can have these pieces of junk for a hundred bucks each." I've been using the hell out of them since, and one thing I use them on is drums.

It's a chorus and delay.

It's a delay unit. Within that, you can get chorus and phasing. See, the most important thing for me in recording is taking care of the fundamentals. The physics of sound are so simple, there aren't really that many things that you can do with it. You can change the level, the amplitude, the phase—anywhere from 0 to 360. And you can change the time—you can delay a sound. That's it.

Everything you hear in the studio comes from those fundamentals. If you look at phase and use it to your advantage, being aware of how time can relate to phasing and being aware of amplitude, as far as the Fletcher Munsen curve—all that stuff—you can create the effects you want. You've got to be aware of the basics. For example, I use a sound pressure meter when I work.

That's pretty rare in a recording studio.

Well, the optimal level for mixing is 84 dB. I have a mark here [on the monitor pot] where 84 dB is, but I still check it every once in a while.

Why optimal?

Remember, 84 dB on the Fletcher Munsen curve is the optimum between highs and lows, as the human ear hears them. When things get lower in volume, the bass tends to go away, so you'll put too much in. At low volumes, you may also tend to put on too much high end. If you listen too low, when you turn it back up, it may be too bassy and too bright. On the other hand, if you listen too loud, the stuff may come out bass- and presence-shy.

Those fundamentals are the most solid ground you can work on. I think people often overlook that, now. They think in terms of, "This is recording." But it isn't. It's sound. I also like to keep track in a mathematical way of all that stuff. I know what my delay times are from the earliest room sound, all the way up to a half note, and the triplets.

Why?

I don't use reverb much, so how I get a spacious sound if I want it—instead of just slapping on a reverb unit, which may just sound dark—is to use various delays.

Reverb is just reflections, coming from how far the walls are apart within a certain spatial environment. Digital reverbs use algorithms, which are mathematical templates that will simulate a room size with delays. What I do is to take the tempo and meter of the song and set up delays that correspond to those reflections—the earliest reflection in a room sound would be about 30 milliseconds, all the way up to a half note, and the triplets, and the dotted notes.... I set up all these delay times for the tempo of the song. If the tempo changes, I recalculate.

Having the basics down frees you up to be creative.

It's easier to learn a few basic rules than it is to try to learn every piece of equipment. You can spend your time learning how a Harmonizer 949 works, then some day, you don't have one and you want that sound. Well, think about what that 949 is doing. There's so many different ways to solve a problem. You don't need to have a 949 to have its sound.

If I was stuck on a desert island, I'd need something that could delay, and it could just be a tape machine. And I'd need something that you could change the phase with—that could be a soldering iron. So maybe a tape machine and a soldering iron is all I'd need.

When I set up mics, for doing drums, the first thing I'm always thinking about is phase. Will one mic serve better than putting up four mics? I keep that in mind, thinking, one foot equals one millisecond. Sound travels at 1,100 feet per second at 70 degrees at sea level, and a millisecond is one-thousandth of a second, so, basically, one foot is one millisecond.

So, you're using the three-to-one rule to prevent phase cancellation.

There's that, and there's also the other one, the 9 dB one, where you can look at your console meters, and, if you have a mic on the snare, and it's picking up a tom over here, the tom should be 9 dB down from the main snare signal so there are no phase discrepancies.

Uh, do you own stock in Summit?

[Laughs] No, my engineer does. I like the sound of tubes. We use the preamps, compressors, EQ… line mixers, too; there's a full studio in this rack. We mainly just use the console for monitoring and mixing. Even though I use the VCAs on the SSL to mix in the end, and I'm recording on Pro Tools, the first introduction from the outside world into the studio of every sound is always through tubes.

What are your favorite microphones?

Lately, I've been using really cheap mics, like ones that come with phone machines, because there's a color I'm going for. But I do like Telefunken 251s, U47s, and C-12s. As for a desert island mic, probably the most versatile is an SM57, and for a good, balanced condenser mic, the U87, or my favorite, the U67.

What mics do you use on drums?

My setup for drums is pretty much the same all the time, and probably the same as anybody else's. More important than the selection of the mics is the selection of the drums. I use the Drum Doctor,

Ross Garfield, a lot; he's got three snares I like. I mic the top and bottom of the snare with SM57s, with the phase flipped on the bottom. I like a fatter hi-hat sound, almost like a heavy metal hi-hat, so I go for those kind of cymbals, and on that I'll use either a KM84 or a Sennheiser 451, with pads. I always top- and bottom-mic the toms, unless they're concert toms, and I almost always use toms with top and bottom heads. I use Sennheiser 421s on the top and SM57s or 421s on the bottom, with the phase flipped on the bottom. For overheads, C-12's or 87s or 414s, and I try to make sure the ride cymbal is picked up properly. Sometimes, I have the mics over the drummer's head with a stereo technique, or I'll just have them spread out. Sometimes, I'll use various condensor mics, 84s or 451s, as filler mics to pick up china cymbals, or whatever else they may have.

For bass drum, I use an AKG D112. I put a sandbag in there, and usually I have a front head on with a hole cut in it. I like using smaller bass drums. They've got more punch—a 22- or an 18-inch kick sounds great to me. A 26 is good if you've got the right room for it and you want to go for a Bonham sound, but if I'm going for a sound like that, I use less mics and a lot of compression with Fairchild 670s, going for that classic "Andy Johns" drum sound. But usually, I stick to smaller kick drums. And of course, I compress everything when I'm recording.

How do you mike electric guitars?

A 57 angled in at 45 degrees, coming in somewhere between the center and the edge of the cone.

That's quite a large road case your amp heads are in.

I prefer to have the amp heads in the room when I record. I had the cases designed by Anvil. We hook them all up, and I can go through them, boom, boom, boom, and see what we want to use.

Do you triamp the speakers?

What you mean, I think, is what I call triple tracking—I approach guitar sounds with highs, mids, and lows. So, instead of bringing all three up with one sound and one amp, using EQ, I'll use an amp basically dedicated to lows, one delegated to midrange, and one for high end. I might use a Vox, or a Matchless cabinet like an AC30 with a Big Muff. That will give a big bottom end, especially with a Les Paul. Then for midrange, I'll use some kind of Marshall, a 50- or 100-watt lead, or a Bogner, and for high end I'll use a Soldano or another Bogner for a more piercing sound. The basis of the sound is the Marshall in the middle, and I'll bring the others into the mix. I don't mix them onto one track. They stay on separate tracks all the time—for some reason, it just sounds better. I'll use three amps for the bass, too, when I'm tracking.

To split the tracks, I use something called the Lucas Deceiver, which is a box that takes care of the ground problems. It's an active splitter, with an op amp. Terry Manning builds them down in the Bahamas. I love the Deceiver. People ask me all the time how I split the signal; then they try to do it without one, and they give up because of all the ground buzzes and stuff.

Do you own a lot of outboard gear?

What I own is more musical stuff—amps, synths. I do own some EQs—Trident A range, a Neve Prism rack, Massenburg, API 550s—but the outboard tools I use are pretty simple. When I mix, I have only a couple of things plugged in on the board: an H3000 Harmonizer, my AMS DDL, and maybe a long delay. All the other effects have already been recorded. It's not like some guys, who have to have 100-input boards because they have all this stuff set up.

I understand setting up a bunch of equipment and just seeing what's going to happen. I've done that. But in the mixing process, there are already a lot of creative decisions to be made, so I believe that when you get to mixing, you're not recording anymore, you're not creating in that sense anymore—you're creating in the sense of putting together the song.

Do you still spend a few days in the studio getting comfortable before you record?

When I'm recording a whole album, there's a period where I'm trying to acclimate the band to the studio. I get them used to the headphones, the smell of the studio, what the coffee tastes like. It only takes a couple of days. The point being, if you are going to do something important in the creative world, you have to look beyond just pushing around faders. There has to be a bond made between the producer, the band, and the engineer. It's almost like a family, and you have to understand each other and establish trust.

Also, recording should be fun. It shouldn't be this arduous process of 18-hour days, seven-day weeks, to where you've totally lost perspective and you're completely burned out. It should be fun, like going to play a baseball game.

Bill Szymzyck once said to me his philosophy in the studio is, "If you're not having fun, it's time to go home."'

I agree. I don't have any problem going all night if everybody's having a good time and it's working, but how I generally schedule my work is six days a week, eight hours a day. Now that's the hours I'm in the studio. The engineer will be here more hours, making backups, etc. But the eight hours I'm here are all focused work. I've got a goal for the day, and when I'm done with it, we go home.

I saw a quote from you in *HiFi* where you said your style as a producer is to do your job and to let everybody else do theirs. But you didn't say what your job is.

When people ask me to produce a record, that means, to me, to make a record by whatever means. I may be a psychiatrist, a technician, a musician, but the overlying important thing is that I have a point of view all the time. The main job, which may include all those other duties on top of it, is to be a person who has a point of view and maintains it on the whole project. I let the musicians make the record and do their parts, but it's in the framework of a point of view that we've all agreed on. Because productions can get lost really quickly if the objective has not been maintained.

To do this, I use my initial reactions as a listener, and I ask questions. What do I expect to hear from this person or this band? What is the essence of this band? That is, stripping away everything they're not, and then looking at what's left. We get in agreement, musically and stylistically, about what they are, and we form a general image of what it's going to be, the theme. We fine-tune as we go along, but we're always moving toward the objective, so at the end of the day we can say, "Yeah, we made the record we wanted to make." That's the job.

Kevin "KD" Davis

Selected Credits

Eric Benet
A Day in the Life,
True to Myself

Blu Cantrell
So Blue

Coolio
"Gangsta's Paradise,"
Dangerous Minds Soundtrack

Destiny's Child
The Writing's On The Wall,
Survivor

Montell Jordan
Let's Ride,
Montell Jordan

Mya
"Case Of The Ex,"
Fear Of Flying

N'Sync
"It Makes Me Ill,"
No Strings Attached

Pink
"Just Like A Pill,"
M!ssundaztood

Tupac Shakur
Me Against The World

TLC
3D

Usher
"You Remind Me," *8701*

Quick Hits at an Early Age

"Wunderkind" is probably the most appropriate label for Kevin "KD" Davis. Still in his early twenties, Davis is a one-man mix factory, working six to seven days a week at his favorite Los Angeles room, Larrabee North's Studio 1, where he focuses on cranking out pop and r&b chart-toppers for the likes of Coolio, Montell Jordan, Brandy, K-Ci & JoJo, Adina Howard, Somethin' for the People, Keith Sweat, SWV, Chante Moore, Oleta Adams, New Edition—the list goes on and on.

Maybe Davis relates so well to what the kids out there are buying because he's not that far away from being one himself. Or maybe musicality just runs in his genes; both of his parents were professionals in the music business. Trying to get some hints about the secrets of his success, I dropped into Larrabee one afternoon for a visit and found Davis to be low key, friendly, and modest to the point of shyness when discussing the subject of his early-in-life achievements.

You were a recording studio rugrat.

Yeah, I was born into the music business. My father, Mark Davis, is a producer who worked with people like Sly Stone and Natalie Cole, and my mother, Ivory Stone, is a songwriter. She also sang backup for Smokey Robinson. She's been doing that since I was three or four years old. I was always around studios, playing in the game room or, many nights, sleeping on the couch.

And I always had some kind of musical equipment around the house that I was trying to have fun with—keyboards or drum machines. Being around studios as a little kid, I always wanted to touch all the buttons, and get in there and do something. At age 14 or so, I went out on tour with my mom as a roadie, learning the live end of the business, setting up the stage, doing bags, whatever. I did that for a few years, and then one of the sound guys suggested that I go to recording school, to take what I knew and apply it at a professional level. So in '91, I went to the L.A. Recording Workshop. I knew

Photo: Maureen Droney

before that that I wanted to work in the studio and make records, but I didn't know how to get there.

What was your first job after recording school?

I started at Cornerstone Studios in Chatsworth as a runner/assistant. That was a good thing, because at the bigger studios, you have to start out as a runner and work your way up to get to be an assistant. But at that type of studio, it's so small you just do everything. I was hired as an assistant, but if somebody needed food, I went to get it. I was there about a year, and I got a great deal of knowledge. Then I moved to Soundcastle, and was a full-time assistant for about a year-and-half, and then I went independent.

That's pretty quick to go out on your own.

I had a couple of clients I was working with a lot, tracking for, at Soundcastle. A lot of times, people would come in, they didn't have an engineer, and they would need someone to help them track. I built up a good relationship with some of those people who kept coming in, and I just started urging them to give me a shot at doing their mixes. In my early stage, it kind of sounded strange....

You mean it sounded strange to ask them?

[Laughs] No, I mean the mixes sounded strange! Because I was just trying to get the gig. But the clients heard that I had something, so they kept going with me, and I still work with a lot of the same people today. Some of my main clients are the same people I started off with. Somethin' for the People, Laney Stewart, Tricky Stewart—we all got our start together.

So you were developing some clients, doing a few mixes. How did you go from that to being so in demand?

I don't know, word of mouth? I hope it's people hearing what I've done and liking it. But it's a blessing, really; it just started snowballing.

You have a lot of loyal clients. Why do you think they stay with you?

A lot of my main clients, we just relate well together, and they know me from when they started, when they weren't as good as producers, and I wasn't as good as an engineer. We've come up together, so at this point it's like, they're a little bit more successful now, I'm a little bit more successful now, why change it? It's not broken, so why try to change it up?

Do you think you're easy to get along with?

I think so. If a producer comes in here and doesn't like what I've done, I'll change it. My main thing is I want the song to come off cool. I mix a lot of songs, and not every song is gonna be a hit; it's not gonna happen—you just can't make every song be a hit. So, I'll try to make the producer happy enough so he'll say "Kev is cool to work with. I like what he did with the song, and I know he'll get the job done."

When I was an assistant, I saw a lot of producers and engineers that were hard to get along with, and I always wondered why. I try to keep everything organized, but still be laid back. Because really, this job is so chill—I don't have a mean boss, I live right around the corner, I just don't have that much trouble. You know what I mean? There's just no reason to stress out too much. I do really try to keep things organized.

There can be stressful moments, though; for example, what do you do when you're working with a producer and you know that he or she is going down some wrong path that's going to keep you up all night?

[Laughs] There's different techniques to head that off. Engineers have their tricks, but we're not going to give them away here.

Do you work mostly on singles or on whole albums?

Both, right now. Earlier on, I did mainly singles—one song here or there because my clients were just getting to do one or two songs on an album. But now it seems like five or six songs at least on an album. Lately, I've built up more of a relationship with labels and the A&R departments. I've met a lot of producers through A&R, and it seems like when you get more label connections, you're more likely to get the majority of an album.

What makes an r&b hit? There seems to be such a formula today among songs—what do you think gives a tune that edge that makes people hear "Buy me!"

That's a good question, because, right now, to me, r&b is in bit of a lull as far as the creative element goes and having something new that sounds great. It's like you turn on the radio and hear a sample of something old, over and over again. I think the formula right now for a hit is something that makes the public remember from the old days. That's why these samples and remakes are selling so much and are on top of the charts. There's something familiar in every song that brings people back and makes them think of when they first heard the original song. Then, when they have their favorite artist, a rapper like Jay Z or a singer like Mary J. Blige or Faith Evans on the record, it's just all that much more—their favorite rapper with the old song that they used to love, together all at once. Right now, that's a hit formula.

Do you think you have a feel for when a song will be a hit? Say when you mixed "Gangster's Paradise" for Coolio.

Now, that's a funny one. We were mixing at Encore, and Coolio decided that he didn't really like the drums on tape, so at about two in the morning he changed all the drum sounds up. We were still mixing at six in the morning, and finally, when we were finished, we were so tired that we didn't even listen to the finished mixes—I just had the assistant print them after we left. The next time I heard it was on the radio, and then it seemed like it was everywhere, and I was like, "That's the song we did? Sounds pretty good." So no, I didn't know it was going to be a hit. But you do get a feel about a track sometimes when you put it up.

Do you have to do a lot of "mixing as arranging" — muting things, compiling vocals, making decisions about what stays and what goes?

It really depends. Sometimes I deal with producers who are organized, and sometimes I deal with producers who are unorganized. I guess it's about half and half. Sometimes I get a producer who's got great sounds, everything's arranged, the backgrounds are comped, everything's done, and all I've got to do is just push up the faders, add a little of my thing to it, and get the right balances. But sometimes, I have to fly vocals around, change drum sounds, and really get into it. Which I don't mind, if it's a good song. I can get excited about it because I'm adding to what could potentially be a hit. But, when it's just an "okay" song, and it's really got some work that needs to be done, those are the days I wish I could be at home instead.

My main clients for the most part are pretty well organized, things are set and done, and we may just add a few things here and there.

When you get tracks, what kind of shape are they in? A lot of engineers these days complain about track sheets, tracks that haven't been cleaned....

We do get some real crazy stuff, sometimes. But I've got a real good assistant here, Steve Macauley, and we just rip up their track sheets and redo and relabel everything.

Do you work mostly from analog or digital masters?

Usually, analog 48-track, although lately a lot more has been coming in that was cut on 48-track digital. But I also might transfer tracks to a hard disk, like the Akai DR16. I might transfer the vocals, because it takes SMPTE so quick—it locks up instantly, and when you don't have to wait for the two machines to lock up, it makes the work a whole lot simpler and quicker.

What format do you mix to?

I mix to Quantegy half-inch tape—30 ips at +9.

Do you work alone a lot, without the artist or producer being there?

It varies. I like to work alone to a certain point where they can come in and say, "Do this," or "That's fine," and a lot of producers will give me that liberty to do what I do. They come in after 6 or 7 o'clock and make a few changes. With my main clients, we tend to have a relationship. I already know how they want it to sound, and they know what I'm going to do, so when they come in there will be just a few things that we have to do.

Do you usually leave your mixes up overnight, spending a day-and-a-half on them?

It depends. With my main clients, I usually knock it out in a day, if it's just a straight mix. If we have to change things or put on more vocals, I like to get that leisure of taking a day-and-a-half, but sometimes, certain clients' budgets aren't to that point.

You're mixing mainly for radio. How do you keep up with the competition?

I listen to a lot of stuff in the car, both CDs and the radio. I don't listen too much at home because when I go home, I'm not really thinking about music. But being in Los Angeles, you spend at least an hour a day in the car, so you can be taking care of business when you're rolling around.

At the studio here, they have a Sony digital satellite system that broadcasts a lot of the music channels —r&b, rap, blues, jazz, '70s, soft and hard rock. I'll listen to those channels sometimes just to get familiar with what's playing. I have a MiniDisc player in my car, so to listen to my mixes, I record a MiniDisc at the studio.

Why MiniDisc instead of CD?

It's just easier. Also, the CD thing gets expensive. With a MiniDisc, you can record over and over, and you don't scratch them up as easily because they're in a case. CDs, you always scratch up. And you can label the MiniDiscs, so you know which one's playing. The MiniDisc doesn't sound as good as a CD, but it sounds a lot better than a cassette does. Like most engineers, I truly hate cassettes.

I'll burn a MiniDisc through an Apogee filter off of the console stereo bus, and in the car, I can get an idea of how it sounds. I know mastering is going to do a little something different to it, but it's still gonna be in the ballpark.

What do you monitor on in the studio? Do you use the big speakers?

I do a lot of my work on NS-10s—the old style, not the studio version. And I like my little Bose Freestyles that Barney Perkins turned me on to. I think Bose stopped making them for stores, but there's a private stock if you call the company. I love the way they sound. I often use a mono Auratone for vocal rides, and I do listen some on the big speakers. One of the things I like about this room at Larrabee is that you can throw the mix up on the big speakers and cruise for a while. It doesn't really hurt your ears.

You don't do much recording these days. Do you miss it?

Not at all. If you're working with a live band, it's a whole different story. That's fun when you're in there trying to get the right sounds. But if the music is coming out of a keyboard or a drum machine and you're just getting levels, waiting for it to lock up, and then dumping it—no fun.

When you first put up the tape, how do you know what you're going to feature? Like between the bass and the bass drum on a particular track?

It's just feel, and it depends on what the bass is doing patternwise and how it sounds, what sound each producer has chosen. The bass and drums have to be hitting to the point where you really feel the track, and you have to understand what the singers are saying. You can't have the track with just the bass and drums driving where you don't understand what the vocals are saying. In my early mixes, that was the big problem for me—trying to get a happy medium between the two. Now I always kind of put my vocals on top, and second you'll hear the kick or bass. Really, the main focal point is just vocals. That's what sells the song. Because if you're listening on a bad-sounding radio, what's important is for somebody to be able to sing the song, rather than to know what the bass drum is doing. It's work, though, because at the same time you've got to have the track hitting.

You always mix on SSL consoles.

I'm hooked on the 9000. It's hard for me to go back to a G. I like mixing on Neves also, but for me it's hard to find a Neve room that sounds good. I've been at Larrabee for a few years now, and when I go to other rooms it takes me a day-and-a-half to adjust. When I work here, I always know what it's going to sound like. It's true, when you play it loud on the big speakers and when you play it in your car.

A lot of tracks you've been working on lately have that really low, woofy, rubbery bass sound. What might you do to give it enough definition in the mix to work well with the drums?

I like to use the Distressor on drums, and I'll also use it on the bass; I'll just change the attack and release of each. The Distressor is great because you can manipulate it so much. And, on the kick, I might use an API 550A EQ—I love the sound of those—and on the bass something like a Pultec.

So, a tighter EQ on the kick, and more of a wash on the bass. And you might tie them together using the same type of compressor.

Yes.

When your tape comes in, what's the first thing you do?

I put it on and throw up the faders to see what's goin' on, see what kind of song it is: Is it a good song or not, does the singer sound right? Then I'll listen to it instrumentally, see what's not good, so I can take it out or throw it far back in the mix or fix it! I'll listen for what's good that I can feature and see what I can do to make it better. Sometimes, you can't really do much. No matter how much fixing you do, it's just going to be what it is. Then I'll lay the board out how I want it, see if I have to crosspatch.

Do you listen to rough mixes of the song?

If they have one they like. You can hear the song how it was when they first wrote it. Sometimes, it doesn't sound great, but they like the way it felt.

What's your favorite gear to use on vocals?

I love the Avalon 2055 on vocals—it's smooth. I also like to use LA-2As and Summit compressors, and maybe a Focusrite Red 3 compressor/limiter. I like GML or API EQ on the backgrounds.

Do you use much board EQ?

I'll do a lot of taking out of stuff that I don't like with outboard EQ, then I'll use the EQ on the board to bring out stuff that I do like. I love being able to use the E selection EQ on the J Series board.

Do you use the SSL stereo compressor?

No, I think it makes things sound a little small. I do use the Focusrite Red 3 across the stereo bus a lot. Focusrite is the smoothest; it seems to warm stuff up a lot. It doesn't seem to squash things, but overall, it makes it sound like a record. I also use an NTI as a stereo EQ.

What gear do you own?

The Akai hard disk recorder, the Bose Freestyles, NTI EQs, and I just ordered the Avalon 2055 and a Red 3 Focusrite.

What effects do you like?

I like the Sony D7 as a stereo delay, and of course, like everybody else, I have to have my PCM42s. The Sony V77 is pretty awesome, and I've been using an old Mutron a bit on bass tracks lately.

What do you listen to for fun?

I like Faith Evans, some of Eightball, and Jay Z is one of my favorite artists. I like R Kelly, DJ Quik, TQ, Outkast, and I love A Tribe Called Quest.

Do you want to produce?

Most definitely. Actually, I'm getting ready to start a project for an artist named Soleil that I'll be co-producing. That's got to be the next step. But it's hard, because I do love what I do. And I love that when the mix is done, I'm done working. I can go home, and I don't have to think about anything else.

Do you have any engineering heroes?

Well, I have a lot of people whose mixes I like. Tony Maserati and Steve Hodge both do a great job. I love Jon Gass's work with Babyface. Manny Marroquin, Dexter Simmons. . . . When I was coming up, I listened to a lot of Dave Way, Barney Perkins, Jon Gass—they were the guys I wanted to be like. I wanted to be as busy as they were, so I was listening to what they were doing, trying to see what it was about them that made them get the kind of work that they did. I wanted to have my own style, but at the same time, I wanted to be commercially acceptable.

What were some of those things that they did?

Some of the effects and tricks that they were using then were really cool. There was a lot of trickery that engineers were doing in the late '80s and early '90s with drum sounds, delays, gated reverbs, and stuff like that. Music has changed now, and mixing is a much more straight-ahead situation these days. It seems like lately it just has to hit, and it's got to hit hard.

So, what's a trick you might use?

[Laughs] Sometimes, I try not to listen from a mixer's perspective, but rather to listen to the song from a regular person's perspective, as if I just like the song. I try to figure out what it is I like about the song, not, "Is the kick hitting at 150 Hz?" I just listen to the song and what it feels like, because the average person wants to know what it feels like, and if they can sing it, and that's what's gonna make it come together.

Leslie Ann Jones

Doing It All

AUGUST, 1999

A master of the art in the classic sense, L.A. Jones is, first and foremost, a truly musical engineer. Highly respected by her peers, she's the kind of professional that clients come to depend upon—for her uncompromising dedication to quality, her no-nonsense attitude, and most of all, for her educated ears.

Not someone whose work is all over the pop charts, Jones is a bit of a well-kept secret. It's the producers, composers, arrangers, and musicians she works with who know her true worth. And that's why she's one of the busiest people you'll ever meet. Known particularly for her jazz, big band, and orchestral recordings for artists like Michael Feinstein, Wayne Shorter, and Herbie Hancock, and for her impeccable vocal recordings of artists like Rosemary Clooney, Bobby McFerrin, and DeeDee Bridgewater, she's also recorded some of the funkiest stuff around with seminal r&b artists like Maze, ConFunkShun, and the Whispers.

In person, Jones is generally quite thoughtful, serious, and businesslike, but a puckish sense of humor underscores her get-the-job-done mentality. Those in the know appreciate her relaxed approach to even the largest and most complicated sessions.

Although she continues as a hands-on recording and mixing engineer, Jones is also Director of Music Recording and Scoring for George Lucas' Skywalker Sound complex in Northern California. This year, she's also added to her workload the position of Chairwoman of the Board of Trustees of The Recording Academy. With such a non-stop schedule, I was lucky to catch up with her between sessions at Skywalker.

You actually started out your musical career as an artist.

Yes, I got a Sears Silvertone guitar for Christmas when I was about 14 and started playing it. Then my cousins and I and a friend formed a group, kind of like a teenaged Fifth Dimension, and that was pretty much how I spent my high school years, performing and recording.

It was the classic Hollywood story. Every time we'd bring home a record contract, everybody would get excited and think we were going to make it, and then we'd get dropped. We got signed to Columbia by Gary Usher, which was great because we got to hang out at Columbia recording sessions, then Gary Usher got fired so we were dropped. Then we were signed to Johnny Rivers' Soul City label along with the Fifth Dimension, but when the label was bought out, we were dropped. It would have been a sad story, except that we were having so much fun the whole time!

Your father was the famous musical parodist Spike Jones. Was he a big influence on you?

I think he was influential to me in a peripheral way. Because of what he did, I was exposed to all different kinds of music at a very early age. But actually, I think it was my mother, whose professional name is Helen Grayco, who more directly influenced me and the kind of live, big band music that I ended up doing a lot of work with. She sang in my father's band, and I watched her perform every night. Also, through her, I was exposed to really great singers. She had one of the first Muntz 8-track players in her car, and we'd listen to Mel Torme, Barbra Streisand, Frank Sinatra....

How did you make the transition from artist to engineer?

I ended up in an all-woman Top 40 band, playing electric guitar and singing backgrounds. When we went on tour, I was the one who put the P.A. together. Then when the band split up, I owned the P.A! By then, I was thinking about what to do next. I'd done recording sessions, and I realized that it took something more than I had to be a great musician. I'd never taken lessons or anything; it always came very easy to me to do things like cop Stephen Stills' guitar solos. And that's fine up to a certain point, but if you want to be really good, you have to do a lot more. So I started working with other people's bands, helping them arrange their background vocals, sort of semi-producing their live shows, and then I started mixing their sound.

So you were producing and arranging even before you were engineering.

Yeah [laughs], in fact I never really wanted to be an engineer, I wanted to be Peter Asher: a producer and a manager. I thought that was a great combination of skills for me because the producer could be the creative side and the manager could be the anal business side.

Meanwhile, I got together with a couple of guys, pooled equipment, and started a P.A. company. Obviously, it was very hard work, and I really knew nothing. Thank God they were patient with me! Then, in 1974 (I know that year because this is Tascam's 25th anniversary year, and I was reminiscing with some of the guys there!), we bought the first Tascam Model 10 console, which was a 4-bus console, and the half-inch 4-track, the 80-8, I think it was. We set up in the basement of my house, and we also had the idea of putting this stuff in a truck and going to clubs to record bands live and get their demos done that way.

No sooner did we start doing that then my partners got other jobs. Meanwhile, I had a day job at ABC Records in publicity and artist relations. I decided the path I wanted to pursue was to produce and manage, and I thought it was important, if you were going to be a good producer, to know something about what a good engineer does. So I went to Phil Kaye, who ran the recording studios for ABC, and asked him for a job. He wasn't quite sure, but he said, "Let's hire you and see what the clients think." He was very willing to put me on with the understanding that it was extremely rare to have a woman engineer, and that if the clients didn't dig it, I'd be gone. So, twenty-five years later, here I am!

At ABC, I worked for six months as a production engineer doing tape copies, and then started assisting. There were two rooms that had just been redone with one of the first inline automation consoles ever built — Frank DiMedio consoles with API/Allison automation. It was the kind of automation [Ed. note: before SMPTE!] that you couldn't record on an edge track; you'd record on one track, and you'd bounce that to another track. Basically, you'd bounce it back and forth until it screwed up. I spent most of my time on that first project in the tech room asking a bunch of questions and trying not to look too terribly stupid.

A year and a half after that, I was doing a lot of dates with Reggie Dozier and Barney Perkins, who were two very popular black staff engineers. They were always working on more than one project at a time, so it was great for me. They'd be mixing, and I'd get to do their overdubs, or I'd get to help them track.

Then I assisted on a John Mayall album, and when it became time to do his next album, he asked me to engineer it. There was something about me being able to tweak tape machines that he liked. I don't know how you make that leap from tweaking tape machine to engineering someone's record, but that was the first record I did.

At ABC, you often worked with Roy Hallee, one of the all-time greats.

That was one of the best things about being there. I learned so much from him. Not just the nuts and bolts of getting it on tape, although all of that too. Learning to punch in fast, how to work with musicians and the conductor, aligning the tape machines absolutely perfectly, putting tones through the faders so you knew your echo returns were absolutely right —because Roy would not accept anything that was less than perfect. It wasn't just about making sure it was tweaked, it was about making sure it was perfect so you could then go on and be creative. You didn't have to go back and check things. But I also learned from him in a real creative engineering kind of way. The wonderful textures he creates—working with him was really pivotal for me. Go listen to Paul Simon's *Hearts and Bones* album, the album before *Graceland*. There's a song on that called "Train in the Distance" that's a wonderful example of Roy's work.

You went from ABC to David Rubinson's Automatt Studios in San Francisco, and then back to Capitol in Los Angeles.

There were a lot of politics and changes at ABC, and it became time to leave. But I was in that funny place that so many people are in—you've done just enough work as a first engineer that you don't want to go back to being an assistant, and you don't have enough credits to be a first engineer. I don't envy people who find themselves there. It's very tough to know when to make that break.

When I was ready to move on, *Mix* magazine had just come out with studio listings, and I started sending my resume out. I saw Fred Catero's name listed as David Rubinson's engineer at The Automatt. Fred was another icon; I'd always admired his work, all the Big Brother records and Blood Sweat and Tears, and I knew he and Roy Hallee had worked together at CBS in New York. I figured it was a shot in the dark, but I sent my résumé up, and three days later they called.

David had just taken over CBS/San Francisco. He'd had one studio in the complex, and when CBS closed, he had to either take over the building or lose his studio. So he found himself with three studios and a mastering room, no studio manager, and no staff. They couldn't offer me a job as a first engineer, but I took the job because I knew I was capable and that opportunities would present themselves. And that's exactly what happened. Not long after I started, somebody needed strings done, and they didn't have an engineer. Because of David Rubinson, who managed Herbie Hancock and other artists, at The Automatt, we were on the cutting edge in a lot of ways. We were the first studio in San Francisco to be automated, we did the *Apocalypse Now* soundtrack, we did Santana's *Swing of Delight* album on one of the first 3M digital 32-tracks with Carlos, Herbie Hancock, Ron Carter, and Tony Williams. I worked with so many really great artists there like Herbie, Carlos, Maze, ConFunkShun, Angela Bofill.... There was always a lot going on. The Automatt closed in 1984, and after that, I was an independent engineer in the Bay Area for three years until I took the job at Capitol.

I once heard a well-known horn arranger come out of a session with you and say, "Her ears are amazing. She really gets it." Do you think you have perfect pitch?

No. [Laughs] I can say that because I know people who do. I think I have really good pitch, but with me, it's something more like what you might call multitasking. My brain is somehow able to do a lot of things at the same time, and I'm able to keep an ear open to the performance constantly, no matter what else I'm doing. That makes it possible for me to hear things pretty readily. For example, if we're doing horn overdubs, to hear if somebody comes in wrong, or there's a bad note, or somebody didn't play. That's probably why people started asking me to produce.

Speaking of horns, what are some of your favorite horn mics?

I like RCA DX77s or Neumann TLM 170s on trumpets, U87s or RCA44s on trombones, and U67s on saxes.

Would you tend to compress trumpets or saxophones when you are recording?

Generally, I don't anymore. I used to when I first started out, because I didn't know how to record. I used it as protection, and because I was working with people who maybe weren't that great at controlling their own dynamics. Working with great players helps because they set their own balances quite well.

But that means you're doing a lot of riding while you're recording.

Yes, especially in softer sections, if the trumpets change to mutes or something like that. I try to bring them up when I'm recording. If I don't, every time we play the tune back I have to make a level ride for people to hear it the way the arrangement is supposed to be heard, and I'm too lazy to do that!

Obviously, you don't get that many rundowns. Do you know what's coming up from reading the score?

From reading the score and watching the band.

Watching the band to see when they're going to play softer or louder.

Usually, I don't worry about it when they're going to play louder, only when they're going to play softer. I try and get my loudest level right away and then work from there. Same thing with saxes. If we're cutting a live solo, I can't record the section too hot, because when the person goes to take a solo, I don't have any more headroom. I have to record the saxes lower and all the rest of the horns lower, so when the solo happens, I've got enough headroom to bring it up. People need to walk into the control room to hear the playback and know that they played it perfectly, so I record it that way. It's not that hard, really.

Any tricks for recording saxes?

No tricks, but sometimes an RCA 44 sounds really good on an alto or soprano sax, especially if it's a real nasal or reedy type sound. Also, when I'm doing trumpet solos, if I'm using a DX77, I'll put it in omni for the mute work. It makes it sound more round and less harsh.

What are you listening for when you record a big band?

The internal balance of saxes. Making sure there's enough lead trumpet. Also, the bass has to be articulate.

I've heard you quoted as saying: "When you're an assistant, think like an engineer, and when you're an engineer, think like a producer." Many engineers just record whatever they're given. But you've always acted more like a producer on that end—speaking up if something wasn't right.

I suppose that's why a lot of people feel comfortable going into the studio with me without a producer, or why some producers like to work with me. They know there's a certain thing that I can take care of that they don't have to pay too much attention to. They know that I'll catch it if something is wrong. That's just always been part of what I do.

What consoles do you prefer to work on?

I work on Neves because that's what I'm used to. I've never been an independent long enough to have to learn a lot of different consoles, which is

sort of a blessing and a curse at the same time. When I was at the Automatt, we had Harrisons and Tridents, and then I was at Capitol for nine years and all the consoles were Neves.

So, obviously, I'm very comfortable with Neves, I like the way they sound. The one we have at Skywalker is the new VXS, which I think is outstanding. It's an upgraded V-series with improved power supply distribution, improved mix busses, and an eight-by-eight post panel for film and 5.1 mixing. As far as automation goes, I think Flying Faders is still one of the best automation systems around. It's very easy, very fluid.

Is there any equipment you can't live without?

Well, for tracking or mixing, I would have a very difficult time without my speakers. They're Tannoy Limpet 8s—the self powered dual speakers, PBM 8s with the Canadian Limpet amplifier on the back. I own two pair so that I can do LCR with them.

There isn't anything else I really have to have, although I'm getting close to buying an original 224 for myself. They're getting very hard to find now, and none of them have been kept up very well, so I'm thinking of getting one of my own. I find there's something refreshing about older reverbs that haven't been so tweaked to death, in terms of their algorithms. They're a little more pure, a little more natural sounding. That's probably why the EMT 250 retains its popularity. It's got only four settings, and you can do maybe a total of sixteen combinations with it, but it has a sound that for something artificial is pretty remarkable.

You're known as an expert vocal engineer. How do you go about choosing vocal microphones?

I don't think I do it differently than anybody else. With experience, you get an idea of what the characteristics of certain mics are, and if I have the opportunity, I'll stick a couple up and hear the person sing on that particular song. With the song, not a capella, of course. You can't really hear what a mic is going to sound like on someone's voice if they're not singing along with the band. There are too many characteristics that may not show up. It might sound fine if they're all by themselves, but then you stick them with the track, and it'll sound completely different. There are some mics that don't sound good on women, and some mics that don't sound good on men. I find 249s or M49s on women sometimes don't sound good because they're a little too bright. When women sing, particularly in their midrange, or when they have to sing out, their voices tend to get a little thin, and those mics may accentuate what you don't want to hear. A lot of times, I'll go with the tube 47, and since the 149 came out, I use that quite a bit. So, my group of three would usually be a 67, a 47 tube, and the 149.

Do you have a desert island vocal compressor?

Since I bought the Avalon 737, I've been using that almost exclusively. I love the way it sounds, I love the control that it gives me, and I like having everything in one box that I can duplicate, if I need to, wherever I am. The side chain in it is great, as well. It leaves the low end and the high end free to be used for EQ and allows you to use the two midrange bands as side chains. So, if you have harshness in the midrange, you can compress it and still have top and bottom end EQ available.

Besides that, it would be an LA2 or a Summit. The rest I use for special applications. Like, I tend to use an 1176 on bass quite a bit, usually when I'm mixing, because it really seems to bring it out in the track more than anything else.

You record to analog.

I used to record at Capitol to the 32-track Mitsubishi, which I wish I still had, because on most of the big band stuff, I could really use a couple of extra tracks. Now, I drag along a DA88 with the 24-track analog, and I usually put the room mics on the 88, or anything else extra that I need. I find the DA88 to be quite an incredible tool. I think Tascam has very good sounding converters, and it sounds fine. I use it when I'm mixing now, if I have to make an intro separate from the song, like for a practice edit. I'll mix the pieces to half-inch, lay them over to DA88, and time the crossfade right. I use 88s for that kind of stuff constantly.

What other new equipment do you like?

Well, at Skywalker, we get into the more esoteric stuff, and I'm getting a bit spoiled. For one thing, I've been kind of stunned at the difference cables make. I used to think it was a lot of voodoo, but when you get into a place where you can really hear the difference, it's not such voodoo anymore. Not that I would take $7000 cables with me wherever I go, but I definitely think it contributes to why Skywalker sounds the way it does. We use MIT, Cello, and Canare Starquad.

I also love the Pacific Microsonics Model One converter. It's really difficult now for me to use another converter when I'm mixing direct to 2-track. I use it as a 16 bit to mix to DAT, or I use it 88.2/24 bit when I'm doing something high bit on the DA88.

So, I'm kind of spoiled, but we need those things. We do a lot of direct to 2-track recording and a lot of really kind of critical-listening records—the kind of music where that equipment makes a real difference,

What engineers and producers do you admire these days?

Well, Don Murray, of course, does great work. And Al Schmitt, obviously, as well as Shawn Murphy and Keith Johnson. I also really like Mike Shipley's work. Shania Twain's record sounds fantastic; it's wonderfully tough sounding. I think some of Bob Clearmountain's work is absolutely astounding, like Jonatha Brooks' *Ten Cent Wings*. As far as producers, John Levanthal and Larry Klein are two of my favorites. Both of them are so talented on their own, but you don't hear their contribution when you listen to the records that they produce. They really enhance the artist that they work with and bring out the best in them without making it seem like it's their album. That's really hard to do.

What's your secret for juggling all your different jobs?

[Laughs] I have a very understanding partner and a good dog. Seriously, the easy answer is because I want to do it all. I took the job at Skywalker because I don't want to give up engineering. I really love it, but I don't want to spend ninety hours a week in the studio, any more. And I think continuing to be a recording engineer is part of what makes me a good studio director. If I don't keep my hands in, then it's kind of hard for me to have real conversations with other engineers who come in. It isn't easy to do it all, and I'm really lucky that Skywalker has been supportive of me being so active in the music community. They see it as a positive thing for

Skywalker and the studio. And it's certainly a positive thing for me. Being back in the Bay Area and doing a combination of all the things I love is just about perfect.

Jimmy Douglass

OCTOBER, 1999 ## From Classic Rock to Hip-Hop, in Touch With the Times

Jimmy Douglass seems too young to have done so much. His past credits include work with icons such as the Rolling Stones; Led Zeppelin; Emerson, Lake & Palmer; Aretha Franklin; Stevie Wonder; Hall & Oates; and groundbreaking records with Slave; current platinum projects include Timbaland, Ginuwine, Aaliyah, Lenny Kravitz, and Missy "Misdemeanor" Elliott. The explanation? Obviously, when you start off working at Atlantic Records' New York studios while still in high school, you get a jump on the business. And maybe having two personas makes a difference; Douglass is credited on Elliott's *Da Real World* as two people: engineer "Senator Jimmy D" and mixer "Jimmy Douglass." If you're two people, you can get twice as much done in half the time, right?

In person, Douglass is a winning combination of very cool and very warm. Although he's not a native New Yorker, he has spent most of his life there, and it shows in his fast-talking, East Coast style. Besides the aforementioned artists, his recording career includes work on pop/electronic projects like the System's "Don't Disturb This Groove;" jazz recordings by George Duke, Alfonso Johnson, and Stanley Clarke; projects by musical wild cards like Frank Black,

At Manhattan Center Studios, with Timaland and Mike Daddy in background

Photo: Jimmy Douglass

Vernon Reid, and Willy DeVille; and chart-topping r&b tracks by Jodeci, Jay-Z, and SWV.

Mix caught up with Douglass for a series of conversations that took place at his New York recording domicile, Manhattan Center Studios, on breaks from working the night shift with rapper Jay-Z.

You were literally just a kid when you started in this business.

I started out in high school. I was a musician, and I wanted to be a producer, but I didn't know what a producer was. I happened to know some people who happened to know some people at Atlantic Records, and it was someone's good idea that I could work at Atlantic's studios. The concept was that I could work in the evenings making tape copies—dubs for foreign countries, things like that. Put the tape on, copy the tape, pack it up, and while the copies were running, I could be doing my homework. It was a good idea on paper, but the part of the building I was working in was two doors down from the main Atlantic Studios, where you'd have Aretha recording with Tom Dowd. You'd have Dusty Springfield, the Young Rascals, Cream.... I never did get to do any homework. I'd put the tape on and run down the hall. The length of the tape was half a side, about twenty minutes, so for twenty minutes or a half hour, I wasn't there.

Could you sit in on recording sessions?

Oh yeah. This was in the early '70s, and it was a whole different world. For instance, Tom Dowd didn't have assistants. It was ... you just did what you did, and whoever was there was there.

You kept working for Atlantic and kept moving up.

Absolutely. I started working with Tom at night, when nobody else was there. I was just kind of watching and trying to figure out what he was doing, until it got to where I was able to help him. And to where he insisted that I was probably pretty good at doing other things besides tape copies, and that they should move me along the ranks—at least as much as they could with my schooling still going on. Tom also encouraged me to try stuff. Like, I'd drive into the city in the morning before school, take old tapes, put them on the machines, and figure out how to work things. Stuff like that. Nobody minded.

Because it was Atlantic's studio, it wasn't like the studios were really there to make money. They were there to service Atlantic artists. It was Jerry Wexler, Ahmet Ertegun. I was there in this great arena with all those legends who were doing it for the love of music—something you don't really see that much anymore. And it was a simpler time. They had the power to make decisions. There weren't as many people that you had to go through to decide if something was all right.

Eventually, I got better, and they started trusting me more, and I started doing more.

It seems much harder now to get started—the field has narrowed.

Well, technology has changed the whole thing, and I have a perspective, because I was there then and I'm here now. Back in the late '70s, people would come to me specifically for what I did. They knew I had a certain talent, and I could do things to sound, but they had no clue how I did it. Really, they had no idea. Oh, maybe every once in a while, you'd get a wise ass who'd say, "Why don't you put some 5K on that?" and you'd look at this guy and say, "Okay, what engineer did you hear that from?" Because they didn't know what they were talking about. It was just something to say.

But, today somebody with a couple of dollars can go to Sam Ash or Guitar Center. For $3,000 to $10,000, you can have a pretty technically amazing studio. Musicians can play with the buttons and knobs and get a basic flow going and a general idea of how it all works. So now, when a guy comes and sits next to me, I have to look at him and think, "You know, this isn't magic to him." I have to look at him a little differently, and my role becomes a little different. I have to respect him more and include him in the process of what I do.

Of course, there are still guys who spend the money and don't know what they're doing! But I have to have a very open approach to everybody. I believe everybody has something to contribute in this process, hopefully! And I treat them like they do until they prove the other way around.

How do you maintain that open attitude? When you've been at it a long time, it's difficult to avoid becoming closed and cynical.

I've noticed that gets you nowhere in life. There are so many ideas out there on this planet, and you never know what will work. One thing about me, even when I'm producing a record, I was never one

of those people who would have to say, "That was my idea, therefore it's good."

I don't care where the idea comes from. To me, the process of making a record is that the best ideas are put forward. Some get thrown out, and some we try even though we know from experience that may not be the way to go. That's always a hard call. Sometimes, you know that you're going to go a long way to get maybe another five percent; and maybe that's not what you want to do that day, budget-wise, and so on. But every now and then, somebody will jump up and down and say, "This is really important to me," and I'll say, "Okay, I'm going to spend this extra three, four hours." And you know what, sometimes I get fifty percent. That's the part that you never know, and that's part of the attitude to being open.

Would you say you have a certain sound?

Definitely. I don't know if I can describe it, but you can hear it in all my records. It's solid, and I've always liked vocals up front. To me, they sell the song. Some engineers forget that when they make mixes.

I've always looked at records like movies: the record producer is the director, and the engineer is a great cinematographer. And I've looked at the song as a script, and the instruments I look at basically as sets. I don't mean I look at it that way all the time, but when I sit back, it's like, that bass is so loud it's obscuring the vision of the actor. We've got to push the set back a bit and tone the color down—that kind of stuff.

You work at Manhattan Center Studios a lot.

Yeah, it happens to be one of those anachronisms in the middle of Manhattan. Growing up in a house studio like Atlantic, I got very used to being able to leave stuff set up, and to have more freedom with scheduling. You go to the big boys, every two minutes, they're like, "What are you doing tomorrow; what are you doing now; when are you doing this?" At Manhattan Center, they allow us the kind of flexibility to not have to know every exact thing that we're doing, and if we miss a beat, they won't kill us.

They have two great rooms. I work mostly in Studio 4, which has a [Neve] VR. My preference is definitely the Flying Faders system; I think I've mastered Flying Faders.

You like to record and mix on the same board.

If I can. If I'm really lucky, I'm able to go from soup to nuts. It makes life a lot easier.

Especially in hip-hop, they do a lot of building in the studio, as opposed to thinking about it before they come in. They build the tracks and the ideas and the parts of the song there. It used to be, on a lot of records, people would use their imagination to know that things would be right later, and they didn't have to hear everything to do their part. But in hip-hop, they can't go on unless everything is there—they can't create the next idea. So, if you're fortunate enough to be building in automation, when it comes time to mix, the mix really isn't the greatest deal in the world. We build the sound that they want as we go, and all you have to do is just embellish it a little bit.

You've been working with Timbaland a lot the past couple of years. How did you two hook up?

It was a side effect. I was invited to do Jodeci's last album by this studio upstate. I had done some work for them previously—kind of bailed them out on a three-day marathon where people came up, about five acts and three sets of producers. I did all the sessions, and they were kind of impressed with me. So, when Jodeci booked in and they didn't really have an engineer, the studio called me. The side effect was that Timbaland was in the crew with Missy, Ginuwine, Player—they were all just kind of up there. I took a liking to Timbaland and what he was doing. It was very innovative and different, and he was very free—free of worry about where it was going. There were two studios, and he and I ended up spending most of our nights after Jodeci was done just working on more stuff.

Do you two rent a lot of gear or are you self-contained?

Between my outboard EQ and effects and everything, his equipment, and MIDI equipment

that we share, we have six to eight roadcases, and wherever we go we set up shop. All we need is a VR.

What is the main composing tool when you're working together?

He uses various sequencers—he uses the Ensoniq ASR a lot, and I have an array of MIDI sound modules.

Was *Da Real World* written all in the studio?

Missy could be one of the fastest writers that I've ever worked with, and Timbaland is one of the fastest track/beatmakers. Between the two of them, they can do a song in half an hour.

They come in with just an idea?

[Laughs] They'll just come in.

Okay, then they're laying parts down and you're bringing feeds up on the console and making it sound the way you all think it should . . . .

Temporarily. Then she'll write a song around it, and then we'll go back and rethink the track and then redo it, and she'll rethink it. It's a give and take. "Oh, you did that. Well, I'm gonna do this! Oh, you did this. I'm gonna do that!"

What are some pieces in your rack?

I use an Akai S3000 for vocal flying—that's my sequencer. And of course, I have the ASR10X, which I like for the effects and the resampling ability. All the sync boxes are mine. That's my area—I'm Mr. Sync Man.

How do you lock everything up?

We'll stripe some SMPTE. I steal whatever tempos he's dealing with, and I become the master tempo man, and I let all the sequencers slave to mine. Everything slaves to my SMPTE, to my master sync box.

Is a Lynx the main sync box?

Yes, actually, I'm still in the old days. I bring my own two Lynxes wherever I go, because some studios don't have them. They have these new things that they need for video capability. But the Lynxes are so simple. I don't need the video stuff. I just need to simply offset things.

So, first the crew will be just composing and you're getting sounds, and after a while, you roll the tape and record some sort of basic track.

Yeah, like a "glop track," I call it. There it is, a glop of it, so something can be written around it. Then I do the vocals.

There are a lot of vocal tracks. How do you combine parts?

I try when I can to keep them totally spread. I try not to comp them. I've found that leaving all those doubles and quadruples open instead of just comping them and making them one stereo pair gives me this amazing ability to have extra space when I'm mixing. It's a track killer, but when I can have it, it makes things a lot easier.

What mic do you use on Missy?

Usually an 87—mostly for consistency, because I end up recording her so many different places and because she does things so on the spur of the moment. She doesn't have the time to wait for some special setup. Really, she's very quick; when her mind is moving, it's moving, and all you have to do is capture it. She'll switch three songs on you in two seconds, and she'll want to punch in. This way I can always find my way back to where it was.

You probably don't EQ much to tape.

I try not to EQ—except, of course, for those telephone voices she does. I do those right to tape. She insists on hearing it that way then and there. She can't get the vibe if it isn't that way.

What format do you record to?

I like to do the tracks analog, and when we can afford it or I'm in a place where it's available, I do the vocals digital on the 3348. I also have a DA88 setup that I use for flying vocals if I don't have the luxury of the 48. If I just want to fly eight tracks of the vocals and use them for the hook or something, it helps to keep the autonomy of the tracks and still fly them.

You're not recording to hard disk?

I sometimes use the hard disk stuff to fly parts around. I usually have Pro Tools sitting in the room that I lock up when I need to. I'll just fly to the Pro Tools and fly back. I do that a lot especially to create the clean versions that we have to do a lot of these days—to get the curse words out or flip them around or whatever.

Personality-wise you're an interesting combination of speedy and relaxed. Even though a lot of the people you work with can be very fast about writing, there still must be hours of working out parts where there's not so much to do and you have to just kick back and let things happen.

Absolutely. That's part of the phenomenon of the way r&b and rap is often done these days. A few years ago, I had some training in this area. I started working with some people, and they'd say, "Tomorrow at one o'clock." I'd come at one, and nobody would be there, and nobody would do anything for three, four, six hours. And after a while, I'd start saying, "Hey, this is ridiculous, let's get moving!" And they'd go, "Jimmy, just chill." And we wouldn't get rolling till seven, eight, nine, and get out at three or four in the morning. But after a while, I realized, nobody was in a hurry but me! So, it was calm down, just relax, and let it happen, because it is what it is, and that's the only way it's going to happen.

What do you do for those hours in the hang?

Take care of whatever business you can. You do whatever writing you need to do. I have a little sequencer set up and a couple of modules, so sometimes I'll be writing. And of course, you get to really learn your equipment! That's one way I got to learn the VR so well. I was sitting there many, many days, and I'd read the manual over and over. I found stuff that people didn't realize was in there.

What are some of your strengths?

I really enjoy depth in records, space in records. Even when it's crowded, there's still a way to get space in there somehow.

What do you do to create that depth?

One of the things I try to do is to look at left, right and center and not to get too hung up on places in between. It's something Tom Dowd told me years ago: "There's a left, a right and a center—the rest of it is all crap." [Laughs] So, I try to work with that instead of spending time putting things in every little space across the spectrum. And I try to create depth by putting delays that send stuff back into the speakers, making it more concave from my perspective instead of left and right.

The quiet parts of your tracks are really quiet. How do you achieve that dynamic range? Hot levels?

Yeah, I'm a squasher. Everything is slamming. I record at +9 [tape alignment level: +9/185 nanowebers], and I hit the tape really hard. It's a holdover from my rock 'n' roll days. I like the sound of it. And I try to punch in only when I need to. I don't leave mics open and tracks in record. That's probably a big part of it too.

How long does it take you to mix a track?

If I'm lucky enough to be doing soup to nuts, I've already been mixing as we've been going along so all I basically have to do is recall from where I left off. That's a method Tim and I developed in Rochester, because we were doing so many songs every night for so many different people. He'd

have to take 'em up and put 'em back, take 'em up and put 'em back, and I had no assistant! One of the things I learned how to do was to minimize my effects, because to document them all by myself and then to change the tape over was too hard.

Living in the same room a lot, I was able to have everything always lined up the same way, so I developed a method of storing the recall right in the actual mix, without a big deal.

So you don't have to try a lot of things in the mix.

No. I sit and play with the vocals and really get them nice and put effects on them and work on the spacial differences and the spread. Then we do the drops.

You mean like cuts, muting parts, and creating arrangements.

Right.

You've had ups and downs in your career. Have you developed some kind of general philosophy about the business?

I really believe if you're any good at this, you're going to continue to be good at it. It's not about the million dollars you might make today because, in my experience, the money has always come after the love. If you're really digging what you're doing, and you really put your heart into it, and you are doing the best job you can, you may not have that hit today, but eventually you are going to have that hit, and the money will come. Maybe I'm a bit of a romantic about that.

We don't always hit a home run. There are albums I made with people that didn't happen, but we made a really fine, quality product. They didn't sell like they should have, for whatever reason—the record company, the management, yada. But the point is, these people I worked with I know for life, and I love them for life, because we experienced something together—a creative bonding that's irreplaceable. And that's as important to me as the successes I've had.

Brian Malouf

Secrets for Crossover Success

Selected Credits

Everclear
Sparkle And Fade

David Gray
"Babylon,"
"Please Forgive Me"

Macy Gray
Live EP

Lit
A Place In The Sun

Lisa Loeb
Tails

Madonna
Breathless

Sarah McLachlan
"Terms of Endearment"

Pearl Jam
"Even Flow"

Queen
"Fat Bottom Girls" from *Jazz*
Innuendo (two singles),
Live At Wembley

Smokey Robinson
"Love, Smokey"

There's a real art to making successful transitions, whether in a career or in a life. Brian Malouf has managed to gracefully make more transitions than most: from musician to busy live sound man, r&b hit mixer, successful alt rock producer/engineer, and talent scout. These days, he combines what he's learned from all these roles into his job as Senior V.P. of A&R at RCA Records, where he supervises recording projects and does hands-on producing and mixing for artists such as Lit, Danielle Brisebois, Eve 6, the Verve Pipe, and Hum.

Malouf's credits range wide. He was a recording engineer on Michael Jackson's *Bad*, mixed Extreme's monster ballad "More Than Words" from their multi-Platinum *Pornograffitti*, and mixed singles for Madonna, Expose, Roxette, Slaughter, Gin Blossoms, Pearl Jam, Ugly Kid Joe, and Bon Jovi, among many, many others. His more recent work includes mixing and co-production on Everclear's breakthrough *Sparkle and Fade* and mixing for Kid Rock, Tonic, and Lit's *A Place in the Sun*.

A thoughtful fellow with a realistic point of view and a penchant for detail, Malouf seems to take nothing lightly. This is not to say that he doesn't laugh or have a sense of humor — he definitely does. But his serious demeanor makes it obvious that his natural inclination is to think before acting.

Malouf is a bicoastal hybrid. He's originally from Los Angeles and is now based in New York City; on any given day you're likely to find him behind a console in either city.

How did you get your start in L.A.?

I was a musician — a drummer. In high school, I also experimented with other instruments; I played trombone and euphonium and upright bass. I learned a lot of instruments because I wanted to be an arranger as well as a musician. But in college, I went back to playing the drums.

You knew early on that you were interested in musical arrangements.

Yes, I wrote for the big band in high school and got into learning band instruments. But doing that actually ill-prepared me for college; when I applied to Cal State Northridge, I was rejected. I'd applied as a percussionist, going back to what I thought I knew, but I didn't really know it very well at all. Getting rejected was a real turning point for me. I spent the summer after that studying, re-took my juries, and got into the school. By the time I finished at Cal State Northridge, I was the principal percussionist in the symphony orchestra, which was the principal chair of the department.

Meaning you played tympani and hand percussion?

Just tympani. That's what you work toward as a percussionist. Every section has a principal player, the first chair, and the first chair in the percussion section is tympani.

So by the time you graduated, you were first chair.

Right. And entertaining the notion [laughs wryly] of being a legit symphonic percussionist. I was almost good enough to do it, but I eventually got tired of counting rests. In my fifth year, I left school and went back to playing drum set in bands.

I was always the guy in the band who did the P.A., and liked that sort of thing. So when I quit playing, five or six years later, I went full force into sound engineering. I did live sound at the Bla Bla Cafe and for a couple of Top 40 bands who could afford to rent a P.A. from me.

You had your own system?

Actually, I had three. I rented some equipment back from the band I'd just left, I bought some on my own, and I built three systems. I was making good money, and I kept very busy. During the day, I also apprenticed with Dave Jerden at El Dorado Studios. He's the guy who taught me studio engineering. I apprenticed with Dave for about a year, during the time he was working with Brian Eno and Bill Laswell and Material.

Photo: Cindy Malouf

Malouf in front of New York's Electric Lady Studios

I left around '81 and went to Can-Am Recorders. The place was for sale; [owner] Larry [Cummins] was very disenchanted with the business and was ready to call it quits. Then I showed up one day, with all this energy and all these ideas for how to rework the room, and we set about doing that. We tore the whole studio apart and rebuilt it. I was the chief engineer, the assistant engineer, the gofer — I was everything and so was Larry. We built up quite a nice little clientele.

Michael Jackson walked in one day with his brothers. That was a pivotal thing for me, because that's how I started working with Michael. He came to me on one of their sessions and said, "Hey Brian, I want to come back tonight and do my own stuff. Can you do it with me?" And that was the beginning of working with him for a year and a half on the demos that were the beginning of the *Bad* album.

It was pretty heady stuff, very exciting, and it led to lots of other things. I remained at Can-Am for ten years, until in '91, I started doing more work at other places.

Working with Michael started you off on a career in r&b and pop. But, unlike many other engineers, you've been able to transition into rock. You didn't stay pigeonholed as only an r&b engineer.

Actually, I was severely pigeonholed, and it was r&b and pop for a long time. One of the things that helped me break out of that was a group called Slaughter—that was really the first rock thing I did. They called me because they'd heard my r&b stuff, and they wanted a big fat bottom end on their record. I mixed seven or eight songs from that record, and the songs that I mixed were the singles that broke that band. And then I did the "Even Flow" mix for Pearl Jam that helped get them rolling, then Everclear and Lit. I've managed to get in on the ground floor with a lot of rock acts. Now, it seems like that's all people call me for, so [laughs] I'm pigeonholed again.

How did working for a record company come about?

I told my manager, Steve Moir, that it was something I was interested in. At that time, I'd been in studios day and night for thirteen years, and I thought, "Maybe it's time for me to do something different; maybe a more social existence would be preferable for the quality of life."

But now you spend thirteen hours a day in the office and the studio, right?

No, I'm in clubs seeing bands at night, and in the office or the studio during the day, but it's not the claustrophobic, total studio environment where that's your hive from 11 A.M. to 11 P.M. That got old for me.

Whereas many people end up in a job by chance, you've made very conscious decisions about your life and career.

Yes. Well, the breaks happened, but one of the things I've always believed in is that opportunity knocks for all of us. Maybe not regularly, but often enough to take advantage of, if you're prepared. It started in college, when I wasn't prepared to take that first jury. I decided that was the last time I'd be

caught with my pants down. So from the moment I got into college until today, I've been prepared for whatever was the next thing that was going to happen. If the Philadelphia Philharmonic had called me on any Saturday, any time after my second year of college, to come and audition for them on Monday, I would have been ready to do it. That meant I had to practice every day, and maybe that phone call never came, or maybe I wouldn't have taken [the job] once it did, but I was prepared. That's what I mean by being ready when opportunity knocks.

I also made conscious decisions, sometimes, to take a step back in pay, like when I went from being a live sound engineer to being a studio engineer. I sacrificed a lot of income to go back and become an apprentice in the studio, because I decided that the real future for me was doing studio engineering.

I made a similar kind of reduction when I came to work for RCA. Maybe not that drastic, but it was significant, because I looked at it as an opportunity to do more with my life creatively.

At the time, I'd been an assembly line mixer, just like the guys today who are doing it. Every day is a new tape, and it's somebody else's vision, somebody else's baby that they've brought up from the cradle. You're handed it for a day or a week, and then it's gone out of your life. And that's great. There's nothing wrong with that. It's a really good living, and it's really fun to mix. I loved every minute of it, and I'm very lucky to still be able to do it. But after a while, I thought, "God, I'd really like to do it with my own group and work on music that I'm completely accountable for."

So, to prepare to get the job I have now, I went out to the clubs and to the publishers and to the other sources—managers and attorneys—and I began doing my own A&R, either when I wasn't in the studio or at night after a session was done. Because I wanted to go back in the studio and have fun. Like the first time I took a band into El Dorado because Dave said I could, to get my chops down on a weekend—I took a band in and had the time of my life. I hadn't done that for so long. So that's what I did. I looked for acts to produce. That's when I found 1000 Mona Lisas and Everclear and took them into the studio. By the time the job was offered to me, I'd been doing it for a year already.

You recorded demos with Everclear, and you mixed their hit album *Sparkle* and *Fade*. How did you originally hook up with them?

That was a result of a meeting with a publisher named Andy Olyphant Steve Moir said I ought to get to know. Andy, who now is in A&R at Almo Sounds, was an up-and-comer. We sat down and played each other a bunch of stuff, and neither of us was particularly turned on by anything the other guy played, although we were being polite and getting along well. As I stood up to leave he said, "I've got one more thing to play for you. I'm trying to sign this but my boss doesn't like it. What do you think?" It was Everclear, and I flipped out. I thought it was the most vital music I'd heard all day—actually, in years.

They had no record deal at the time?

No. Andy wanted to publish them, and his boss didn't get it. And I said, "I know why he doesn't get it—it's a little too rough around the edges. I'll take them into the studio and make some demos that might sound a little different to him." So we did. And it was the classic story: They came, they slept at my house, we worked in a little studio out in Westlake Village, and we came up with some demos that got them the publishing deal. That was right about the time I was going to take the job at RCA and actually had a meeting with Art [Alexakis] for him to come to RCA. But he'd already been excellently seduced by Gary Gersh and was on his way to signing at Capitol.

On to your productions, then. It's always interesting how people choose to balance guitars vs. drums and vocals. Your records have different placements, rather than a consistent style. How do you decide what gets featured?

I always desire to feature the vocal; that's always my starting point. I try to get it as loud as possible without taking away power from the track. So that's my focus, and if the placement sounds different from song to song, it's really the presence of the vocal that counts. Some of it is real loudness, and some of it is apparent loudness. And getting apparent loudness on the vocal has, I think, a lot to do with the arrangement that's underneath it. If a song is arranged in a great way, everything sounds loud. So actually [laughs], the key to being a great engineer is working with a great arranger.

If the vocal sounds back or forward when you compare one mix of mine to another, it's safe to say that the arrangement of that song forced me to put the vocal where it is. But always know, with me, the vocal was as loud as I thought it could go without ruining the track. And what I listen for is timbre.

What I do in terms of levels and so forth all has to do with the timbre of the individual voice and how it relates to the other elements in the track. Generally, I try to have the bass and vocals be the counterpoint to each other. I try to make the apparent level of each be equal, and everything else hopefully falls in around that. I look at those two elements of the track as the central melodic components.

Not to make an '80s-type fetish of it, but you get some really cool snare sounds, like on Lit's *A Place in the Sun*. Your snares punctuate but don't dominate, feel good but don't overpower.

Yeah, I listened to that record the other day and thought, "Oh good!" Some [snares] are more compressed than others. Some of them I really laid it on, just to get the snare to sound unique, like a couple of the tracks that have horns.

What compressors do you use for that?

I do the same things everybody else probably does; like a lot of guys, I usually mult off the snare. Then I use the SSL board compressors, and I also use the Distressor—that can do quite a lot. That's about it. I think I used a Joemeek compressor on snare a couple of times on the Lit record.

More info, please.

Well, compression oftentimes does equal punch and impact on drums. But, like with most other things, I really don't overdo it. Instead, I do a lot of mild compression—multistage compression, with each one set to mild gain reduction.

Typically, the dry snare channel will get a touch of either the SSL compressor or the Distressor—not too wacky—and a bit of the SSL gate as well.

I do run all of the drums, in almost every rock mix that I do, through a separate stereo compressor. Sometimes I use Joemeek, or there's a stereo dbx setup that I like, or maybe the Focusrite Red 3, or that stereo Neve [33609] two-rack unit—some sort of stereo compressor that all the drums go through.

On the [SSL] 9000, there are four stereo busses that are selectable from several sources: the large fader, the small fader, and the odd and even effects sends. I'll send from the large fader directly to bus A, so the exact levels, post fader, that I've got up on the console, are sent to that stereo limiter, and the small faders are freed up to be other sends.

There's a little compression there, there's a little on the original track, and then I'll often route the snare to a separate audio channel where I get kind of crazy with it—distort it, or ridiculously compress it. One of the things you can do for a lot of punch is set a compressor to a very fast attack so it actually clips off the first part of the sound. The very early envelope gets hit really hard, and that combined with the open channel can add up to something pretty cool.

Another thing is, you can get a lot of great snare drum from leakage into the overheads and the tom mics. If you look for the snare sound in a lot of different places, you generally can find what you're looking for. Which is why I don't use samples any more—I think they take away from the performance. Sometimes, the drum sound on tape isn't what you would like to have, but you just keep working with it until you get it as likable as you can, and you go with it.

You're often mixing songs you didn't record. When you put up a mix, what do you do first?

I put everything up. I put all the faders in a straight line, somewhere in the middle of the fader range—between minus 5 and minus 10—and just listen. I sort of look at it as a big jumble, then with each pass I do little things. I usually don't start soloing individual instruments for a good two hours. In the meantime, I'm looking at the big picture. I'll do some obvious panning moves, then the pans change with every pass, the levels change with every pass, and the EQs start to change, although EQ is the thing I try to do last. I try to work for the longest time that I can with level, ambience and panning, before I start pressing dynamics or EQ buttons. It varies. On some things, obviously, I press in an EQ or a compressor or gate right away, but generally I try to take as much time with the naked track as I can stand. [Laughs] I make the music make me do things. I don't start out doing things from the get-go.

My favorite mixes are when I look at the board and see twelve or twenty buttons pressed on a 96-input console. Because that means it's well recorded and well arranged. And by not pressing all those buttons, I'm not introducing all the nasty artifacts of the signal processing.

Do you mix a specific way for radio?

No. I really just mix for the speakers that I'm listening to. What I listen to does indeed affect how it sounds on the radio, though. I'll often find myself mixing for an hour or so in mono on the little speaker on the Studer 1/2-track machine. That, I think, helps make it sound good on radio. And you're not so influenced by the panning you've done. Oftentimes, I'll find that when I come back to the stereo near-fields after I've been on the Studer speaker, things that I've panned way out to the side sound really loud. I don't change that, and that gives my mixes a nice, big stereo feel.

Do you move the Studer with the speaker closer to you?

No. [Laughs] It stays wherever it is in the room.

What other speakers do you use?

Ninety percent of the time, I'm on Yamaha NS-10 studios.

How do you balance lots of guitars and still keep the midrange under control?

I mostly use the older stuff for equalizing and compressing of guitars: LA-2As, LA-4s, 1176s. On acoustic guitars, I love the old RCA [BA6A] compressors.

Guitars are so compressed anyway—there's nothing more compressed than a distorted guitar right out of the speakers—so you don't really need that much. Instead, I do a lot with subtractive EQ and panning.

I've never considered myself a connoisseur of great guitar sounds. I don't own twenty guitars, and I haven't played with every vintage amp. These days, if I'm not happy with the guitar sound, I tend to put it through the POD, which actually reproduces a lot of really great amp sounds. I use it on bass as well.

You use it right out of the patchbay? You don't have to do any level matching?

The POD does all the gain changes necessary. You can plug a guitar straight into it as well.

Naturally, the cleaner the guitar sounds going into the POD, the more influence I can have on the amp sounds coming out. I'm not always able to effect exactly the sound I want. But between EQ, panning, compression, and spatial things like chorus and flanging, I can pretty much get what I want. However, I've never considered myself a true expert on making guitar sounds from scratch. I generally rely on the player.

When I'm recording a guitar, I really just try to get the full range from the speakers that are being played through. I set up a couple of mics and try to get one to capture all the low mids, and one to capture all the highs. I blend those, and there you go. I never record a guitar with any EQ and never with any compression. Unless, of course, it's totally clean, and then I can do whatever I want. [Laughs] It's open season on the guitar, if it's a clean sound.

Your vocal sounds tend to be dry and present with a lot of impact, but they avoid that danger zone of knife-edged brightness. What do you do to create that necessary presence?

I find that dry vocals cut through without much manipulation. When it's really dry, you naturally have a very direct-sounding instrument. In a rock band, most everything else you're putting up has either gone through another transducer before it hits your microphone, or the mic is at a greater distance from the source (e.g., a room mic on a drum). Even the close mics on a drum set can't be as close as when the vocalist's lips touch the windscreen. So a dry vocal will naturally cut through pretty easily without much else going on.

I think I pretty much do the same thing as most people. One of the great things about being an A&R guy is that I get to watch the other guys mix. I've actually picked up on a lot of tricks and techniques that way, like from Tommy and Chris Lord-Alge. But, of course, nobody can make a mix sound like them. You could copy down every one of Tom's settings from front to back, and try to do it yourself, and it won't sound anything like him.

It's the same with anybody else—it just doesn't work the same.

But, that said, I do pretty much the same as most people. But what I don't do is much of the really super-compression that mixers like TLA will do, putting it through one or more devices and really sucking it in. Although I experiment, I generally find my way with the SSL compressor or an outboard device like an 1176. Or I use a dbx 160X a lot with the over-easy switch for peak limiting vocals; I think that compressor design is still pretty tough to beat.

Sometimes, super-compression is the answer. I admit I've cranked an 1176 to where the gain reduction meter is pinned to left, but that's the exception rather than the rule.

Obviously, you have a love for emotional rock and an appreciation for clever lyrics. What else are you looking for in a band?

You always look for a songwriter who writes melodies that you can remember—that combined with the lyrics become hooks. Then I always prefer to sign a band with a killer drummer. And also, I like to see two stars on stage, I like to have Mick and Keith, John and Paul, Axl and Slash. A lot of my favorite rock bands have two stars in them. It's great to have at least two focal points.

I like fresh chord progressions. I love it when I get surprised by a change, and I love innovative rhythm tracks.

Your job is not an easy one. It's pretty rare to find all that.

[Laughs] Well, actually any two of those things will do!

ALAN MOULDER

Selected Credits

BT
"Shame"

Elastica
Elastica (seven tracks)

The Jesus and Mary Chain
Honey's Dead, Automatic

Loudermilk
"California"

Marilyn Manson
Portrait of an American Family

Moby
Animal Rights, I Like to Score

My Bloody Valentine
Glider, Loveless, Tremelo

Nine Inch Nails
*The Downward Spiral,
The Fragile, The Perfect Drug*

Remy Zero
Villa Elaine

The Smashing Pumpkins
*Siamese Dream, Mellon Collie
& The Infinite Sadness,
Machina/The Machines of God*

The Sundays
Reading, Writing & Arithmatic

U2
"The Lady With The
Spinning Head,"
"Mofo," *Pop* (various tracks)

From Trident to Nine Inch Nails

FEBRUARY, 2000

An ochre harvest moon rises over the eastern rim of New Orleans. It rotates smoothly across the black sky, and just before it sinks below the horizon, the door of a nondescript building (a converted mortuary, actually) creaks open. Soft light from inside briefly illuminates two night creatures, who exit and go their separate ways, eager to reach shelter before the morning sun burns their pale skin. That was how I first pictured Trent Reznor and Alan Moulder, at work at Reznor's Nothing Studios. Okay, it's a bit heavy on the Anne Rice, but listen to Nine Inch Nails' latest release a few times and see if your thoughts don't drift toward the dark side. The sound is elegant, wicked, and occasionally blood curdling—by turns both open and claustrophobic. A line from *Rolling Stone's* review puts its controlled insanity into perspective: "In a pop year silly with baby talk and plastic mambo, the thundering overindulgence of *The Fragile* is not a trial, it's a f**king relief!"

Yes. Well, co-producer, recordist, and mixer Alan Moulder is no stranger to this kind of creativity. In addition to *The Fragile*, his lengthy discography boasts numerous other credits best described as "intense." He was co-producer and mixer on the Smashing Pumpkins' *Mellon Collie & the Infinite Sadness* and mixer on their *Siamese Dream*. He also mixed NIN's *The Downward Spiral*. Delve a bit further and you'll find Moulder was behind the desk for works by singular artists such as the Jesus and Mary Chain, Moby, My Bloody Valentine, Marilyn Manson, Erasure, U2, Shakespear's Sister, Curve, and neither last nor least, Tom Jones.

Just off a two-year stint at the New Orleans studio where *The Fragile* was constructed, and hoping for some holiday time in his English homeland, the affable and rather soft-spoken Moulder instead found himself hard at work. I nabbed him for this phone interview during a week when he was mixing projects for both NIN and the Pumpkins. (Like I said, intense!) We got our conversation started when he took a short break from sorting takes at London's Rak Studios while Trent and the boys were off shooting footage for a video.

How did you get started in recording?

I started off playing guitar. I'm from a small town in Lincolnshire, where I was in a band and very interested in music. After I was done with school, I managed to get a job at Trident Studios in London as a runner — a tea boy, as we call them. But I left after a month. I hadn't quite finished being in bands, and I realized that if I was working in the studio, I'd have no time for it. Instead, I went to work in the Ministry of Agriculture, doing research into plant diseases. It was a job that gave me the freedom to play in bands at night and on weekends.

After four years of that I thought, "You're not going to make it, and being in the studio is more fun anyway!" Meanwhile, the guy who used to be head engineer at Trident had bought the studio, so I rang him up. I got lucky and walked into an assistant's job without having to go back to being a tea boy. Which was a bit difficult, actually, because I jumped over three tea boys who'd been there six months; I wasn't very popular in the beginning. Fortunately, two of them got fired very quickly and the other got promoted, so after a month all was sweet. But I was starting quite late, you see. I was 24.

God yes, so old. Well at least you had that training as a musician.

That's true; it was very good learning. It gave me the musical point of view, and it also gave me the knowledge that I'd done that route, and was making a decision to put it away and go for another career. I could put one hundred percent into engineering, which you need to do. You have to be committed or you won't get on.

Was Trident still all Trident consoles at that time?

When I first arrived, there were three rooms. Two of them had old Trident consoles and one room had an SSL. So, yes, we used the old A Range Trident board, which was great, but I ended up spending a lot of time in the SSL room, which was mainly for mixing.

Trident was a fantastic studio for training; we had an incredible staff when I was there. There was Flood, who I used to assist a fair bit; we had Mark "Spike" Stent, Paul Corkett, and Steve Osborne. A lot of people would use the house engineers, and part of the job of the house engineer was to train the assistants. Also, Trident pushed you into engineering very quickly. It was a baptism of fire. They'd toss you off the deep end, and you sank or swam.

That concept of having staff engineers is almost extinct these days.

Yes, that's a big demise I think, a real shame. I was very lucky [at Trident] because they gave you so much freedom and you were encouraged. It was very tough, of course; if you did mess up, you were out. But at least you were given the chance.

What kind of music were you working on?

A cross-section. There was a company called Record Shack that did high-energy disco that we all used to end up cutting our teeth on. It was mainly drum machines and DI stuff. You didn't need fantastic technical expertise to record it. And they worked very quickly, so it made you get your speed together.

And then, because it wasn't a particularly high-tech studio, and it was cheap, we used to get a lot of alternative bands. They could get the studio at a reasonable price, and they'd get the house engineer included. I remember Flood doing Nick Cave & the Bad Seeds, stuff like that. I stayed there about four years. Then the studio changed hands, and I went freelance.

Once you went freelance, how did you get work?

I'd met Dave Stewart of Eurythmics because my wife, Toni Halliday, is in a band called Curve that's signed to his record label. I started doing work with Dave and some of his other bands. He signed me to his management company, where I worked with Karen Ciccone, who is still my manager now, and I had a few clients from Trident. Actually, I was doing a lot of dance stuff at this time, and it looked like I was going to be a dance mixer.

Moulder with Trent Reznor at Nothing Studio

I also knew Alan McGee from Creation Records. Alan managed the Jesus and Mary Chain. That's how I'd got to work with them. They asked me to do *Automatic,* and when Alan heard it, he asked me to do some of his other bands like Ride and My Bloody Valentine. So, I took a bit of a change into the kind of music I was actually into and then went on that way.

Still, the dance music wasn't bad training.

No, I enjoyed doing it. It was when they were beginning to construct tracks up from just solo vocals.... You were re-creating everything, and in a way it was kind of punk rock—you could throw everything at it. It was great fun, and it helped me get my low end together.

How did it help with your low end?

Club stuff has to have heavy bottom end, and you have to get it tight and punchy. I grew to really like that. When I went to work with rock bands, I tried to incorporate that kind of low end, which is probably a more American-type sound—rock with a big, thick bottom. It's just having the bass and bass drum loud, and getting them to sit without compressing them too much, which takes the low end out. Also, normally with SSLs I put a Focusrite EQ across the mix and add a bit of low end, as well

as a bit of high. The Focusrite seems to work really well with the SSL board.

Meanwhile, you also had an affinity for guitars.

That helped I guess, doing bands like the Mary Chain. I loved working with them. Their sound was so irreverent and abnormal.

Yes, you seem to have an affinity for that as well.

[Laughs] One thing has led to another. I've been fortunate, I must admit, in the bands that have picked to work with me. You're only as good as the bands you've been working with.

Trent Reznor's studio really is a converted mortuary, right? What's it like?

Amazing. He has two rooms—the main room is an SSL G-Plus with Ultimation. The main thing is, it sounds good—no surprises when you leave. It was designed by Steve "Coco" Brandon, and despite the fact that it's a large control room, the big monitors are really good. The mains are Tannoys built into the wall. Then, Trent decided that he wanted to get some of that "Jeep going past" kind of thing, so he's got 18-inch JBL subwoofers and a 2K amp just to drive them. When you turn the subs on, your back starts shaking. It's great!

Equipment-wise, you've got every piece of gear you could want, and there's two of nearly everything. Also, everything is very accessible. Brian Pollack, who looks after the studio, is an engineer, so it's set up the way you like to work.

In general, you stick to SSL consoles.

I like the way they work. I know some people are funny about the sound, but I think it's good. I'm not tied to SSL. I'll work on Neves or pretty much anything. I think all desks have their good and bad points, so it's best to focus on their good points, and there are plenty of good ones on SSLs. I know some people think they're not as open, or as deep, or whatever. I've never had a problem with them.

Do you like them for both recording and mixing?

It depends. If I was doing a live band, it wouldn't be my console of choice. I find that old Neve recording with SSL mixing is a happy marriage. Although, I haven't used the J Series yet. That might change my mind.

Really, I use whatever. I think that's more of an English thing as well, by the way. We don't tend to have the finances or resources to be quite so fussy; you have to go with what you've got. I used to work a lot on indie bands who didn't have large budgets. I've been stuck with a band in a tiny studio with a desk I can't even remember, and all I had was SM57s. You have to make a record with that. You can't start complaining because you haven't got the right Neve modules.

I think a lot of American engineers are lucky enough to be spoiled in that way, whereas we've had to rough it a bit. You're given a budget that's low, and you have to get on with it and make the best of it.

Can you describe the process of making *The Fragile*?

The process changed, as you can imagine. Trent had some demos and a list of atmospheric territories he wanted to attack in different ways—electronic, or more organic and funky. So, we just started experimenting. When we'd gone through the demos, we started doing new stuff, which would involve, sometimes, just making sounds. We set Trent up in a room with a whole pile of junk, really, and four mics, and he'd just hit things and we'd record it. Sometimes, we'd play a loop of something and he'd play along on different boxes, or big plastic water bottles, or shakers. He'd pick up whatever appealed to him. We spent a long time cutting that together, and we made quite a few songs out of it. Sometimes it was based on him playing to the loop, and sometimes it was just based on the samples.

Then we'd build on it—put some basses on and guitars—and then we'd move on. We never got stuck on anything for too long, we just kept moving. What was good about that was, when you'd come back, after not listening to it for a month, it was a pleasant surprise—much better than we thought. We were having a lot of fun creating stuff, and we kept doing more and more. The down side was we ended up with something like 117 tracks. I knew definitely then that we were into it for the long haul.

One hundred seventeen tracks.

Yes. The strong ones survived. We just kept going round, improving, and then we'd have big review sessions where we would go through everything and say, "No, that one's out." Sometimes, we'd get bored and have lab days, making percussion banks or putting drum kits in different rooms and running them though P.A.s. A new piece of gear would arrive, and we'd spend half a day exploring it. You know how it is, when you get a new toy, you always get fantastic things out of it, in the beginning.

Well, you ended up with a lot going on for the vocals to cut through. How did you record them?

In the end, it got down to two main chains: the 58 for the more loudly sung, cutting vocals, into a Neve 1066, then into a Distressor. Everything went straight into Pro Tools, and it wasn't 24-bit. Twenty-four bit came out when we were in the middle and we thought, "We're committed, we're

not going back, forget it!" We did go through an Apogee, the stereo one. Some of it was self-limited, and some of it wasn't.

For the other chain, for the more breathy, high-sounding vocals, Trent has one of the new AKG C-12 valve mics, and we also used the Sony— the one with the big hairdryer heat sink, into an Avalon VT737P. Sometimes, we'd use an 1176, but those were the main chains. Trent always sings in the control room. We just turn the speakers down and put headphones on. It's the quickest—much easier for communication.

You've got piles of guitars to deal with. I suppose stereo placement is one of your tools to make them all work.

Yes. Rather than just going for "down the middle" or "hard left or right" or "9 o'clock," you can find little bits; just by wiggling them around a bit you'll give them a different space.

This is really dull to say but, generally, on guitars in the mix, I do absolutely nothing. A little bit of EQ to separate, if there's a whole wodge of them, and a very slight board compression. I use the channel compressor on the SSL set so it's hardly working. That gives it a bit of warmth or fatness.

I do use filters a lot, probably more than EQ. On guitars, I sometimes find that if you put the high-pass filter in slightly, it can clear out a lot. Also, sometimes I filter the top off.

I know you used all sorts of different guitar setups on *The Fragile*, but isn't there something basic you'd start with?

I don't have a particular setup. With other bands, it's what the guitarist likes to use. Then, if we're struggling, I'll suggest something. In this case, Trent had a few preamps; in particular, we used the DigiTech 2112 a lot. It's stereo, and you can route a tube preamp to one side and a solid-state one to the other. We'd do that, then send them to a Boogie power amp and out to a pair of Boogie 4-by-12s. It sounds really wide with different preamps on each side.

Distortion is one of the main artistic lynchpins of the record. What are some of the things you used to get it?

We'd go on pedal-buying trips a lot. Swollen Pickle was very popular, by Way Huge. They don't make them anymore. We used Lovetime, Big Cheese, Fox, The Tone Machine, and some things were done on the Eventide DSP 4000.

There's a pedal called the Fuzz Factory we liked, and we used the Shinai fuzz/wah, which the Jesus and Mary Chain used to get their thin, wiry distortions. There's the Roger Mayer Voodoo Axe, the Danelectro Daddy-O. . . . I could keep going on. Also, often they were strung together.

With so much going on, and so many different kinds of distortion, how do you carve out niches for each part?

I suppose some of it's done by taste and fine-tuning while you're recording. You get a sound that works with what else is there. The way Trent works, you're always trying something different. He'd want to do a guitar overdub, without particularly having a part in mind, so we'd grab a load of pedals and plug them together—either plug the pedal chain into a valve DI, or sometimes we'd put it into an amp through speakers, or sometimes through an amp into a speaker simulator. He'd get a sound and go, "Well, that's quite interesting," and he'd come up with a part based around the sound, which is quite a liberating way to do guitars.

That's opposite to how a lot of people work.

It is. On this album, there was no real agenda or plan. It all kind of unfurled as we went along. In hindsight, when I listened back to it, it seemed that we knew what we were doing, but we didn't. We just didn't want to pull out the old tricks. For a lot of the sounds that Trent had gotten in the past, particularly on *Downward Spiral*, people seem to have created plug-ins that do them immediately. So, he couldn't use those, he had to move on.

It really was a different way of making a record. We both said we were glad we did it, and that we enjoyed it, but we wouldn't do it again. Both of us were, I think, at a point where we wanted to have that indulgence. Especially as an engineer, it's a dream to be able to indulge yourself in sound as much as we did.

What did you mix to?

DAT, 16-bit. Through the Apogees. In hindsight, I would have liked to have gone to half-inch, but since I thought we would be doing more post-production, going digital back to Pro Tools, I thought we should go to DAT.

Do you think you have a special talent for working with people with strong personalities?

My preference is working with people with strong personalities. They know what they're doing; they're not looking for you to give them a sound. You work together, which I like; I always work as a co-producer. I believe in working with bands that inspire me. It would be a complete con to take solo production on any of these bands' records because they have such massive input. You're there as devil's advocate, somebody to push them, as a sounding board, or to give them ideas. A lot of the time, you're there to filter through their ideas. A lot of the people I work with are not short of ideas or parts. They've got too many! They just want somebody to go "That one!"

To help sort it out.

Yeah. So, if somebody says, "The guy in the band's a control freak," I think, "Fantastic." Because, for me, they're much easier people to work with.

Is there a piece of equipment you can't do without?

I've got a Forat F16 that I use to trigger kicks and snares. Most people don't admit doing this, but I'm going to put my hand up and go, "I do." I don't use them to replace; I use them to put behind, because I don't really like reverbs on drums. Instead, I'll put a low, whoompy-sounding kick beneath the kick drum to give it sub. Sometimes, you can't EQ that in, or if you EQ it in, it gets muddy. I find it works with a blend, with the recorded kick drum as the main sound, the low one underneath, and then you just sneak in the subharmonic dbx on that.

The dbx boom box?

Yes. You don't have a lot of bleed going on and you can get a very present kick drum. So, I'll have a whoompy one or sometimes a clicky one, just to give it a bit of definition. And just behind the snare, I'll put an ambient snare sample instead of using a reverb. A lot of people are a bit Luddite about samples, but I don't see the difference between putting an ambient snare sample behind the snare and using reverb. Some people reach for the same reverb to put on the snare all the time. They think that's fine and a sample isn't. I don't see the difference, apart from the fact that, to me, the snare sample sounds more natural than the digital reverb.

You use the Forat because you have sounds in it you've collected over the years.

I use it because it's quick. I have got a lot of samples in it that I can quickly flick through and see which ones suit the track. I don't like replacing sounds using MIDI maps because I find they drift. Especially with kick drums, the attack's not the same. The next thing, I suppose, would be to record it into digital audio and move it so it's spot-on, but at this stage, I find the Forat much quicker. Also I can change the tuning, adjusting it as I go. I got into it early on, working with the indie bands who would get me in to mix records that had been recorded incredibly quickly in very small studios. The drum sounds weren't as good as they could have been, and they always wanted the guitars deafeningly loud. The only way to get the drums to cut, without having them loud, was to have a sample going underneath to give it some kind of presence and definition. The Forat's done me well. I think there are only two in England now, and every time I reach to turn it on, I hope and pray that it's still working.

It's a bit surprising, but I like listening to *The Fragile* at low volume.

Yes, I definitely try to make a mix sound good quiet, as well, so I tend to mix very quietly. I have it loud at the beginning to get the general vibe—the feel of the rhythm and the drums—but once I'm happy with the basic way it's sitting, most of the balancing is done on the Auratone.

A single Auratone.

Yes. Also, the Auratone makes me mix the guitars louder.

What other monitors do you like?

KRK 7000s. Butch Vig and Billy [Corgan] were using them on *Siamese Dream*, and I got into them. Before that, I was using NS10s, as everybody was. I grew to really like the KRKs. They have, since I've got them, time-aligned the bottom end, and what on earth possessed them to do that, I can't imagine. I know at least five people who are cueing up for the old ones and don't want the new ones. Of all their range of speakers, and they've got loads of them, to me these are by far the most accurate. They're not particularly flattering, but for balance, I find them great. Everybody I work with likes them and wants a pair, and they can't get them because they don't make them.

Any new gear you're impressed with?

It's an amazing time, I think. There's so much great gear that's come out. Trent got one of those Virus keyboards, which was fantastic, and there's a sampling box—I think it's the SP808 Roland—which has inboard effects that we used a lot. There's Distressors, and the TC FireworX is good.

I've also got a dbx160S, which I really like. I can't remember a time when so much good gear was coming out. It's expensive trying to keep up.

Do you find yourself doing less in the mix than you used to?

Yes, I'm not that keen to reach for the EQ or the compressor. I think that's something you learn, to try to make what's there work best on its own. I've learned that from the artists I've worked with, who are precious about their sound. They've spent a long while getting the guitar sound, and you're just coming to mix. They don't want you to steam in and ruin it. So, panning, sometimes a bit of slight compression—I guess that's dull really, isn't it?

Trent Reznor has said that the random button on a CD player is his enemy. Obviously, the sequence on *The Fragile* was very important. It's interesting that you brought in an outside person, namely Bob Ezrin, [Pink Floyd, Lou Reed] to help sequence the album.

We were just punch-drunk really. I tried sequencing, and it took me three hours to get the first four. We thought we hadn't any objectivity left, and it would be great to get somebody else to help. The running order was crucial. We knew if it was wrong, it would be a very arduous journey.

It's definitely an album, one of the few these days, that sounds better when you listen to it all the way through. A lot of time was spent getting that right.

Making a whole album is a lot of work in itself. You've done two doubles, *Mellon Collie* and *The Fragile*. Any hints on keeping up the stamina to get through them?

[Laughs] I don't like double albums. But I go back again to my training. Working at Trident was almost like being at boot camp. From the beginning, you were thrown into the long-hour deep end of sleep deprivation and of being able to keep it together. Stamina-wise, I can only think it's enthusiasm that keeps you going. On both of those albums, I was working with fantastic bands. You couldn't ask for more inspiration than you got from them. Every day, you wake up, and it's not a drudge to go into work. You're lucky to be there. It's really just enjoying it and loving it.

DAVE WAY

APRIL, 2000 ## Mixer on a Hot Streak

Dave Way is no stranger to hot streaks. He's had more than a few in his career, from his early days with kingpin hip-hop producer Teddy Riley, to hit mixes for TLC, Whitney Houston, Babyface, Boyz II Men, Spice Girls, Bobby Brown, Michael Jackson, and Toni Braxton, including Braxton's Grammy-winning single "Breathe Again." His latest hot streak places him once again at the top of the charts with mixes for back-to-back number ones: Christina Aguilera's "Genie In A Bottle" from her five-times platinum LP, and "I Knew I Loved You" from Savage Garden's latest platinum endeavor, *Affirmation*. In addition, Way both recorded and mixed the CD that appeared on so many pop music critics' Top Ten of 1999 list, Macy Gray's debut, *On How Life Is*.

It takes only a quick listen to note that the Aguilera, Gray, and Savage Garden tunes all sound completely different from each other. Obviously, Way isn't the kind of mixer who churns out hits by imprinting his signature stamp on every project. When you talk to him, it becomes clear that this is no accident. He spends time and thought delving beneath the surface and takes great pride in helping to bring out just the right emotions and feel for each piece of music he's involved with.

Way's reputation for being an easygoing, all-around nice guy precedes him. In conversation, he shows himself to be a true music lover, with a ready smile that shows a quiet enthusiasm for the projects he's involved with. It takes a bit of effort to make him talk about himself and his work, but, once primed, he has a lot to say. His ideas and theories on sound and the art of mixing are fully formed—the product of time spent listening, playing, studying, and, of course, behind the console.

I first met with Way for this interview on a day when he was holed up at Larrabee North's Studio One, mixing tracks for Quincy Jones' latest pop project, *Young Americans*.

Selected Credits

Christina Aguilera
"Genie in a Bottle," "What a Girl Wants," "Come On Over"

India.Arie
"Ready for Love"

Babyface
"When Can I See You?"

Michelle Branch
"You Get Me," "Something To Sleep To," "Sweet Misery"

Toni Braxton
"Breathe Again," "You Mean the World to Me," "Seven Whole Days"

Foo Fighters
"Next Year" radio/video mix

Macy Gray
On How Life Is, The ID, The Trouble With Being Myself, "I Try"

Mick Jagger
"Brand New Set of Rules"

Paul McCartney
"Loving Flame," "Lonely Road" radio/video mixes

Pink
"Don't Let Me Get Me," "Eighteen Wheeler," "Numb"

Savage Garden
Affirmation, "I Knew I Loved You"

TLC
Ain't Too Proud to Beg, "What About Your Friends," "Red Light Special"

Congratulations on all your recent hits, and extra kudos for the Macy Gray record. I think it falls into that rare category of "What Is Hip?"

Yeah, I'm pretty proud of that one.

You usually just come in for the mix these days. How did it happen that you recorded Macy's CD?

When [producer/manager] Andy Slater played me the demos, I was really floored—by Macy's voice in particular. We started talking about what kind of record he wanted to make, and it turned out to be exactly the kind of r&b soul music, based on live players, that I've wanted to be a part of for a long time. He talked about Matt Chamberlain playing drums, and having John Brion come in, and it was like, "I've got to record this stuff—it's going to be great!" Plus, because I've spent so many years now just mixing, with only little bits of recording here and there, I thought it would be good to get my chops back up, to make sure I haven't lost anything. It was exciting, and it was a lot of fun, but it also made me realize how great just mixing is. [Laughs]

You'd forgotten how much work recording and mixing a whole album can be.

Recording and mixing … you get so inside of the record, it's very intense. When you're just mixing, it's all been done. [Laughs] There's a nice rough mix for you to listen to, and everybody's excited for the song to be done at the end of the day. You do your thing, and a couple of days later, you're on to the next one. It's creative, but it's a lot easier on your mind and your psyche than doing the whole thing. At the same time, having done the whole Macy Gray record gives me a lot of satisfaction. But I don't know if I can do that process more than once in a while.

You must bring your mixer's perspective to recording.

Yes, you're constantly thinking about the mix as you're recording—at least I was. So when it comes time to mix, you're just trying to fine-tune the rough mixes. On Macy's record, we did a lot of referencing to the roughs because they were really good. They were what everybody at the record company was excited about. We spent a long time seeing if we could make them a little bit better here and there, but basically, we wanted to keep the raw quality that we had from them.

You worked on different consoles than the SSLs you're used to.

We recorded almost all of it at Sunset Sound, and it was the first time I'd worked there. It was great. The API consoles they have sound amazing. We did most of the tracking with the drums in Studio 3,

Way on the Patio at Larrabee North

which is the little room in the back where Prince did *Dirty Mind* and some of his other earlier records. Then we moved to Studio 1 and did some mixing and some more overdubs. Then we went to A&M and did some mixing as well on a Neve.

From the start, you had a sound in mind that you were going for.

Absolutely. As I understood it, we were looking for a Stevie Wonder sound, like from *First Finale* or *Inner Visions*. That kind of dry, in-your-face, honest-sounding record, with people coming out of the speakers, rather than machines. And number one was to have Macy at the front of all of it, so that the focus was on her. We wanted her to be captured by this fun, almost family-like atmosphere going on around her. And I think that's almost exactly what we got.

What did you do to accomplish that?

Number one, we used hardly any digital gear, no digital reverbs....

In tracking?

In mixing, too. When it came time to mix, we used plates and chambers, and we set up some mics and an amp out in the room at A&M's Studio A, the big live room. We used a lot of compression to make things sound like they had a lot of room on them, and we really tried to stay away from anything digital—anything that would take away from the warm, analog, not-so-state-of-the-art sound. We wanted to make a record as if it had been done in 1973.

It doesn't sound like 1973, though. It sounds totally contemporary and very cool.

The modern stuff comes from DJ Kilu, who did scratching and from loops. Rami [Jaffee, Wallflowers' keyboardist] used a Casio keyboard that he'd run through an Echoplex and this weird Univox filter and all kinds of other crazy contraptions. We'd just put a mic on the amp. So from the source, there were some digital links in the chain, but outside of that, it was pretty much all microphones and tape.

Let's go back in time. How did you learn engineering?

I went to school—Berklee College of Music in Boston.

To study music?

No, engineering. But when you're at Berklee, you're a musician. For about the first two years, you don't even step into a studio. You're taking theory courses on the studio side and practicing your instrument—taking harmony and arranging classes. Because, if you want to get a degree like I did, a Bachelor of Music, you've got to pass your proficiencies on whatever your instrument is. My instrument, when I was there, was bass.

But how did you even know that there was such a thing as a recording engineer?

I grew up listening to the Beatles and Stevie Wonder. I spent years listening to all of their records with headphones on, dissecting them, and listing to every note. It's hard not to be aware of the engineering and production side of music when you're listening to "I Am The Walrus" or something like that.

And, growing up in bands, I was making demos. I had this quarter-inch Sony tape machine that we used. It actually sounded really good. I remember recording, with this little Radio Shack mixer, our version of the Eagles' "Best Of My Love" on that quarter-inch machine, and when we played it back, it sounded great. Just the sound of the tape saturation and everything else—it was amazing because you sounded a hundred times better than you did in real life due to the medium you were recording on.

Then, after school. . . .

I sent my out my resume and ended up at the Hit Factory for a few months, and then went to work across the street from it at this little one-room studio called SoundWorks. Shep Pettibone and Teddy Riley were working there all the time, just at the start of when they were becoming well known.

For a year, I worked a lot assisting and doing engineering for both of them. Then, stroke of luck, Teddy asked me to do a mix with him, one day. He liked it, and I kept working for him. I joined up with Teddy just as his career was starting to skyrocket. I learned so much watching him; he's just an amazing sponge of creativity. The way that he was making hip-hop/r&b/new-jack-swing records then was so revolutionary. It's the way records are commonly made now, but then it was making everybody sit up and look.

For somebody to be sampling these little bits of James Brown and all kinds of snare drums and kick drums and vocal samples and playing them like a drum machine. . . . He really was making music in a different way, and he influenced everybody. He changed the face of r&b music.

Bass is key to most songs, and especially to the r&b-based pop music you often work on. Do you have any theories about how to make it work properly?

When I think of bass, I think of length; like how long a note should be. Because you can make a note longer by boosting 20 or 30 Hz. Those frequencies are so big, they ring out in the room longer and make the note actually longer. Sometimes you want something to be really long and to hang over, sometimes you want it to be tight and clipped. So, you might have to clean up the bass and take out some of that 20 to 30 Hz to make it tighter. After that, I'm looking at the detail and the high end of it to make sure that it's poking through.

If you are listening on an Auratone or something that doesn't have a lot of bass in it, can you still hear what the bass is doing?

Sometimes, on r&b records, the bass is like a Minimoog thing, where it's almost all low end and fundamental; there aren't a lot of harmonics to it. That's fine when you're playing it on the big system, but when it comes time to listen on the Auratone, you've got to come up with some tricks to make it audible on the small speaker. That might include splitting it off and trying to find where you can get the attack on it, then compressing and EQing that and adding it in on top.

So you spend time listening on a single Auratone?

Sometimes, or I'll listen on the Studer speaker.

What are your main monitors?

Generally, here at Larrabee, I'll tend to listen to the big speakers more, because they're really good, but I do listen to them at a pretty low level. At other studios, I just work on the nearfields.

I have a pair of Tannoy System 8s that I've had for a long time that I love. And just recently, I've gone back to using the regular [Yamaha] NS10 studio monitors. Before, I had a pair that had a custom crossover in them. I like the NS10 studios because they're not quite as bright. I like to have a nice full bass and a good amount of midrange—but not to be too hyped on the high end.

I'm constantly trying to listen to speakers. At home, I've got a pair of NHTs that I really love. I went to a hi-fi store and heard the NHTs with a Sony amp. They sounded great. I love to listen to music on them. They've just started making some studio monitors.

Yours are high-end consumer monitors.

Yeah. They've got domed tweeters and a small

midrange speaker—about five or six inches—
and a side-firing low speaker. It's like a sub that
comes out the side rather than the front. It adds a
different kind of spaciousness that fills up the room
in a very nice way. I love taking my CDs from the
studio home and listening on them.

I love speakers, and I try to listen to a lot of them.
I have a pair of KRK E7s that sometimes I like,
sometimes I don't like. Recently, I've also listened
to the E8s with a subwoofer, and I'm starting to
like them.

You've got to be careful about getting new
monitors. You've got to break them in and get to
know them before you start to rely on them. So, at
this point, I've also got these little Bose Freestyle
speakers that I got turned on to at La Face by
Barney Perkins, the engineer there. They still
sell them; they sound like a little boom box with a
surprising amount of bass coming out of them.
They do have a really hyped high end, but between
them and the NS10s and the Tannoys, I feel like
I've got all the bases covered.

You have all of them set up in the control room when you're mixing?

Yes. I do a lot of switching between them, then
listening off the Studer. Then, like I said, here at
Larrabee, I use the big monitors a lot, and then I
go out to the car. I always take a CD out to the car
before I put it down, and then I play it at home.
[Laughs] If I can't figure it out after all those
speakers....

Do you always leave a mix up overnight so you can take it home and check it out?

Lately, I've been really appreciating the value of
that extra half a day on the second day—that extra
two or three hours in the morning after you've
listened at home and listened in the car and slept
on it. To be able to make it that extra five or ten
percent better really does make a difference.
Sometimes, of course, it sounds great, and you
come in the next day and just print it, but it's nice
to have the luxury to know you've got it right.

"Genie In A Bottle" sounds present and punchy, but
avoids getting attention by being super-bright.

The super-bright thing doesn't work for me when
I'm trying to make something hard and punchy.
Super-bright works when you want to make
something sound nice and pretty. So, on something
like "Genie In A Bottle," too much brightness can
actually take away from the attitude.

I try to think of frequencies and mixes, in general,
on emotional levels. What kind of feelings and
emotions are you trying to bring out of this song
or this artist? That was a song that we wanted to
be hard and fun and to have it catch your ear from
the very first intro.

You think about frequencies in terms of emotion?

Absolutely. For instance, bass frequencies seem to
fill me up with warmth, and they kind of resonate
down here [points to stomach]. Ultra-high
frequencies translate to me in terms of pretty and
sweet. I don't think it's a coincidence that we say an
EQ that has high end on it sounds sweet. If you're
mixing a ballad and the lyrics have something kind
of naïve or pretty about them, you might want to
kind of accentuate those frequencies.

Whereas, with a warm ballad that's maybe a
little serious, I would tend to steer clear of those
frequencies that make it too pretty. Then, for me,
midrange frequencies equal a more jarring kind of
energy. It equals "bold" in a big way, and you use it
if you want something to really grab your attention;
if you want the artist to come across saying, "This is
how it is!" You want to make sure the midrange is

screaming to you, saying "Hey, listen to me!"

Now, the song "I Knew I Loved You" [by Savage Garden] is not one of those songs. That's a sweet song. So if you were to compare that song with "Genie In A Bottle," you would definitely hear differences between the high-end information on both of them. There's also probably a little more bass on the Savage Garden song. Bass on a funky track like "Genie" can have a lot of energy also, but it's not ultra low. The ultra low stuff would be more on Savage Garden, because it would fill you up with some warmth.

That's why I don't always try to make every mix and every song sound the same frequency-wise. They're not trying to say the same thing, and they shouldn't sound like it. I'm trying help get across what they are trying to say and to pick the frequencies and effects that work for that.

Anything unusual happen during the mix for "Genie In A Bottle?"

Well, one interesting thing happened after we'd done a mix and listened—all of us—and agreed that there was something in the rough mix that was missing from the final. We determined that it was because the rough mix was all done in Pro Tools—all digital. But, the night before we mixed, they'd dumped everything onto two-inch tape for the mix, and that had changed the sound. Particularly the drums and background vocals, which were softened somewhat—having lost those transients going to tape, it was hard to get them back. So, we ended up bringing the Pro Tools rig back down and taking most of the drums and some of the vocals right off of it, and the rest of it off two-inch. That's what ended up in the final mix.

That leads us to the eternal question, digital or analog?

I embrace all. Like, for Macy Gray, I wouldn't have picked anything but two-inch tape. [Laughs] Well, maybe I might have picked two-inch 16-track or 1-inch 8-track, if we had those options. On that record, we mixed to both half-inch and DAT with a dB Technologies converter at the front, and for the mixes we did at A&M, we used the custom converters that they have there, which sound really good. I'd say on probably at least half of the songs, we mastered from the DATs. We'd listen to both, and one format would work better for some particular song.

I've got to say, though, that recently I've been mixing more directly off Pro Tools. In the last few months, probably sixty percent of the things I've mixed have been right off 24-bit Pro Tools, and they've sounded great. Especially coming through an SSL 9000 console.

Don't you ever worry that things may end up sounding too much the same if everybody ends up recording in the same format, e.g., Pro Tools?

You still have control over what goes in on the front end. You're free to manipulate as much as you want. It's not going to make things sound more "all the same" than when everybody was putting everything on two-inch 24-track. Plus, the console still makes a lot of difference. More, in my opinion, than the recording format.

As a busy mixer, how do you avoid doing the same things all the time, thus, ending up with the same sounds?

It's easy. I don't use the same gear all the time, and I constantly try new things. Like lately, I've been using a Pendulum Audio compressor that's really pretty good. There's a certain sound to all these things—an EMT 250 sounds different than an AMS RMX. They might both have a long 3.5 reverb time, but they have different qualities, and depending on whether I want something that jumps out of the track or sinks into it, I'll choose one or the other.

I hope that all my mixes don't sound the same, because if they did, I'd feel like I hadn't done my job. Macy wouldn't have sounded right, like Christina. They're two totally different artists. Why should I impose what I want to say on what they want to say?

Up Close on a Dave Way Mix

In a second conversation, I prevailed upon Way to get specific about what he was doing on a few channels of the mix he was doing for British pop band S Club 7. He demurred at first, insisting that the mix was too simple to be of interest, but his basic good nature won out, when I persisted.

Let's take a look at what you're doing on the bass.

This is definitely a single-sounding mix. It's got a funky beat with a bass that primarily moves around with the kick drum. Also, the bass is more staccato in the verses and legato in the choruses, on the same channel, with basically the same notes and chord progressions through the verses and the choruses.

So, I did have to do some things in order to make it more dynamic between the verse and the chorus. I did some mutes, on both the bass and the kick drum, to help the overall dynamic of the song.

On the bass, I tried different compressors, like the Tubetech, which I use a lot, but when I compared it with the uncompressed sound, I preferred it uncompressed. I did the same thing with a Motown EQ that I often use to put a lot of low, low stuff in, but it didn't sound any better either. I always compare to how the signal is originally, and if it's not better after fudging with it, I'll go back to the original sound.

I ended up with just a little bit of board compression on the bass. I do have a good amount of EQ compared to what I normally put on — mostly accentuating midrange and upper stuff. I also added some [Line 6] POD distortion to bring out a little more harmonics and make it a little more buzzy.

You have that on an insert?

No, it's on a bus, and I'm mixing it in. It really seemed to jump out of the track when I added the POD on top of it. It's the kind of thing you don't necessarily hear in the track, but you feel it. All of a sudden, it seems to have more presence without having to EQ the midrange on it. That's nothing new, a lot of people do it.

Yeah, I'm seeing PODs in every control room lately.

Guilty, as charged.

Okay, drums.

On the kick drum, I've got a 550A on the insert, just to give it a little more knock. I like those because they're particularly hard-sounding — almost shiny. I'm boosting 2 dB at 5K, 2 dB at 1.5, then taking out a little at 300 [Hz], and the high shelf filter is in.

There's also a little bit of an enhancing reverb on it — a very, very, short room from the [Eventide] Orville, one of my favorite boxes, these days. It's so short, it's actually more like a chorus.

Backgrounds.

This song has a nice airy feel. The chorus is mainly background vocals that are kind of light and breathy, fairly sweet on top of this funky beat. I tried to go with that, and put this airy reverb on the background vocals in the chorus to exaggerate that quality in the vocals, using the Orville program called Ghost Air. I also brightened them up considerably. There's also a judicious amount of delay on the vocals, [laughs] in keeping with the British approach to mixing, which maybe has a little more reverb and delays than I would normally use. Because they are British, and also I'd heard tracks from their last album and from this one, and I think that sound is part of their appeal that I don't want to change.

Steve Marcantonio

Keeping It Real

JULY, 2000

Engineering country music is a special balancing act. Take a roomful of musicians, then double or maybe triple the guitars, add piano, stacks of keyboards, some strings, high-profile background vocals, a pedal steel, and perhaps even some electronic percussion. There's almost always a lot going on, but somehow you have to make it all sound simple. And you still have to hear the bass and keep that all-important lead vocal way out front.

Steve Marcantonio is a master at the task. Given his trademark punchy drums, well-placed guitars, and tastefully present lead vocals, it's no surprise that the client list of this former Jersey boy reads like a Who's Who of country. His work encompasses classic Nashville as well as the edgier side of the genre, including projects for Rodney Crowell, Deana Carter, Billy Falcon, the Nitty Gritty Dirt Band, George Strait, Alabama, the Warren Brothers, and Vince Gill, among others.

It wasn't easy to catch up with Marcantonio. There are a lot of good studios in Nashville, and he seems to be spending time in most of them, juggling projects and producers. We finally caught up with him on his cell and arranged to talk between mixes for Montgomery Gentry at Ocean Way Nashville and Deana Carter's latest at Sound Kitchen. It's a noteworthy comment on Marcantonio's personality and vibe that, even though our conversations were by phone, his enthusiasm and honest enjoyment of his work came clearly over the land lines.

So how does an Italian guy from Jersey end up as one of the busiest engineers in Nashville?

I grew up at New York Record Plant; I started there in '78. But really, it was pretty much a fluke the way I got started in the business. I come from a musical family, and one of my cousins, who lived with us, was in the Four Seasons. I used to go to a lot of concerts when I was a kid, and I always read the backs of album covers. So I knew about engineers, and I said, "I want to do that." Then, when I was a junior in high school, I took a course in record engineering. But during that

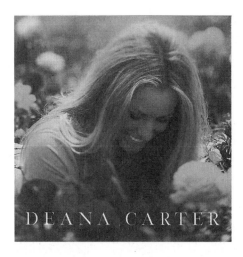

DEANA CARTER

was a great time to be there. I didn't know a thing about recording when I started, but Roy wanted people like that because he liked to teach them his way. You came up through the ranks, you paid your dues. It was a great school. I was addicted to that place. I was there all the time. I slept there. I truly loved it. As tired as I was, every time that I went there, I felt rejuvenated.

How did you move up to engineering?

I worked with Dave Thoener a bunch, and he really helped me out a lot. He was working with Rodney Crowell, and he used to let me do overdubs for him.

One day, I did an overdub for Rodney where I had to match a vocal sound. It was a bit difficult, but I did it, and he was really impressed. A year or two later, out of the blue, he called me up in New Jersey, to come down here [to Nashville] to work with Rosanne Cash, who he was married to at the time. So I came down to do a record, which was called *King's Record Shop*.

I did Rodney's record after that, with Tony Brown producing, and I started meeting people. Back then, it seemed like I was like the only person from New York around here. So, I think I was looked at as having a different sort of attitude, and a different sort of sound.

What was the difference?

When I first came here, they were doing things like recording drums direct. I'll never forget walking into Sound Stage Studios where they were recording Russ Kunkel, and he was playing pads! That seemed so bizarre to me. They did it, I think, because the control room was not isolated from the studio. There was no wall, so in order to record drums, you had to either listen on headphones or record direct.

But, overall, I think that at that time, in Nashville, the sound was a little bit more tame than it is now. And my sound, coming from New York, was a little bit rougher than what they were used to. I think, in general, my drums were a little louder, my guitars

course, I realized I was in way over my head. Everybody else in the class was already either a technical engineer or a musician. They were a lot older, and they were asking questions that I didn't know anything about. I just wanted to make music. I didn't play an instrument, but I listened to records and radio all the time. I would key in on certain instruments and just really get into their sound.

Anyway, I pretty much gave up on the idea of being an engineer after that class, although I kept on being into music. After high school, I went to work at the General Motors assembly plant.

That's so Jersey.

[Laughs] Yeah. Well, at the plant, there was a time each year while they changed over to make the new models, and everybody got laid off for a few months. During that lay-off time in '78, my cousin Joey happened to get on the phone with Roy Cicala, who owned the Record Plant. I'd read Roy's name on albums, and I knew who he was. I guess that impressed Joey, because he said, "Let me see what I can do for you." Long story short, Roy took me under his wing, and I worked there until '84 when I became freelance.

Who did you work with at Record Plant?

Just the staff. But the staff at that time was like, Dave Thoener, Thom Panunzio, Jay Messina.... Jimmy Iovine was still there then, and I got to do a couple of sessions with him and Shelly Yakus. It were a little louder, and there was more 'verb on the drums. People seemed to like it, and that's how I got started. Then I met Josh Leo, who'd moved here from California at around the same time. We're both Italian, and we hit it off immediately. I worked with him for about eight years. We did Alabama and a bunch of other stuff... and here I am.

Some people specialize in tracking or mixing, but you seem to do both equally.

[Laughs] Well, there are fewer acts now, and a lot more engineers, so it's a good thing I like to do both! I always love to mix, but tracking is sort of why I started engineering in the first place.

If you get it down really good on tape, then mixing is that much easier; that's my philosophy. When I track a record, if I know I'm going to mix it, I assume that what I'm hearing in my basic tracks is going to be the record—just maybe a bit more polished or fine-tuned. A lot of people have told me that my rough track mixes sound like records, and I take pride in that. It's the birth of the song right there in tracking, and that's really exciting for me.

So, if you know you're going to mix a record, you prefer to cut the tracks.

Absolutely. Even the best tracks that you get, you always say, "I wish I could have done this or that." I just feel more comfortable with my tracks. I think most every engineer would probably feel the same way, don't you?

Can you describe your day today?

It's funny you ask that, because I just came back from mixing in New York, and on my way to work today, I was thinking about how good we have it here in Nashville. It's so easy to drive to this studio [Sound Kitchen]. It's easy to park, it's easy to get in and out. I live ten minutes away from where I'm working today. This morning, I was reading the paper at home at quarter after nine, and I knew that the producer was getting in at about ten. I'd been thinking about a couple of changes to make in the mix, so I threw on my clothes and came over to do them before he got here.

I usually like to get a mix to a certain point at night and then close it out the next day. I don't see how these guys do two, three songs in a day. I'm kind of jealous of them, I guess, but for me, I like to spread it out a bit. I can't stay in the control room too long. I like to get up and walk around, and stuff like that.

So, I had this mix up last night, and I was able to do a few things to it this morning before he got there. In like ten or fifteen minutes, I was able to do a dozen [level] rides, and within an hour the mix was done.

When you listened to your ref CD at home, you made some notes about what things you'd like to change.

Right. I used to write stuff down, but now I usually don't. [Laughs] As bad as my memory is sometimes about other things, I can always remember that in the fourth bar of the first chorus, I need to raise that one snare hit.

So that's what it was like today. I got up and went to the studio. I did my changes. I came home, I showered, and I went back. By that time, my assistant had put down the multiple versions. I don't know what they do in California, but here we put down a lot of versions of the mixes.

You mean like vocal up, backgrounds up, bass up? Doesn't everybody do that?

Well, certain guys I know don't. But here, you can do anywhere from six to twenty different versions. I stay to make sure it goes down right for the first master, but after that, usually the second engineer will cover it, because it's just a matter of running it onto tape. The second engineers down here are really good; they've got it together. That way, you get about a two-hour break in between each mix.

What consoles do you prefer to work on?

I go back and forth. When I came here to town, I'd never worked on an SSL. But now that I've worked on SSLs, I like them a lot—especially the G Series. And I like Ultimation a lot. Which is good, because this is very much an SSL town.

On the other hand, I really love the [Neve] VR console. There's something about the VRs—to me, those consoles are more rock 'n' roll, and the bottom end sounds bigger. The SSL is a little bit more pop. Like I said, I go back and forth, because the SSL can sound more punchy. Just a little. It can sound like there's more attack on everything in general. I know it's kind of a vague statement to make, but that's the way I feel.

The 80-input VR at Ocean Way Nashville, I totally love. I also like Trident 80Bs. And I'm excited about the new APIs. Sound Kitchen is putting in an 80-input inline Legacy; I know the sound of those consoles, and I'm sure it's going to sound great.

I love the old Neve [80-in 8078] at Ocean Way; it's one of the best sounding consoles I've ever worked on. When you lift up the fader to get a sound on something, it's almost as if you don't have to do anything to it. Old Neves can be like that.

Sometimes, your tracks sound better just running through them. I guess lately, that's my console of choice. Also, since I do a lot of recording, I own a few API preamps. I also rent things. There's a cartage company down here called Underground Sound, which has a 12-input Neve sidecar that I use to record my drums through.

I hear you're a wizard on the Sony 3348.

I love the machine. There are some Studers around town, but I demand the Sony. It's just so much easier to use. I do a lot of flying, and I'm pretty quick at it.

To me, the 3348 sounds great. And it's great on country records when you're recording eight or nine musicians, and you're gonna be using thirty tracks, and you're gonna be punching in—it's not uncommon that I'm punching in a whole band. I can rehearse the punch, then do auto-punch. You can't beat it. [Otari] RADARs are becoming popular here, and they sound pretty good, I must admit. They're easy to use. But I love the 48. You get great, punchy drums.

When you're recording, what mics do you like to use on them?

I use a lot of the same mics all the time on the drums. A Neumann 47 FET on the kick, and I might use an AKG D12 or D112 with that. I'll put the 47 outside and a D112 a little bit inside. I stay away from using gates. A lot of guys don't like any leakage on the kick, but I like the sound of the area around the kick drum, and I use the 47 to get a little of that air in there. I usually don't gate any drums in tracking. If I gate, I'll send it in a mult-in mixing, so I have an additional gated track to mix in.

With the snare, I go with a 57 in general, but it depends on what studio I'm at. I'll find out what kind of mics they have there. I've used 414s on the snare, and one time the drummer brought in a Beta 57 that sounded great.

Photo: Sharon Corbitt

Do you mic top and bottom?

Yes, I do. When I first started miking the bottom, I got in trouble because I had too much bottom—too much rattle. Now, I tend to use just a little bit of the bottom or put it on another track.

On toms, I go back and forth. I've used 421s in the past, and at Ocean Way they have Sennheiser 409s, which are great. Recently, I bought these really tiny Sennheiser MD504s, and I've been using them. Even with those, though, I try to place the tom mics a little farther away—maybe eight inches off the head—once again, to get in a little of the air.

On hi-hat, usually a KM84. On cymbals, KM84s, sometimes. Or 414s, 67s...I treat my overheads sort of like a stereo drum mix. There are a lot of cymbals in them. I try to get the sound of the drum kit in the overheads. Sometimes, I'll start with those mics and build my drum sound from that.

Then, depending on where I'm working, I'll use some room mics—M49s or 67s. Over at Ocean

Way, they've got RCA77s—the old ribbon mics; I like those for the room. And also, I've used the Coles. At Sound Kitchen, they have four Audio-Technica mics wired into the ceiling that come up in the patchbay. They sound incredible, sort of like a nonlin-type room [nonlinear reverb effect setting]—a tight, short decay that's good for rock 'n' roll.

Sometimes, I'll also put a center room mic down low, or sometimes, I'll put a mic behind the drummer. I'll print them on separate tracks. If I have the tracks, I like to print three or even four tracks of room, to be able to blend them later.

You compress the room mics.

Definitely. I love the 1178s and the Fairchilds for that. If I can get hold of a nice set of Fairchilds, I'm happy. I also love using the Distressor on room mics. Actually, I'll use a Distressor on almost anything.

When you get to mixing, what's the first thing you do?

I'll listen to the overheads, blend stuff into them, and try to get back what we had when we were tracking. Then, what I'll usually do is run a submix of the drums through a Fairchild or an 1178 and bring that back on two faders to make it real punchy. I like that real compressed, 1178 sound, which sounds so cool by itself, but if you blend it in, you get a little more apparent level without getting too much VU in the mix.

What settings would you be likely to use on compressors?

It depends on the song—the rhythm of the song. With the 1178, sometimes I'll press all the buttons in, and it does "infinity" or something like that. That can be really cool. Generally, I'll use the slowest attack and then a quick release, which gets them pumping. But it does depend on the tempo of the song. I'll mess with the attack mostly. The release, I'll keep quick.

With the Fairchild, there's only one knob, and I usually tend to keep it on 1, which I think is the quickest. If I use Distressors, I usually put them on Nuke or Opto.

What mics do you use on guitars?

I like 57s. Coles are cool, but sometimes, they almost sound like the compressor is in already, giving a real attacky kind of sound. Royers are good on guitars, and I also like using an 87 a little farther away, in conjunction with the close mics. A FET 47 also sounds great on electric guitar.

If I'm recording a straight-ahead guitar sound through an amp, I'll either put an 1176 on it at 4:1, with the attack about medium and the release on quick; or the Distressor at about 6:1, or maybe the Fairchild. Sometimes, on certain guitars, if you put the Fairchild on three, they'll sound really smooth. When I cut tracks, I usually run the acoustic guitar through a Fairchild. I like mixing it up and trying different things. If I go to a studio I've never worked at before, I'll ask the guys who work there what they have that's cool. Some guys don't like to do that, but I do.

What do you usually mix to?

I always mix to half-inch.

Do you prefer a Studer or an Ampex?

I use an [Ampex] ATR, although if there's a Studer available, I'll use it. Sound Kitchen just purchased two of the older Studers—I don't know the model, with the scissors and the little speaker. I just did my first mix yesterday on one of them, and it sounded great. I really prefer using half-inch when I mix, although I'll always run a DAT as a safety. And, you never know—if the mastering engineer prefers to use the DAT tape, you will. But most of the time, it's half-inch.

What kind of tape?

Quantegy 499, at +5 over 250. And I put some hefty level onto the tape.

Do you carry your own speakers around?

I have Genelec 1031As. Lately, I've been going back to NS10s, too. I go through different speakers when I'm mixing. Like today, I have the big KRKs, I've got the Genelecs, and I've got NS10s. The other thing I rely heavily on is my old Sony jam box.

How long have you had it?

It's 14 years old, and I must've put a few hundred dollars into it, just fixing it. It sounds great. There are many times during the day I'll have it on, in front of the console or somewhere behind me. It does wonders. I mean, you can't really judge a mix on it, because there's a lot of high-end stuff that sounds really loud on it.

But it's like the radio.

Yeah. We used to do that at the Record Plant. There was an engineer I worked with a lot, Bill Whitman, and he used to crank up his compressors and listen to it on a radio speaker. So, I took that idea.

What else do you own?

When I first came here, everyone had their own gear, but back in New York, no one owned anything. So, I fought it for years, but now, I finally have a rack. It's a low-tech kind of rack, though. I've got some TC gear—the M2000 and 3000. I like them because they have two engines. I've got this BSS dynamic EQ. And I bought an 1178. I love an 1178. I'd like to get a couple of 1176s, too. Oh, I also own two Distressors. To me, they work similarly to almost every kind of limiter. A Distressor can be like an 1176, or, at times, an LA2 or a dbx. I'll use them on everything— drums, vocals, bass. I've got some [API] 560s as well. And I've got a [Roland] Space Station. I picked that up real cheap, years ago.

Why do you think the engineer-manager thing, which is so ubiquitous in L.A., doesn't seem to exist in Nashville?

I think it's just smaller and more personal here. For example, Tony Brown is the president of MCA Records, and he produces a lot of major acts. I can call him up tomorrow, and if he can't take my call, then he'll call me back in five minutes. You have personal relationships with everybody in town— the producers, the production assistants.... It's more one-on-one in Nashville. It's more of a community. Here, I think, you go by your reputation and by word of mouth.

Do you have any theories on what makes a good-sounding record?

Well, I'm old school. When I listen to music on the radio, I try to picture the band actually playing. I listen a lot to oldies, and when you hear those records, you can almost see them in the studio. Nowadays, often you hear records, and it sounds like, that guitar is "here" and something else is "over there"—it almost sounds like it's pasted. It doesn't sound real. I take pride in getting stuff on tape as good as possible, in just capturing the performance of the musicians without messing with it. And then, putting it out in its rawness. To me, that makes a good-sounding record. I don't care if there's a mistake or if you can hear a car going by outside. You need to fix some mistakes, but if it sounds natural and real, that's a good-sounding record.

Any words of wisdom for people starting out?

You know, my motto is that I always try to remain professional. I realize that it's a job I'm doing, and it's a job that I really like. I'm paid well, I get a credit. Sometimes, things don't go your way, but you can't have everything. I know I could be on the assembly line again. And that's the perspective I keep.

DAVID THOENER

Memoirs of a Mixmaster

These days, you hear David Thoener's mixes everywhere. There's Santana's "Smooth" of course, the blockbuster single that spent twelve consecutive weeks at Number 1 on the *Billboard* Hot 100 and propelled sales of his *Supernatural* album to thirteen-times Platinum. Then there's matchbox twenty's "Bent," the Number 1 most played song in the U. S. for over eight weeks, and the left-field "Teenage Dirtbag" by Wheatus, a Top Ten single on Alternative.

You've heard a lot of his other mixes, too, from Aerosmith's 1998 smash "I Don't Want To Miss A Thing," to Meat Loaf's "I'd Do Anything for Love (But I Won't Do That)," John Waite's classic "Missing You," John Mellencamp's "Pink Houses" and "The Authority Song," and AC/DC's "For Those About to Rock." Not to mention those tracks he did way back as a young whippersnapper: the J. Geils Band's "Freeze Frame," "Centerfold," and "Love Stinks."

Wait, there's more: Thoener has mixed records for Billy Squier, Kiss, Sammy Hagar, and Billy Joel, and has recorded and mixed country

Photo: David Cline

artists from Brooks and Dunn to Rodney Crowell, Travis Tritt, and Ronnie Milsap. He's also known for his live recording and mixing with Aerosmith, Shawn Colvin, the Neville Brothers, Woodstock '94 and '99, Bob Dylan's 30th Concert Celebration, and the double CD *Concert for the Rock & Roll Hall of Fame.*

And all of that is just a partial discography. It's obvious that Thoener has what many engineers aspire to, but few achieve: a career that has both diversity and longevity.

He rarely does interviews, but while attempting to schedule this one, it quickly became apparent that he has plenty to say and a vast stockpile of great stories. It was also readily apparent that with Thoener, as with a great musician, it was best just to place the mic, roll tape, and get out of the way. So that's what we did. Now, heeeere's Dave, taking it from the top.

I started at the [New York] Record Plant on April 4, 1974. I remember going for my interview in platform shoes, huge bell-bottom pants, and of course, a psychedelic polyester shirt. Ed Germano [now owner of New York's Hit Factory] was the manager. When I left, I didn't think I had the job. But as soon as I got home the phone rang; he wanted me to start the next day!

Just the atmosphere of Record Plant at that time was enough to excite you. The carpets were shag; the walls in Studio B had a weird map that looked like Bullwinkle. Records by Jimi Hendrix, Yes, Jackson Browne, Grand Funk Railroad, Don McClean, the Raspberries, John Lennon, etc., lined the walls. The year before, I'd worked for a demo studio on 7th Avenue where I'd learned disc mastering and engineering, but Ed G. started me out as a tape copier anyway. I remained in the copy room for about three months. The turning point came when I was asked to take a piece of music and make a cassette where it repeated over and over. I guess management expected me to record, rewind, and record again, but I had a different plan.

I went into Studio C, took several mic stands, then created a huge loop that went from the copy room down the hall, past the rest rooms and back. When (Record Plant owner) Roy Cicala went to the restroom, he had to pass my loop! The next day, Roy called me into his office. I thought I was getting fired, but instead, I was made an assistant.

Lucky for you Roy appreciated initiative. And attitude.

Jimmy Iovine and I were assistants at the same time, and Roy made Jimmy his personal assistant. The chief engineer was Shelly Yakus, and since Roy had Jimmy, Shelly took me. That was great, because Shelly was one of the hottest engineers in New York. I got to work on some amazing projects. One of the first was the Raspberries with Jimmy Ienner producing. Then there was Johnny Winter, Edgar Winter, Rick Derringer, Chick Corea, Blue Oyster Cult, and John Lennon, just to name a few. As time passed, Shelly would let me do some overdub engineering. He had me do the piano interludes with Chick Corea on "Where Have I Known You Before." I was only twenty-one at the time, so this was really great! Then Jimmy got the chance to engineer Bruce Springsteen's *Born to Run* album. I remember him coming to me after a session, telling me the news, and asking me to assist him. Of course, I said "Yes!" All of the staff at Record Plant, especially the assistants, were very close, and we were happy when one of us got a break. One funny story that I hope Jimmy doesn't mind me telling was the night we were recording the lead vocal on "Jungleland." Jimmy had been working late for many days, and that night he fell asleep. He had his legs up on the console, and he just dozed off. Jon Landau and Mike Appel were producing, and Bruce was ready to sing. They looked at me and said, "Dave, you can do this, right?"

I said, "Sure," picked Jimmy's legs up, slid him over to the end of the console, and recorded Bruce's vocal. It was an incredible performance; sitting in the control room watching Bruce deliver that vocal was a moment I'll never forget.

Soon, Jimmy started giving me gigs—sometimes full recording and sometimes overdubs. I was very grateful to get anything. Not long after that, Jimmy started producing, with Shelly engineering, and the rest is music biz history.

Now you were on your own.

I started getting booked with outside engineers because the management knew I could engineer, or at least explain how things worked to a visiting engineer. One was Martin Birch, and I did Richie Blackmore's *Rainbow Rising* album with him. Then, I worked with Harry Maslin on David Bowie's *Young Americans*. But the engineer who introduced me to the band that would change my life was Bill Szymczyk. We worked on an album called *Hotline* by J. Geils in 1975. Then in '76, Bill was busy with the Eagles, so the Geils band called Roy Cicala to engineer, and he booked me as his assistant.

On the first day of recording, I set up the band and set the console so Roy would just have to come in, sit down, and hit the record button. As the band started recording the first song, Roy looked at me and said, "I'll be in my office if you need me." Then he got up and walked out of the control room! I'm standing by the multitrack, like the assistant is supposed to, and I'm thinking he's joking, that he'll be coming back in to see if I'm cocky enough to sit down.

At the end of the first take, the band looks in the control room and asks if it was a good take. By this time I've worked on a lot of albums, so I give the typical producer response: "I think you should try it again!" They look at me, then at each other, and Stephen Jo Bladd, the drummer, counts off for another take! And I can't believe what's happening!

We recorded two more takes and the band walked in the control room to listen. They asked where Roy was, and I answered, "He's in his office, do you want me to get him?" They said, "No, you'll do just fine."

That's a "Glory Days" kind of story.

That album was *Monkey Island*, with a hit called "I Do." I thought I'd arrived. But that was my first album, and there weren't any bands lining up for me to do another. The management of Record Plant decided to put me on an assisting gig, but by this point, my ego was too inflated, so when J. Geils asked me to go on tour with them, I quit the Plant and went on the road.

Well, that's a different perspective.

The road is a very good way to realize what's important. Example: at a show, the first priority is monitors. The band has to hear themselves and be happy with their monitors, if they're to perform. Second is the FOH [front of house]. Sometimes, as FOH guy, I was able to get a rehearsal, and sometimes, if we were the opening act, I didn't. "How can you get great sounds without hearing the band?" you might ask. The answer: you wing it.

From previous shows, you have a good idea of what the survival EQ should be — the EQ that can get you started.

Okay, we know every show is different, but how about an example of what survival EQ might be.

For drums, maybe, roll off some low bottom, roll out a few dB at approximately 500 on the kick and toms, and add some 4.5 to 5K on the snare. You might roll out a few dB of 200 on overheads, roll out 200 to 300 Hz on hi-hat, and on the vocal, roll out between 300 and 800 Hz. Just a few dB, nothing radical. I'm more likely to take out than add. If something isn't bright enough, rather than adding top end, I'll find out what's making it cloudy and take that away.

Then you see where everything else sits. The most important fader is the lead vocal. If the drums are a little muddy, there isn't enough bass, or the guitar EQ isn't just right, they can wait, as long as the lead vocal is heard. You can buy, like, three minutes, which is your first song. You better get it right by the end of the first song, where the enthusiasm of the band going on stage with all the screaming will help cover the fact that you're making the mix better. FOH guys have it down to a science. I have enormous respect for them because I know first hand how hard it is. That's why I don't do it anymore! In fact, I quit after the first leg of the Geils

show because I thought they should use a more qualified person. I felt I needed to go back to the studio where I belonged.

But that experience paved the way for the live recording work you later got into.

The live recording engineer gets even less time than FOH. If the FOH guy needs time to get his mix together, his needs take priority. Sometimes, while he's getting his sounds, you can get yours. But if he needs to focus on a problem area, you may run out of time before you get your EQ together. How does an engineer get great live sounds if there's no soundcheck? Same answer as before, you wing it. Along with your knowledge of survival EQ, the most important focus is to make sure everything's going to tape!

It's always best to EQ on the monitor side of a live recording. Make sure everything is going to tape clean and at a proper level. It doesn't matter whether you're recording analog or digital; you need to maximize level to get the best signal on tape, and you need to make sure NO distortion is coming from your side of the equation. As with FOH, it's best to get your act together in the first three minutes. That means EQ, compression, balance, effects ....

If you're doing a live broadcast like when I did *Woodstock 2* and *3*, the pressure is even greater. Your instant mix is going out to millions of people who have no idea what you're up against. Some of the *Woodstock* performances happened so quickly, many of us in the recording trucks only got a line check — you know, when a roadie goes out on stage and scratches the mics so you know they're live. Sometimes, I've lost a mic just before the band goes on stage — talk about heart failure! The only thing you can do is have your stage engineer try to locate the problem and switch out the mic, or the cable. And to do it between the time the lights go down and the band walks on! It has happened to me, and we've fixed it before the first note played. It's a stressful gig, to say the least, but it's also a tremendous thrill when it's all going down. You get an adrenaline rush, probably the best high I've ever experienced. And when it's over, the relief is just as strong.

Meanwhile, back at the studio....

Right. Well, after being on the road with J. Geils, I went back to Record Plant with my head hung low and asked for my job back. To my great surprise, they gave it to me. It was back to assisting, temporarily.

But soon, David Johannsen, who now goes by Buster Poindexter, asked me to do his album. It was called *Funky But Chic* — you might remember it? It got a bunch of airplay in New York, as David was in the New York Dolls, kind of a cult New York band at the time. After that, some more albums came along, and suddenly, it was the next year and Geils was ready to record *Sanctuary*.

This was the first of three albums we recorded at Longview Farms in Worcester, Mass. Longview presented a few challenges. It was a house, not the kind of acoustically designed place I was used to. We all lived on the premises, which was good because I didn't have to wait for the band to arrive, but bad because they also didn't have to leave. There were many long nights.

But that's a part of recording, and I love recording so much that it was more fun than pain. Also, the band treated me like a band member. I traveled with them, ate with them, partied with them. We were a family. I had great admiration for them, and they trusted and respected me and what I had to say about the work we did. I always tried to push the envelope, sonically.

Like back at Record Plant, when we were doing *Monkey Island*, we'd experimented with putting Stephen Jo Bladd out in the back of Studio A. It had a great sound because the walls were stone, and it was very live. The only problem for Stephen was that the garbage was stored there. We couldn't record there in the day because the sound would travel all over the building. So we started at night, when the garbage from all the offices was piled around him. Boy, did it smell! But it sounded great!

Sanctuary turned out well, but when *Love Stinks* started, I took it to the next level. *Sanctuary* was recorded in the house, which was the way the place was designed to work. When we started *Love Stinks*, we recorded in the barn. Now I say barn, and it was, but it was split into two areas. The barn with the animals was on the top of a hill, and the place where the band stayed was next to it. The barn sounded great, but it had a very old Angus console and was meant to do demos and such. We loved the sound of the room, so I would bring the instruments up the mic pre's of the Angus and send them over line level to the MCI console in the house, which had the multitrack and the monitors. I couldn't see the band at all; I could only hear them. Every once in a while, I'd have to run over to the barn, which was three or four hundred feet away, and check a mic, or explain something to the band that I couldn't explain without seeing them.

I remember putting a new mic that had just come out called a PZM, [pressure zone mic] on the ceiling, experimenting with ambient drum sounds. I was to find out there was someone else experimenting at the same time. I remember driving up to Longview to finish overdubs, hearing what Hugh Padgham had done on Phil Collins' "Something In The Air," and thinking, "Damn, someone's beat me to it!"

Obviously we weren't the first. Led Zeppelin had incredible ambient drum sounds in the late sixties. But the sounds had changed in the seventies. Disco and dead drum sounds were in. Engineers put drums in drum booths — anything to suck up the ambience and create a dead snare, kick, and tom. This was my attempt to bring back the live sound. I didn't have a castle to do it in, so it took some thought and experimentation.

Our guitars were also recorded in the barn, but in the part the animals stayed in. They would go out to pasture in the morning, so we would set up in the afternoon and record power chords full out. I had some of the mics in omni, and sometimes we'd hear a cow mooing over the guitar overdubs, especially at the end of a long sustained note, and we'd have to go back in and punch in to fix it.

At night, we would put plastic baggies over the mics so the bird droppings wouldn't go on the capsules. J. Geils, the guitar player, and his amp head were set up in the house with me, and we ran a speaker cable to the barn. Since there was a driveway people had to use, we hung the speaker cable in the air from the house to the barn. In the morning, you would see a hundred birds perched on the speaker cable. What a sight!

Speaking of guitars, can we talk a little about how you get all those great guitar sounds you're known for?

I initially learned my guitar technique from the engineers I worked with. That was to first go out and listen to the amp, listen for the sound the guitar player was going for. Then, with your experience with different types of mics, you pick one that will come as close to accomplishing getting that sound as you can—flat, no EQ, no compression. Sometimes, it takes a combination of mics, sometimes two up close, sometimes one close and one back. There is no rule, no easy answer. Just listen to the amp, think about the song, and try to create a guitar sound that captures the spirit of the part. When I worked with [producer Robert John] Mutt Lange on AC/DC's "For Those About To Rock," I learned a few tricks. Mutt got guitar sounds like I had never heard before, and I was lucky to work with him and experience his philosophy and approach.

You're not going to tell us what you learned from Mutt, are you? What is it about that guy? No one will ever talk!

Well, I will say it has a lot to do with the perspective of the vocal against the track. It works great for rock songs, but I'm not always recording or mixing rock. So as an engineer who works on different formats, the basic idea is to create a guitar sound that works best for the music you're working on. All of the sounds you record should be focused on trying to turn the artist's and producer's ideas into

reality. Listen to the song. Hopefully there's a demo, or sometimes, as with country, the artist gets out his acoustic guitar, plays the song, and you use your imagination along with the guitar player's ideas of what the song needs. Together, you create a sound that fits the part.

If you're mixing, it's the same concept, except the recording engineer has already established, to some degree, the sound to be used. Your job as a mixer is to take that sound and use it in the mix to make the song happen. EQ, compression, and effects are all a part of that journey. You are responsible to make sure the song is maximized. If a guitar moment, a fill, solo, or whatever, is pushed, it should make that moment in the song mean something.

What's a typical Dave Thoener guitar starter setup? Please don't say Pro Tools and Amp Farm!

No, it's NOT Pro Tools. I'm an organic guy. First, I go out and listen to the guitar sound the player's got going. Sometimes, he might make a suggestion of a mic he's heard on his amp that sounds great to him. I'll check that out first. I'll almost always put a 57 on the amp, and I like Royers a lot. If he's got a thin sound, and he likes it like that out of the amp, I might choose a fatter mic, if it fits better in the song—like an 87 or 67 tube. Sometimes, you're very lucky, and the guitar player is incredible, like Carlos Santana.

Tell us about recording "Smooth."

The "Smooth" session was a live approach. I went into Fantasy studios in the San Francisco Bay Area a day early, and met with my assistant. He'd worked on some of the material Carlos had already recorded, and I asked how the band set up. He showed me the way they'd worked on previous sessions, and I set up the same way. It helps to talk with engineers who have worked in the room, if you're in it for the first time, or haven't been there in a while. They can help with some of the best locations for drums, etc., and this will cut down the time you might use in experimenting.

With Santana, I needed to do two things. One, make the band as comfortable as possible, and two, get right into recording. I knew there was no time to waste. If I took time to move things around, they might get bored or tired, and this would slow the energy level—something you don't want to happen on an up-tempo song.

I went for my usual mic setup, I knew when the band arrived they wanted to sit down, run it through a few times, and record it. [Producer] Matt Serletic also wanted me to be ready to go when he felt they were ready. We recorded about five takes, and we had it.

What is that usual mic setup of yours?

Drums: Kick: D112 outside, 47 FET inside. Outside, build a tunnel with mic stands and blankets to keep cymbal leakage to a minimum. Snare: 57 top and bottom, bottom mic gated so I don't get the kick rattling the snares. Toms: 421s. Sometimes I might throw a mic on the bottom head of the lowest tom for low, low's. Hi-hat: KM84. Cymbals: 414s. Room: C-12s. Percussion: 57s and 451s, sometimes an overhead 87. On bass, a Demeter DI and on the bass amp an RE20. Also on bass, dbx 160s with light compression: 1 dB or so at 2:1.

How did you record Carlos?

Carlos has his pedal that shifts sound from one amp to another with two different sounds on each, and he controls that, naturally. I put a 57, a 421,

and an 87 about three feet back on both amps. Light compression with 1176's. I usually put the mics on different tracks, so that as the song takes shape, I can alter the guitar sound slightly to work with the new overdubs.

What did you record to?

Pro Tools. Mark Dobson is our Pro Tools genius. We also used Apogee Special Edition 8000 converters. Matt Serletic owns his own Pro Tools system—actually the equivalent of three complete 64-voice rigs. He also brings all his own cables; it's Monster Cable on every microphone, and everything else going into the console. Every guitar cable is his own too, the kind by Monster Cable with arrows pointing the direction of signal.

Did you edit between takes?

Yes, we cut between performances, always taking the entire band performance of each section that we used.

Was Rob [Thomas] recording his vocal live with the tracks?

Yes.

So you recorded the basic track on the first day, and then....

The second day, Rob came in and fixed a few vocal spots, and Carlos fine-tuned his solo. The third day, we did the horns and little extras. We flew to L.A. the fourth day and went to Record Plant. It was in the mixing stage that Matt decided to effect Rob's verse vocal with a setting from the plug-in called Amp Farm.

You mixed from Pro Tools too?

We mixed off Pro Tools locked to Sony 3348 HR through an SSL9000, and we mixed through a 96k/24bit dB Technologies encoder to a Genex MO.

There are a lot of parts on "Smooth." Did you have to use a lot of compression to keep everything in place?

I used compression. Not a lot—just enough to keep things retaining their natural dynamic but able to work within the framework of the entire mix. I like the Neve 33609 as an overall compressor, but again just a little. I don't want the balance to shift when I get to mastering. So, I try to do what I can to master as flat as possible. I generally don't use a lot of equipment. I try to capture a performance as true to the natural sounds as possible, and then I try not to fuck it up in the mix.

You mixed "Smooth" pretty quickly.

We mixed it in a day, and sent a copy to Clive Davis to comment on. We got Clive's comments the next day and finished the mix, doing a few vocal level option mixes.

Then we tore that mix down, at about 11 P.M., and at midnight, started a basic track on another project. We'd booked the musicians for that day, not thinking the mix would take long to close out. But things always take longer than expected, so we just kept going and finished around 5 A.M.

So much for having more regular hours after you get successful!

Success has nothing to do with schedules. Record companies have deadlines, and a lot of the time, you're forced to finish a mix or record a song because you're told it has to be done by a certain date. Then [laughs] you turn it in on time, and they sit with it for weeks.

You're originally from New York state, and you travel a lot for your projects. Yet you've chosen to make Nashville your home, and you also do a lot of your work there.

It has been a wonderful experience, living and working in the Nashville community. The pool of talent is enormous. For me, the recording process in Nashville is exciting, as well. It's not uncommon to record eight musicians at one time, and you've got about an hour to get it together. Not only EQ, levels, and compression, but headsets, effects—the whole nine yards.

The producer wants to hear it as a finished record from the first downbeat. If the session is booked as a 10 A.M. start, the musicians get in about 9-ish, and at 10 A.M., the producer is running the song down. It's not unusual for the first take to be the master, so you've got to work hard and make it right the first time.

You're recurring themes seem to be that you like to work with live musicians in situations where there is excitement and energy, and that, after all you've done, you still like to work hard! Any final thoughts?

A big item on my agenda is to thank my wife Linda for her emotional support and faith in me. It's a very hard job, being the wife of an engineer, and she's one of the best. I also have to thank my daughter Austin for her understanding and love, which constantly fuels my creativity.

And, thanks to all of the very talented engineers and producers I've had the great fortune to work with over the years; I draw from the experiences with them often. Roy Cicala, who gave me my start, Shelly Yakus, Jack Douglas, Jay Messina, Jimmy Iovine, Mutt Lange, Matt Serletic, Martin Birch, Ed Germano, and the great J. Geils Band, who took a 22-year-old kid from Yonkers, New York, let him sit in the driver's seat, and made him a part of their family for six of the best years in my life.

For me there's nothing that compares with getting a talented band in the studio and watching the magic happen between bandmembers. That spontaneous creativity is as exciting as it gets. The great part for me is the luck I have to sit and watch all this come together. Record making is a team effort, and when you're successful, the whole team is responsible.

Frank Filipetti

Life on the Digital Edge

Filipetti at the Capricorn desk at Right Track Studios, New York City

A down-to-earth kind of guy with a refreshingly honest style, Frank Filipetti is highly regarded by his peers. He's also an independent thinker, and was one of the first engineers to embrace digital. His credits include mixes for such Number 1 singles as Foreigner's "I Want to Know What Love Is" and "I Don't Want to Live Without You" (which he also produced), Kiss's "Lick It Up," and the Bangles' "Eternal Flame." He's also recorded and mixed albums for Carly Simon, Barbra Streisand, Vanessa Williams, George Michael, 10,000 Maniacs, and James Taylor, whose elegant *Hourglass* Filipetti produced, engineered, and mixed, winning Grammy awards in 1998 for both Best Engineered Album and Best Pop Album.

A proponent of surround sound, Filipetti has numerous 5.1/DVD projects under his belt, including projects for Billy Joel, James Taylor, and Meat Loaf. And lately, this accomplished studio engineer has been taking his chops on the road, recording and mixing numerous live albums including the *Pavarotti and Friends* series, last year's *Minnelli on Minnelli*, James Taylor's *Live at the Beacon*, and most recently, Elton John's *One Night Only*. He's also recorded original cast albums for *A Funny Thing Happened on the Way to the Forum* featuring Nathan Lane, the Grammy-winning *Annie Get Your Gun*, and this year's Tony Award-winning and Grammy-nominated *Aida*, among others.

Mix spoke with Filipetti during Christmas break, when he was enjoying some time off at his New York home before heading to L.A. to begin recording the latest effort by funk/metalists Korn.

As a singer/songwriter and drummer, you actually had a musical career going when you switched gears to become an engineer.

I was brought up in Bristol, CT, where I had a band in high school, whose claim to fame was that we got to open for the Dave Clark Five. When I went to the University of Connecticut, I formed another band, called Park. After college, we made a demo tape, on a 2-track Tandberg, and we took it to New York City. A producer heard it and signed us up, and we ended up moving there. After that, I had a

Selected Credits

Annie Get Your Gun
cast album

The Bangles
Greatest Hits

Al DiMeola
Kiss My Axe,
The Infinite Desire

Foreigner
Agent Provocateur,
Inside Information

Hole
Celebrity Skin

Billy Joel
5.1 surround remixes for *The*
Stranger and *52nd Street*

Elton John
One Night Only at Madison
Square Garden

Elton John and Tim Rice
Aida

Korn
Untouchables,
Here to Stay

Meat Loaf
5.1 surround mixes for
Bat Out of Hell

Carly Simon
Ten albums, including
Hello Big Man,
Spoiled Girl,
Coming Around Again,
Film Noir, and *Bedroom Tapes*

Barbra Streisand
Higher Ground

James Taylor
That's Why I'm Here, Hourglass

couple of minor record deals, and in the process, I won a first prize as a writer in the American Song Festival. That led to a publishing deal with Screen Gems where I was signed to a salaried contract. I also recorded an album for Lifesong Records as a solo artist. Upon finishing the album, I was informed that they'd lost their distribution deal with Epic, and suddenly, everything in my life began to crash. Screen Gems decided not to pick up my option, and my girlfriend and I split up. She got the apartment, and there I was on my 31st birthday: no job and no place to live. I decided that it was time for a new approach. I'd been trying for nine years to make it as a singer/songwriter, and I was always so close to having something happen. But it never really did.

So the next logical step was...

I thought I'd be good at engineering, because I was always interested in sound. So I went to Simon Andrews, the owner of Right Track Studios where I'd done my album. At the time, it was a 16-track demo studio, and I'd gotten to know Simon because he would engineer my demos for Screen Gems there.

I said to him, "I'm thirty-one years old, and it's a little late to be changing careers. I know I can do this, but I can't afford to be an assistant for two years. Would you give me a shot at engineering?"

He said, "Why not?" So, for thirty days, I assisted other guys. Then he started putting me on 4-track demos, and I did very well. After six months, I became chief engineer, and not long after that, I got a very fortuitous gig with Peter Asher.

How so?

By the end of '81, Simon wanted to expand, and he found a pretty large space on 48th Street where we built a room. We didn't know a whole lot about what we were doing, but somehow we came up with something. The recording area was 40 by 50, with, at that point, two iso rooms and an MCI console. We could fit a reasonably large group of people in there, and it was very inexpensive.

Peter [Asher] was producing *The Pirates of Penzance,* and he was looking for a reasonably priced recording space to put the whole cast in. He booked Right Track and asked for the chief engineer, moi, to do the project. He did bring his own engineer from L.A., Niko Bolas, just in case I wasn't any good. But after two weeks, he was able to send Niko home. From that point on, it was amazing. He took me to England with him to mix the film soundtrack, and he also recommended me on several other projects. A year later, he called me about doing a James Taylor album. But first, I had to do a demo to make sure it was okay with James. So, James' band traipsed over to Right Track one afternoon before their gig at Radio City Music Hall. I guess I did okay, because two months later, I was on my way to Montserrat with Peter and James for the *That's Why I'm Here* album.

Once you decided to engineer you had good luck.

For ten years, I was trying to get songs to Peter Asher. Suddenly, I'm travelling around the world working with him.

But did you ever sell him a song?

No. Previously, my whole life was writing songs, but once I decided to engineer, I never looked back. It obviously wasn't my calling and engineering was. And basically, through Simon's and Peter's belief in me, I got my career started.

You were an early proponent of digital recording.

It's funny about my digital journey. Around '85, during *That's Why I'm Here*, we were asked by Sony to try their new digital multitrack. Which I didn't mind, as long as I could double bus. So on the tracking sessions, we had a Sony 3324 and a Studer A800, and the Studer just blew it away. I didn't like the digital at all, and for the next few years, I was very anti-digital.

What changed your mind?

In 1990, [engineer and Ocean Way Recording Studios owner] Allen Sides came to visit me at Right Track. We had a long talk, and I think we both had a sort of epiphany. I was remarking that I didn't go home and play my recordings anymore, now that they were on CD instead of vinyl, because I didn't really like the way they sounded. And I started thinking that maybe the approach I was taking in making them was wrong. With CDs being 80 or 90 percent of the market, instead of complaining, I should be using it to my advantage. I needed somehow to be mixing my records so that whatever it was that digital was doing to the sound, I could at least hear it before it got to mastering.

I mean, we'd be sitting in the studio playing half-inch mixes going "Wow, this is great." And then you'd get a CD ref back from the pressing plant and say, "What happened?"

Now granted, the filters and the A-to-D converters at the time were pretty poor. But I decided that I should mix to a digital format, and also, instead of listening to the console out, I should monitor after the signal was converted to digital—through the machine, so that if digital does add harshness, or take away some warmth, or dry up the ambience, I could compensate for that before I finalized the mix.

So that's what I did, with a Sony 2-track DASH machine that my good friend David Smith at Sony Classical got me. And when we took the project to mastering, Ted Jensen was able to go direct into the 1630. When I got the CD back, for the first time in years, my mix sounded like what I'd heard in the studio. From that point on, I mixed everything digitally.

That was an unusually logical approach to an often emotional subject.

It just made sense. I also started tracking digitally. Because unlike my experience with the 3324, when the 3348 came out, I immediately warmed up to it. I did two projects with both an analog and a digital machine. What I found on the first project was that on tracking day, the analog machine sounded better than the digital. But after two months of running the tape across the heads, the digital killed the analog.

So, the analog vs. digital debate took on a "he said-she-said" kind of thing. And I got used to not having to go in and check the tones every day, and being able to sample and move things around. The flexibility of the 48-track was so much better than locking up two 24-tracks that whatever slight sonic benefit there might be became negligible. Slight benefit is even arguable. Because, while analog sounds wonderfully warm and cozy, there are some areas where digital does a better job. For example, being a drummer, what I always missed in analog

was the front end of the snare and kick. You never get that initial impact because analog is terrible on transients. The digital machine has those transients.

You were recording and mixing to digital tape but still working on an analog console. That led you to the Neve Capricorn.

Right Track was building a new room, Studio C, and I started reading about this Capricorn. The only one Neve had was at the Penthouse at Abbey Road in London. They flew me there, and I brought along some 3348 tapes that I'd just finished mixing. I was there for two days, but within the first five minutes, I had a mix that sounded better than the mix I'd done in New York. It was another epiphany.

What was it that so impressed you?

The flexibility. The idea that you can have a center section where all your work is done, where you can move tracks around at your whim. You never have to move away from the sweet spot to do your EQ or ride a fader. I do a fair amount of 96-track mixing, and when I'd be mixing background vocals on an analog console on track 96, I'd be twenty feet away from the center. On an 11-minute Jim Steinman track, that's a long time to be listening just to the right speaker. On the Capricorn, it doesn't matter if it's channel 23 or 193, you can move it to the center instantaneously. That just blew me away.

You made a move that was very bold for 1994, convincing Simon Andrews to put in the Capricorn. How did it go?

When we got it to New York and started doing real mixes, it was a bit of a disaster. You'd mix for five hours, and the thing would crash, and you'd be down for six hours. Three days later, it would corrupt the mix tree and you'd lose those three days' work. It was a nightmare. But I still had in my mind that if we could get this to work, it would be incredible. Right Track and I both lost a lot of money in billings that year. But I so believed in it, and the concept was so unique and brilliant, that we stayed with it. And at the end of that year, after endless meetings with the tech people, and the R&D people, and phone calls across the waters, finally we had a system that was stable and operating like the console it was supposed to be.

You're now a great believer in staying in the digital domain once you've converted to it.

This was the other reason I went for the console. When I first played my 3348 tapes on the Capricorn in London, I suddenly heard the music in a way I hadn't heard it before. I'd been working on that album for four months. I knew it well. But when I brought up the faders on the Capricorn and heard this wonderful sound, I realized it didn't make any sense to record to digital, then mix on an analog console only to go back to digital again for the CD.

Initially, you sample the analog signal into the digital format of your multitrack. Then, to get into your console, your numbers have to be reinterpreted back into an analog wave form. You've taken your original signal, made suppositions about it, and reinterpreted all those suppositions only to resample and reinterpret further down the line. The more times you do this, the worse the sound gets. What happens between each of those 44,100 samples per second is predictive supposition. Ninety-eight percent of the time, they're right; two percent of the time, they're wrong. And each time you do this, that two percent becomes four, then eight, etc. Whatever anomalies the digital process adds to the analog signal is compounded with each successive conversion.

What about degradation between digital-to-digital transfers?

Copying digitally, the main problems are clock-based. The more stable the clock, the better your copy.

It's true that even under the best of conditions, there are questions about digital copies. But I did a test on a 3348 that was properly set up, where we recorded a piano on tracks 1 and 2, then bounced it down twenty-four times. I then brought up tracks 47 and 48 on the Capricorn and flipped the phase. They cancelled. On a twenty-fourth generation copy. That was good enough for me.

I go to studios all around the world, and I talk to engineers who say that they've tried digital but it just didn't sound right. And then I find out that they're using mic cable for AES lines, or they don't run a word clock source. Or they're daisy-chaining word clock through the AES line. And, of course, it will sound terrible if you don't do it right. Just like analog. We've spent forty years massaging analog technology to work to its strengths, but people expect digital to magically happen without the same attention to detail.

People think they can just run an AES line from one machine to another, and the clock will run along that line just fine. Trust me, AES-derived clock does not work as well as dedicated word clock, and people who are using it are making a big mistake. It amazes me that guys who will wheel in racks of preamps and vintage devices won't insist on a dedicated word clock. One of my pet peeves is that manufacturers are starting to eliminate word clock inputs on a lot of their devices. I'm furious about that, because you cannot have a good sounding digital box without word clock. Period. All you have to do is listen to it to know that. And that's why, in a lot of people's minds, digital doesn't

sound good. Because they may try it in studios that either cut corners or don't know how to set it up properly.

What do you hear when the clock isn't right?

It's that grating, tearing, hard-edged "digital" sound. Also, the stereo width shortens. There's less depth. It sounds smaller, more compressed and harder.

What causes that?

First of all, jitter. Jitter is exactly what it sounds like — the clock source is a moving target. Second, the AES clock actually works something like FM, where there are several data streams piggybacked on the AES signal. If you filter out the audio portion of the AES signal and just listen to the clock, you can actually hear how unstable it is. The absolute, fundamental rule in digital is the stability of the clock.

What I insist on, and what we do at Right Track, is ensure word clock home runs to all of your important digital devices, like your multitrack, your console, your Pro Tools....

You've said that working on a digital console has changed your approach to mixing an album.

For years, especially since the advent of automation, the standard way of mixing has been to work on a single song until it's done. But with the Capricorn, I realized that I could mix the whole album. I work a couple of hours on each song, get great rough mixes, get a vibe for the whole record, then go back and start doing it again. That allows me to hear the whole album as a work, as opposed to individual songs. The old way, you'd mix a record and maybe have to remix three or four songs, because when you'd finally hear them in context with everything else, they didn't work.

Now, I can mix in a sequence, out of sequence, place different songs next to each other — because I can instantaneously get that mix back up, and it's identical. It's not like I have to sit and tweak for two hours to get the mix back.

Some people say they like to get in a zone while mixing. There are times that I do too, and when I do, I stay there. The point is, I can mix any way I want. If I've been working on an aggressive rock number for three hours and I need to clear my ears out, I can put up a ballad, then go back fresh a couple of hours later.

How do you deal with your outboard when you change songs?

The Capricorn has sixteen sends on every channel. In addition, every function on the console is totally automatable. I usually have about twenty-six sends set up, using duplicate sends. For example, send 8 may go to a Sony reverb or a Lexicon reverb, and I mute or unmute them in the mix as needed.

You have a lot of different effects set up so you can switch songs without having to reset them.

I'll have something like two sets of long, medium, and short reverbs. I have several different delay devices, flangers, etc.

What about conversion delay when you use analog gear?

Most of my reverbs have predelays. Or, if I'm setting a delay in time with the beat, I just set it so it's in time when it comes back to the console. If I'm using a chorus and there's an extra millisecond of delay that the A-to-D conversion adds, that's not going to change my chorus, which has a 30-millisecond delay anyway.

For the most part, it doesn't become an issue. When it does, you have the capability of moving things either in Pro Tools or on your digital tape machine to compensate. It's more of an issue when you're recording or setting triggers.

What is your preferred mix format these days?

My favorite mixing box is the Sony PCM9000, a 2-channel magneto optical box that sounds terrific, but which Sony has stopped supporting. There are several new boxes I've been testing out: I like the Alesis Masterlink, but I hate the fact that there's no word clock in. I'm also mixing to Pro Tools 24-bit, to Genex MO, and I'm trying a couple of the new Tascam units. So far, nothing has won me over.

I'm waiting for the multichannel recorder that I can use for my surround mixes that blows me away the way the PCM 9000 did. On the Elton John recording [*One Night Only*], I used a [Euphonix] R-1, which was intriguing. I'd like to spend more time on that.

How did you come to use the R-1 for that recording?

I talked to Randy Ezratty of Effanel, because we'd done *James Taylor Live* at the Beacon with his Capricorn truck a few years before, and I've always considered that my benchmark for live recording. The Cap truck was booked that night, on the VH-1 Fashion Awards, but Randy knew of another Capricorn truck [TNN's], and he offered to split his team with me.

We booked it, and a few weeks later, Randy called up to say that he'd been talking to the people at Euphonix. Their R-1 was ready to go, and they were wondering if we wanted to use it. I discussed it with Phil Ramone, the show's musical producer, and with Elton John's manager Derek MacKillop, and we felt that as long as we could minimize any risk, we should go for it.

So, you said "Yes, if I can double bus."

Exactly. In doing a live recording like this, you absolutely have to assume that whatever can go wrong most likely will.

Because of the complexity of the show, we wanted to lock up two 48-track recorders. Elton has two drummers, up to eight background singers, a percussionist, a bass player, and two guitar players, one of whom also doubles on saxophone. Also, Guy Babylon has a massive keyboard setup, and we were going to have guest stars like Mary J. Blige, Bryan Adams, and Billy Joel, who was to come out with a second piano. There would be no commercial breaks or time for any changeovers. There was a lot going on.

The problem was, two 48s and two 48 backups physically wouldn't fit in the TNN truck. In addition, we had to limit ourselves to 72 inputs. So we decided on one 48 for the main band and Elton, an Otari Radar 24-track for Nigel Olsson's drums and all the guest artists, and a DA88 for the eight audience mics. We duplicated those machines for our backup, and in addition, sent a split to the R-1.

How much rehearsal time did you get?

None. Just an hour sound check on Friday afternoon. There was no chance to go through each song and determine the instrumentation. It was seat of the pants time.

Were your mic pre's on stage?

Yes. I'd hoped to use a fiber optic run from the stage to the Capricorn, which was some 800 feet away, as we had done with James. Unfortunately, the TNN truck wasn't equipped with fiber, but we felt it essential to place the mic pre's as close to the band as possible. If you can't get fiber, you at least want a line-level signal going down that 800 feet of cable. The stage mics went to a splitter that went to FOH, then to 90 Aphex mic pre's. From there, we split to our setup and to the R-1. I combined them as best I could down to 72 instrumental inputs and 8 audience inputs.

You had someone onstage watching mic pre levels.

Yes. As my mic pre's were remote, anytime we'd come close to an overload, I'd get buzzed from the stage. Then we'd coordinate: he'd tweak it down two as I'd tweak it up two. Basically, I was just trying to make sure that I was getting a decent level without overloading anything.

As we were 24-bit, I had a little more leeway than on some of the other live shows I do, which are usually 16-bit. With digital, it's very important to stay as close to full scale as you can, because digital performs poorly as you approach the least significant bit. Every dB you lose translates into a lower bit rate. But with 24-bit, even if you're a couple of dB down from full scale, you're still well over twenty bits.

Wasn't there one of those angina-producing moments during the recording?

We did have a scare about two thirds of the way into Friday's show—a hiccup where the console froze momentarily. Back in my early Capricorn days, one of the first things I insisted on was that the console would always pass audio, even in the midst of a crash. And it did just that. There was some scrambling, but no one panicked. And listening back, there's not even a hint of a problem.

For mixing you ended up going with the R-1.

We only had six days to mix. Edit, mix, fix, everything. From the show to the stores in three weeks.

I think that's a new world record.

It was tight. We got to Right Track on Sunday, and it became clear immediately that locking up all those machines wasn't going to allow us to mix fast enough.

Although I couldn't do a direct audio A/B between the R-1 and the Sony/Radar, I was able to quickly determine that the R-1 was certainly not inferior. And the fact that you can have 96 tracks of 48K on one machine was truly a lifesaver.

On location: Filipetti recording tribal songs and ceremonies in Botswana

A Frank Filipetti hallmark seems to be an open-minded attitude towards the new.

I try to be. I've developed a way of working over the years that I feel very comfortable with. But if someone can show me a better way, then I don't see the sense in resisting it. I'll never forget my first day on the Capricorn, or my first session in a Martha's Vineyard cottage recording James Taylor with an O2R, or my first ISDN.... There are so many exciting techniques and technologies out there. To cut myself off from them would be inexcusable. That doesn't mean you can't be cautious.

Working with the latest digital equipment has been, and will continue to be, a risky business. No matter how often a manufacturer says that something's tested and ready to go, once it gets into the real world, it ain't necessarily so. Because, let's face it, most of this digital stuff breaks down to lines of code. And if the person writing the code doesn't understand all the permutations that are going to crop up on a recording session, you're going to have problems. Invariably, unless the machine has been in the field for a year or two, you're going to run into difficulties.

But you're still willing to move forward through those difficulties.

Absolutely. How boring would life be, if every new day were just like the day before. Last February, I was asked to record the songs and ceremonies of several Bushmen tribes in Botswana. We spent several weeks on safari in the Kalahari Desert catching up with various tribes. Being with these people, under a moonlit African sky as they sang and danced around a campfire was about as far away from a New York recording environment as you could ever get. But I was able to connect with the true spirit of Music in a way that is sometimes lost in our business. It was one of the great experiences of my life. To try something new, to see something a little differently, to embrace change and add it to your repertoire — to simply take a chance... isn't that what life's all about?

ARMIN STEINER

MAY, 2001 ## Tips and Tales From an L.A. Studio Pioneer

Armin Steiner is a self-described "survivor," having achieved the kind of career longevity that, in the music business, eludes all but a select few. A gracious man, with a polite, almost courtly style, he's also highly opinionated, offering an educated and well-articulated point of view that stems from both his past experiences in the recording industry and his current commercial recording work.

Steiner's pop engineering credits include over a hundred gold and platinum albums with major artists, starting in the mid '60s and including hits for Glen Campbell, Neil Diamond, the Fifth Dimension, Bread, Heart, Dolly Parton, Johnny Rivers, Hall & Oates, Helen Reddy, Barbra Streisand, and many more. In recent years, he's returned to the roots he established during his youth as a classical violinist, and has become an in-demand scoring engineer, recording orchestral soundtracks for such films as *Silverado, Home Alone, Born on the Fourth of July, JFK, League of their Own, Witches of Eastwick,* and *Cocoon,* and for television shows from *Dynasty* and *Star Trek: The Next Generation* to *Beauty and the Beast* and *King of the Hill.*

We met for this interview at the Newman Stage on the Fox Studios lot where Steiner was recording a series of orchestral cues for upcoming episodes of *King of the Hill.* Afterwards, we adjourned to the Fox dining room, where, seated beneath historic wall murals harking back to the 1930s, we settled in for lunch and a long chat.

You're one of the very few engineers who started out to be a classical violinist.

Yes, Phil Ramone is the only other one I know of. And I hear he was pretty good! It's true that I went quite far with my music, to the point where I played with symphony orchestras and was a Columbia artist, all while I was very young.

Then I got serious about this end of the business. I decided I wanted more of a normal life—that I didn't want to live out of a suitcase, as I thought I'd have to do if I stayed in the classical scene as a soloist or a concertmaster.

Somehow, with all those hours you'd spent practicing your instrument, you still found time to develop some technical skills.

I always had this technical thing going. I was eleven when my father bought me a tape recorder. He was an international chess master. That was his profession, and he traveled all over the world. But his hobby was disk recording. We're Hungarian, and my father used to record gypsy music directly to disc in our living room.

I used to record myself and my mother, who was a concert pianist and who played accompaniment for me. And it used to drive me crazy that I couldn't record my violin properly, because that old recorder had so much wow and flutter. There was always wavering in the background.

What formal training did you have to be an engineer?

My first job was at Electrovox Recording Studios, when I was fifteen or sixteen years old, where I was actually told after two weeks that I didn't have any talent for the business and should really give up.

After that, I went to City College here in L.A. for two years studying music, and also engineering and physics and chemistry. There, I became friendly with the man who was head of the intercampus radio station. He took me under his wing, and pretty soon, I was recording big bands and opera—all of that at seventeen years old.

I went from there to UCLA, where I was in the music department. I played a lot, and I also took engineering classes. And I did the same thing there, but for a different reason. Even back then, UCLA was an impossible place to park. So in order to get a parking pass, I offered to do recording for them—at Royce Hall, all over campus. I had a big heavy Magnacord machine, and I was carrying this stuff everywhere, but I had my parking pass! Meanwhile, I had also gotten a job at Radio Recorders, which was one of the first independent studios.

It wasn't long before you opened your own studio. Actually, you were way ahead of your time because your first commercial studio, which you built in about 1960, was in your house.

Yes. A bedroom over the garage, which was 10 by 14, became the control room. The studio, in the garage, was 25 by 15, with 14-foot ceilings. I soundproofed and air-conditioned it with a flow-through system. I took the air from the basement, which was cold, and built it so it went through the pipes at a very low velocity, and therefore was quiet. My uncle helped me, and although my mother thought I was nuts, she supported me in every way.

I also put an iso booth in. Studios didn't really have iso rooms then—just portable ones that they moved around. But I actually made a little room that was very bright in sound. It was lined with Masonite, which was very shiny and reflective—an acoustical equalizer. It was wonderful for all the r&b vocals that we did in there. I also built the recording console.

From scratch?

Yes, of course. You couldn't go out and buy a lot of things back then, you had to build them. The console was stereo, and had six faders, three on each side. Later, I added three more faders on each side, without preamps, to use with high output microphones like the [Neumann] U47. Especially with close miking, there was sufficient gain structure with those mics so that it worked pretty well, and I got cleaner sound that way. We also added a center channel mixer, made up of Langevin modules that had three mic inputs, one line input, and reverb sends. It was designed by Sherwood "Bert" Sax, the brother of Doug Sax of The Mastering Lab. He's a brilliant engineer who designed most of the electronics for all of this and put it all together.

One thing that was really significant to that studio, and part of the reason our sound was so good, was that we developed a phase-correcting network that we used on every channel of our tape machines.

Using tape, as opposed to recording direct to disc, made phase-shift properties more apparent. When the fundamental and its overtones don't arrive at the same place at the same time, and the sound is a little bit spread, you don't hear it coming back exactly like you do in the room. What Bert did was design a device we called a "scrambler." So if we had a 3-track recorder, we would have a scrambling device for each of the three channels, and they would be tuned to the characteristic of the tape track. We'd come out of the buss into the scrambler, out of the scrambler into the tape machine. And it would decode itself better. It was a compromise between shifting the high end and the low end at the same time, and it created better transients. We were the only ones who had that.

What other equipment did you have?

When 3-track came out, I had two 3-track machines —Ampex 350-3s, two Ampex 350-2-track machines, and one that was mono, an Ampex 200 — a great big machine. It was a well-equipped place. I even had reverb. One was a combination of three spring devices that I'd made and hung on the wall, and one was a wonderful-sounding live chamber that that I'd built underneath the house.

Your mother let you build an echo chamber in the basement? And run cables through the walls to them?

Yes. She even let me use her Thunderbird to haul the trailer full of tile that I needed for it. My mother was quite amazing. She also let me use her piano, on which we ended up cutting several hit records.

You had no background in pop music before you built the studio. How did you learn about it?

Two people who were very influential in the commercial rock-'n'-roll business helped me, and actually went into business with me: Lincoln Mayorga, who is a great pianist and the arranger for the Four Preps, amongst many artists, and Eddie Cobb, who was the bass voice in the Four Preps. They were producing records for other people, and they taught me. Because I had never really paid attention to commercial music before, only classical.

How did you get clients to come to you?

After the studio was all built, I did a couple of demo sessions, and we thought it sounded pretty good. Then one afternoon, I got a call from the Wilder Brothers, two very nice and crazy men who had heard I had a studio. They came over with a little group called Dick and DeeDee. We cut a demo, and three or four weeks later, it was a Number 1 record called the "The Mountain's High."

From that moment on, word started traveling. Motown got interested, and I was busy all the time. I had Glen Campbell, Billy Strange, Tommy Tedesco, Dennis Budamir — all these guitar players

sitting there at my house. There was Ray Pohlman, one of the truly great Fender bass players, and the first man to actually build a distortion device. Hal Blaine, Earl Palmer, Joe Osborne, Larry Knechtal, Bill Pittman, Mike Deasy, and of course, Carol Kaye. I'd get a call at three in the morning from Herb Alpert saying, "I've got to overdub a tambourine on this piece." I'd be in my pajamas, and I'd walk up there, and we'd do it. That was that. I used to have the Supremes up there, Marvin Gaye — my mother used to cook for them. Stevie Wonder was in when he was nine years old. People think I'm making this stuff up, but it's true. As a matter of fact, I did a film session with Stevie a while back, and he remembered both me and my studio.

It was a different time, a different place. You couldn't do that kind of thing now. The city wouldn't allow it. I mean, it was all illegal. And there was a lot of activity.

Why did you finally move your studio out of the house?

Really, I would have to blame it on the Watts riots. That very tragic happening in Los Angeles that made many people really paranoid. I was recording a lot of black acts there — mostly for Motown. And we would have lots of cars and people outside the house. Most of my neighbors didn't mind, but one who lived across the street called the city.

I was off working at Radio Recorders one day, and my brother called me to say that a city inspector was there, telling him that I had to have the business out within 24 hours. So I did. I'd operated it for a good seven years, and probably had ten or eleven Top Ten records, but I disassembled the whole thing, took all the equipment over to Radio Recorders, and never looked back.

You built two more studios after that.

Yes, I had Sound Recorders from '65 to '71, then I moved across the street where I built Sound Labs, which I operated until 1980. Then I was at Evergreen in Burbank for a year and a half, then Lionel Newman hired me here at Fox.

You've said that out of all the pop music that you've recorded, the Richard Harris epic, "MacArthur Park," is probably your favorite.

That's a subject all in itself. It was seven minutes and twenty seconds long, and we recorded the music at my studio, Sound Recorders. I think that [songwriter] Jimmy Webb was inspired to do an epic by the Beatles' "Hey Jude." The way Jimmy conceives a song is that he sees the whole thing, then goes back and does it. He's one of the few people that can see the whole picture at one time. And that was an extraordinary piece of music because it had chord progressions and melodies that were far more reaching than your average pop record, to say nothing of a great lyric.

So it was conceived as a whole and he wanted to record it as a whole, with absolutely no edits and no stopping, not even within the movement structure; if you remember, it was a three-movement piece. He wanted to do the whole thing as a complete piece of music because he wanted to capture the whole inspiration.

What was the session like?

It was our usual rhythm setup. Hal Blaine on drums, Joe Osborne on bass, Mike Deasy on guitar, Larry Knechtal and Jimmy himself on piano and harpsichord. I can't remember which one did what; they were playing in unison.

We started rehearsing at ten in the morning. We rehearsed and rehearsed, changed, and rehearsed because it was very complicated, especially the rhythms. The slow section had to be a certain mood. It was like a mini movie.

They rehearsed the same piece for six hours, then put the music down and played the entire piece of music from memory in one take. And that was the magic. Anybody else would have taken it and edited — chopped it up in little sections, and it wouldn't have worked.

What did you record to?

It was 8-track. Sound Recorders was one of the first commercial studios to have an 8-track. Columbia had done it, as I recall, by running two 4-track machines together, not even with a synchronizer. It was kind of all makeshift.

But we actually built one. We took an Ampex 200 deck—that huge thing with big motors, built as a monaural machine. And, as I recall, we used Ampex PR10 electronics. The PR10 was two channels in one box, so we didn't have to have so many amplifiers hanging around. So, what we did was add together four packages of Ampex 2-track electronics.

Then we needed heads. We had the idea to take the specs from a 4-track head, and use the same geometry to make one that was 8-track. We found a company called IEM, in Chicago, whose chief engineer, John Pretto, was building 7-channel data heads for telemetry for satellites, and we had them build it for us.

We didn't even have automatic tape lifters on this thing, so we had to pull the head gate back by hand when we did the rewind. Which was difficult to do with one-inch tape. There was a lot of resistance there, but we made it work.

Of course [laughs], after the rhythm section was done, they took the tape to London to record Richard Harris, and they had to go through a similar process. At Landsdowne Studios, they built an 8-track machine out of Scully parts in order to put his voice on.

Do you recall how you miked the band?

I'm a creature of tremendous habit, so I know that, probably, I used two Sony C37 microphones over the drums. There may not have been a snare mic, but if there was, it was a Sony C500. On the bass drum, probably an Electrovoice 666 — you could hammer nails with it. Piano: always a single mic, a [Neumann] U47. The harpsichord would have been an AKG 451E, taped to the stick of the harpsichord. We always took the bass direct. On the guitar, just a single mic—an AKG 451E; I had a series of those and I liked them because I could put a pad in them to take down the level so that we wouldn't have any distortion.

And always, of course, I'd set it up to have everyone sitting close together. That's very important. If the rhythm section can hear well and feel well together, and have eye contact, it's going to be much better for the ensemble and for whatever magic you're going to get from that ensemble.

Would you have compressed the bass?

No, I very seldom use compressors, except for the bass on r&b records. I rarely even use them on vocals. I always feel like I can ride the level myself better. Once I hear the melody, I've memorized it, and I'd rather deal with it that way.

The only limiters that I ever used were LA2As, LA3As, 1176s and, later, the Inovonics. I still like the Inovonics if I have to use one. I think it's the most "unlimiter" limiter that I know. And of course, in the early days, we had the old Fairchild tube job, that brute force heat-producing monster, which adds so much distortion along with its limiting that it creates a "sound."

Mastering a 45-rpm record of that length, which you also did at Sound Recorders, must have been another story unto itself.

We had to get 7:20 on a 45-rpm record. The only other record that had been done that way was "Hey Jude." Cal Frisk, who worked for me and was a super great engineer, did the mastering. It was done manually. We didn't use variable pitch; we opened and closed the grooves manually.

I knew the music so well, you see, that we could maximize cutting it by doing it by hand. When the music gets very quiet, you can close the grooves because it doesn't take up much space. When you have louder sound and deeper bass, you need more land between the grooves in order to reproduce it. Knowing the music, you pretty much know your limits.

In those days, don't forget, it was a real battle of levels with 45-rpm records. It was always about trying to make the loudest disc and defeat all the stuff in the transmitters and the radio stations so that you could produce the loudest single over the air.

There were two factors to consider: the amount of space that is technically allowed—up to so many centimeters from the center—and the distortion factor. Because as you get towards the inside of the record, you have greater distortion. It was art and science at the same time. That was the romance of the business, in those days. And since the masters were all cut by hand, maybe there was a slight difference between each of them. Maybe I made a better one the second time!

These days, the bulk of your work is orchestral recording. How do you prepare for a large scoring date?

The most important thing is to know what it's going to sound like beforehand. You must get a mental picture of that by knowing your composer and his style.

I also try very hard to go over the details before we ever get into the studio. A lot of the composers will discuss with me beforehand the kind of texture they're looking for. To me, that's absolutely the most valuable information.

Normally, our actual setups are going to be pretty much the same, unless you want something special. Like on the *Witches of Eastwick* score, John Williams wanted me to put the tubas next to the French horns because they all played together. Now that isn't something that you would normally do, but it worked marvelously well. He was one hundred percent right, as usual. Those are the kind of things that create a sound. When I did *Silverado* with Bruce Broughton, another magnificent composer, there were times when it was so loud in the room that it was impossible. We had a very small string section, so I decided to put the strings over to one side of the room and then let the brass and the winds have all the space. Then we put up three microphones for them, and came in a little closer with the microphones on the strings. And it worked. Really, it's about letting the music be your guide.

How long before the session do you arrive?

As early as I can get in there and torment people. Let's assume we're going to start a scoring session on Monday that's going to last maybe a week. And let's say it's conventional orchestra, and it's a large one of ninety-plus pieces. I would like to go in there on Friday, if I can, and spend the entire day setting up the studio. I'll strip the studio entirely bare. I'll never use anything left over from someone else. You have to start fresh.

The setup would be standard orchestral, unless there's something unusual with percussion—ethnic instruments or maybe louder-than-normal kinds of percussion in some of the more exotic scores.

Then you go in with a crew and you set it all up. I supervise that and I don't mind pushing chairs and stands and mics around. I've done that all my career. It takes a good long time to do it right. All the cables have to be nicely dressed, because anyone who is stepping around on a break or something can cause you irreparable damage if everything isn't tied down properly. It needs to be as neat and clean as you can make it.

Ergonomics are important. Musicians must be comfortable. They must have enough space around them to play properly, and they have to be able to hear properly. Because it all must start in the studio. I don't care how talented you are with electronics. If it isn't happening out in the room, you're not going to get it in the booth.

On the Newman Stage, where you often work, the console is an SSL 9000. You also like working on the large API console at O'Henry Studios.

Yes. O'Henry's is an all-custom board, with API equalizers — a marvelous-sounding console that was a great product of love and very precise engineering. I do like the SSL 9000, and I work also on the Neve V-series.

You're not a fan of tube mics for scoring dates.

It depends on the maintenance of the microphone. You don't want a breakdown, because it will always come at the wrong time. It will always happen when you're ready to make a take, or you're in the middle of something that is beginning to come together in a most unique manner, and there you fall on your face. Plus the fact that none of these [tube] mics are even. They don't sound similar, and if you're going to use them across the front of an orchestra, with peculiarities and artifacts different for each microphone, you've got problems.

What mics do you prefer, then?

There are great mics by Sennheiser, which I think are the best modern microphones made, and that's the MKH series. Their characteristics are extraordinarily musical and that's what's important to me—how musical they sound, how real they sound. The reason they sound so good is because their off-axis response is totally linear. In a Neumann microphone—for example, an M50— the off-axis response is very jagged, very unlinear. Remember, any leakage you get in the room must combine. That's why it's very important many times to use the same type of microphone, so that the characteristics of the leakage will be the same. It's just logical. Practical physics.

I rarely do any close miking. For TV, we do go in a little closer. But for scoring motion pictures, you want the sound of an orchestra, and you cannot get it by sticking a microphone in front of somebody's face. It will just sound small.

Therefore, almost everything is coming from the overheads, which would be MKH 80s or 800s. I use five across the front. I also use either MKH 20s, or the solid state M50s for the two surrounds, which are placed overhead back from the orchestra.

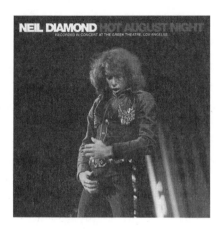

Then, I'll maybe put a couple of MKH40s over the woodwinds just in case I need to accentuate a solo, or change the balances.

For the most part, for a brass section, I'll stick up a couple of TLM 170s at a great distance. I might open them up just a bit and use just five percent of those mics.

What about the percussion?

Perhaps a TLM 170 over the tympani for some accentuation, and perhaps some high, over the overall percussion. I would always rather pick things up in a natural balance. I want to get what you would really hear if you were in a fine concert hall.

You use very little processing when you record.

The only thing I use is a little reverb.

You monitor with reverb.

No, I record with it. Absolutely. I have a favorite that I've used for the last twelve years or better: the Roland R-880. I have a very special program that we developed the algorithm for, on a card that I burned at the factory about ten years ago.

What new equipment have you been impressed with lately?

Nothing, really. At the risk of sounding dated, I'll state that nothing much has really changed in forty or so years. You still have to get from microphone to line level, and what we've done in the interven-

ing years is merely to put a lot of garbage in between them that serves to degrade the sound.

Okay then, is there any old equipment that you can't live without?

No. I use what I have. I don't want to make a big deal out of it. I just need to get the signal properly, and then the proper balance, the sonority. I like to preserve dynamics. If something is quiet, it should be extremely quiet. If something is loud, it should be earthshaking. If the music is exciting, it should come off as excitement, not as something the engineer tries to interpret.

We are not interpreters. We are servants of the music, and all we're doing is taking what the composer did, and hopefully, putting it down in the perspective that he heard.

What advice do you have for someone who wants to become a scoring engineer?

I think he or she should come and listen. Listen to what the orchestra is doing, and after they have that in their heads, they should go in and listen with somebody who has some years of experience.

That's how I learned. When I was fourteen or fifteen years old, I sat with Thorn Nogar at Radio Recorders, who would be doing an Elvis Presley session in the morning and then Henry Mancini in the evening. I saw what he did and learned why he did it. I learned from all of the wonderful staff engineers at Radio Recorders. You can learn so much from observation, if you have a keen ear.

Your job is to try to create the excitement that the artist intended to have in the music. When it gets exciting, your fundamental obligation is to be able to capture that dynamic. It's not only loud or soft, it's all that intensity that happens. It doesn't matter if it's rock 'n' roll, big band, operatic, or symphonic. The most important thing is to let the music be your guide. No matter what you're recording, if you let the music be your guide, you will never go wrong.

JULIAN KING

JULY, 2001 ## Recording Nashville Royalty

Even in the hectic 21st century, the city of Nashville retains its easygoing vibe. In general, people still do talk a little bit slower, and there's an inherent friendliness and courtesy in the way they do business. So it's notable that even among that generally laid-back atmosphere, engineer Julian King has developed a reputation as a particularly groovy guy to work with. King's winning combination of engineering chops and personality has put him behind the board, cutting tracks and/or mixing for everyone from superstars like Faith Hill and Tim McGraw to rising stars such as Toby Keith and Jessica Andrews.

King recorded tracks for Hill's multi-platinum album *Faith* and won a Grammy (Best Country Album) for his work on Hill's *Breathe.* He also recorded McGraw's hit singles "Please Remember Me" and "Don't Take the Girl," as well as Toby Keith's smash album *How Do You Like Me Now* and Jessica Andrews' breakthrough *Who I Am.*

His body of work also includes tracking and mixes for Brooks and Dunn, Clint Black, Randy Travis, Alabama, John Anderson, Clay Walker, and the Neville Brothers, to name just a few.

We caught up with King at Nashville's Loud Studios, where he was taking a break between mixes for a new Toby Keith release. Initially a bit reluctant ("I don't think there's enough to say about me to fill more than a paragraph," he joked), his natural friendliness soon asserted itself, and after a little coaxing, he graciously shared some insights into his engineering style and techniques.

Okay, I can tell that you're a Southerner, but are you originally from Nashville?

No, I'm from Charlottesville in central Virginia.

Did you start out to be a musician?

Well, I kind of hate to say it out loud, but I started as a trumpet player.

Selected Credits

John Anderson
Paradise

Jessica Andrews
Heart Shaped World,
Who I Am

Clint Black
Nothin' But the Taillights,
One Emotion,
D'Lectrified

Brooks & Dunn
Tight Rope

Carlene Carter
Hindsight 20/20

Billy Gilman
Classic Christmas

Faith Hill
Faith
Breathe

Toby Keith
How Do You Like Me Now?
Unleashed

Tim McGraw
Set This Circus Down

Jo Dee Messina
Burn

Randy Travis
Man Ain't Made of Stone

Travis Tritt
Country Club

[Laughs] It's not that I'm ashamed of having been a trumpet player. It's because all I get now about trumpet is "Daddy put that away."

Actually, I did notice a trumpet credit on your Allmusic.com discography.

I have only one album credit doing that, but that one album [Charlie Daniels Band's *Simple Man*] went gold in its debut year! Charlie Daniels is such a generous man. He paid my entrance into the musicians' union so I could play on the one session.

You have a degree in music, though.

Yes, I went to James Madison University. I actually started off as a computer science major, but that only lasted about three quarters of a semester. I got involved in music things there, and they had a music business program. It was a neat program, but it was simple. They didn't have a recording studio, but I met people and made some friends, and I found myself doing live sound for bar bands—that sort of stuff. Rich Barnett, my advisor there, set up an internship for me by way of Merlin Littlefield of ASCAP. They got me in with Jimmy Bowen, at MCA.

At the time, MCA had a lease on Sound Stage Studios, and Bowen was producing, or overseeing the production, of almost everything on the label. So he had a big staff of engineers and assistants, and I did an internship with them. I guess I fit in with what they were doing, and they agreed to keep a job for me until I finished my last year of school.

There were five or six assistants and seven or eight engineers who did all the records—Reba, George Strait, John Anderson, Lee Greenwood, Waylon Jennings, Vince Gill, Steve Wariner, and many others. It was a great place to learn. They used a very structured process, in that it was set up to where engineers were interchangeable. So, frequently, you'd be on one project one day and another the next.

That'll keep you on your toes.

As an assistant, everything had to be very meticulously put together. When a guy came in the next day who hadn't been on the session for two weeks, he could pick up and hit the ground running. I worked with some great engineers that I learned a lot from, like John Guess, Chuck Ainlay, and Steve Marcantonio.

Is it still true that Nashville tracking sessions go really fast?

Well, I'm told that they go fast, but it's what I learned on, so I don't really have a basis to compare.

Typically, we do two 3-hour sessions a day. And in those two sessions, we'll cut at least three, and maybe four, songs. The musicians go from not having heard a note, and with no music notated, to having put together three or four really great pieces of music. I've worked with a lot of musicians all over the place. These guys are among the best. Everything is improvisation, and it's amazing.

You're known for getting a very fat, punchy, drum sound.

That's what I go for. James Stroud, who's a legendary drummer, is my primary client. He played on all kinds of records, everything from King Floyd's "Groove Me" and Jean Knight's "Mr. Big Stuff" to Eddie Rabbit's "I Love A Rainy Night" and Paul Simon's *There Goes Rhymin' Simon*. Drumming was his first profession. When your main client is a drummer, you'd better be able to get drum sounds.

You frequently record tracks in The Sanctuary, Ocean Way Nashville's Studio A.

I love that room. I've been lucky to record in a lot of rooms here and in Los Angeles, and while I have several favorites, that's probably first on my list.

What is your drum setup when you record in that room?

I usually put a FET 47 on the kick drum, and that goes through a module of the big Neve 8078 console that they have in there. I use the Neve 33609 compressor on it and a Pultec EQ. For the snare, I'm pretty boring; I usually just use a 57, with an API preamp.

The API because it's more sharp-edged?

Yes, it's a little more pointed, a little "crackier." Then I end up going back to the line-in on the Neve module, where I still use the EQ. And usually I'll put a dbx 160 on that.

You mean the original 160, with VU meters? How might you set that?

I don't squash the top mic too hard. It hits 2's and 3's at most.

And I put another mic under the snare—typically, an ATM 35, a little clip-on mic. I put it up close to the snares.

Clipped to a mic stand?

No, I clip it on the snare stand itself, so that if the drummer changes the drum and raises or lowers the stand, the mic chases the drum at the same ratio.

Do you put that bottom mic out of phase?

Yeah, I flop that out of phase and smash the you-know-what out of it with another 160. In fact, you don't even want to look at that compressor. If the kick drum isn't triggering the compressor too, then it's not smashed enough. Then I add just a little of that sound in, to get a bit of buzz from the snares rattling.

How about the toms?

The toms have the same mics that I put under the snare drum—the ATM 35s. I clip them right on the rim of the toms.

That's interesting, because your toms don't sound close miked.

Those mics are awesome on toms. But don't print that—nobody else uses them much! They have a fairly tight pattern, and I get them close just trying to get control of the cymbals, so that there's not so much leakage from the cymbals in the toms. They're close, pointed pretty much at the middle of the drum, and then I add a little bit of EQ. They don't require very much, but I end up adding a tiny bit of bottom and taking out a little bit of low middle. No compression on the toms.

Photo: Alan L. Mayor

What else do you do to make it so live?

My overheads help with the fullness of the toms. Depending on how many cymbals the drummer has, I put up two or three 87s over the cymbals—fairly close.

Do you roll off the low end on the 87s?

No, I actually end up adding some low end to the overheads. Again, I take out some low middle, in the 200 to 300 area, but I end up adding some down low in the 100 Hz area. A lot of times, I'll put a high pass in so I don't end up with some 20 Hz trouble. I'll end up cutting out everything under 30, but I'm boosting some around 100, and that helps fill the toms out. You have to be careful, and be sure and audition the phase in several different positions while you are setting it up so that you don't end up making it smaller rather than bigger.

The room mics are what make the drums great in that room. Ocean Way has a great old pair of Telly [Telefunken] 251s. I put them side by side. Do they call that a coincident pair? They kind of point out —one at the hi-hat and one at the floor tom. It's not terribly scientific. They're maybe ten to twelve feet back and nine or ten feet high. They're squashed pretty good too. I usually put the overheads through my API pre-amps and [Urei] 1178. And on the room mics, I'll use a pair of Distressors.

Except for acoustic instruments, the players are in with the drummer, right? How is that set up?

Typically, the bass is direct, although sometimes a speaker is involved. The guitar amps are off in a booth, and we build a big hut around the steel guitar amps that are there in the room, right behind the room mics. The acoustic instruments all have booths. There are lots of booths in that studio.

The typical instrumentation on a tracking session is...

It's usually a pretty big session, if I'm working with James [Stroud] or with Byron Gallimore. There's almost always drums, bass, piano. And the piano player usually is Steve Nathan, who brings an organ and a big synth rig, in addition to the acoustic piano. Then, there's an acoustic guitar player, two electric guitar players, a steel guitar, plus a fiddle player. That's eight. Plus the artist, of course.

How long does it take to get set up?

Typically it takes them a good three or four hours to get it all put together. Just because there are so many bodies that come in the door. [Laughs] The cartage parade alone is lengthy. Usually, by the time I get there, they've got it all set up, and they've phase popped everything.

Speaking of setting up, I'd like to mention that I have five guys and gals in town that I work with a lot who are really the bomb. I am really cranky without them. There's Ricky Cobble, who I have been working with for a long time, Rich Hanson and Jake Burns at Loud, and David Bryant and Leslie Richter at Ocean Way. They all do a great job. When I have an idea in my mind, I look up, and they're already plugging it in. I get to work in a lot of places all over the country, and if one of them doesn't go with me, it's much harder for me.

One of those five leaked to me that you like to use Gefell mics (UM 70S) on acoustic guitar.

I got that from Lynn Peterzell, who was my primary engineering influence. He was my mentor, and I was his assistant. He started me on that mic, which has a really sweet midrange without being hard. I've heard people use them in piano, but I like them on acoustic guitars.

You also often take a direct out on acoustics.

If the guitar has one I take it. It's a texture I wouldn't otherwise have that gives me a choice later. I may do something to it, like split it through Amp Farm and kind of bury it, or maybe put it way out on the edge where it just sounds like a dull double. It has a different dynamic characteristic. It's much less dynamic than the mic, obviously, so with regard to the level of the mic, which kind of goes up and down, the direct holds a more constant path. If the acoustic goes soft on the mic, it may poke out a little more on the direct. And if you pan them away from each other, it kind of makes it move in the stereo image. That all being said, sometimes I don't use it at all!

One place in particular you can hear that kind of sound is in the beginning of "Breathe." Mike Shipley, who did the mix, used it panned out on the edge, and it sounds like there are two guitars playing two parts. You can feel it pulse left to right.

How do you record piano?

I carry a pair of Audiotechnica 4050s, and I have a pair of Calrec RQP3200 modules that were Lynn Peterzell's. They have a mic pre, a line in, an EQ, and a compressor, all in one module. I love them on piano. They're very hard to find; I've tried to rent them out in L.A., and nobody has them. I end up carrying them out there when we work with Clint Black or do movie stuff.

Generally, I use three mics: the two ATs close up over the hammers, low and high, and then I put an 87 back in the middle of the piano, pointed up at the hammers. I add just a little of that to fill in the middle. I set it, for lack of a better description, right over the ass of the piano. And, rather than pointed down at the strings, it's kind of pointed up like it's looking right at middle C. I use a little bit of that because sometimes piano gets "phasey" when you put stereo mics over the hammers. If you add a little bit of that to fill the middle back in, it doesn't vanish, if they are playing something in the middle of the piano. I compress that with a pair of the Neve compressors that are in the console—I can't remember the model—[laughs] the little in-line guys everybody wants.

You've been mixing on the Sony Oxford console a lot lately.

I prefer to mix on the Oxford, absolutely. When James [Stroud], Blake [Chancey], and Paul [Worley] told me they were putting it in here at Loud, I didn't want anything to do with it. George Massenberg calmed me down by spending a little time with me, right at the beginning, and the more I got into it, the more musical it became to me. The automation works perfectly. It's so simple. It doesn't look like a regular console, people walk in and say, "Oh my gosh, I don't want to learn that thing." [Laughs] But I'd really just as soon they not come and learn it, because then they'll be working in here, and I won't be able to get in!

What about the learning curve?

Once you understand the simplicity of it, it's not a problem. You get a good snapshot set up, or have a good starting point on the console, and it's awesome. You can automate anything. If you want an EQ sweep, or if you want an EQ to pop out, you can set two EQ curves on any EQ, and it has an A/B switch that you can automate. Which is great, if you have a soft textured verse of a song and you want to make a little different EQ for the verse without having to set up a completely separate module.

The automation and recall is the best, and that's a real asset, particularly with some of the producers I work with who wear a lot of hats. Several of the prime producers here in Nashville are also label heads. They have to do all the things involved with that plus make records, so their time is really at a premium. With the Oxford, I can mix for a series of days, and since I have total recall ability, they don't have to be here. I can mix five songs, then they can come back for a day, and we can close all five of those songs together in a day. It's also great for artists who tour a lot for the same reasons.

You've been doing some producing yourself lately.

Here and there. I'm so busy engineering that there's not a lot of time. But there's a band I've been co-producing with James Stroud on Dreamworks, called Emerson Drive, a very talented bunch of young guys from Canada that I'm really excited about. They played every note on the record themselves, which doesn't happen with too many groups out of Nashville. It's a 6-piece band: electric guitar, a keyboard player, bass player, drummer, a singer, and a fiddle.

Oh, I forgot to ask you how you mic fiddle. You know, we don't get that many fiddle players out in L.A.

Big vintage mics sound great on fiddles, like a 49 or a 47. We tried one of the Neumann 249s—the new version of the M49—the other day, and loved that.

Do you put it close?

Fairly close, maybe eight inches. Most of the guys work the mic a little bit, depending on the part they are playing. When I'm working at Ocean Way, it goes through the console, but I use a Distressor and a Pultec. I take a little bit of 5K out and add a little bit of 10K.

With all those players, what do you do to help give them each their own space in the track?

The hardest ones to separate are steel and organ, because they end up getting in the same bandwidth a lot. It can be tough to separate them, sometimes. I try to pan them away from each other, if I can, so they aren't fighting for the same place in the middle all the time. And hopefully, there are some subtle EQ adjustments you can make from one to the other, on a song-by-song basis, to try and make them fit.

Do you tend to filter more or add EQ?

I end up doing some of both. The FET 47 [on the kick], for instance, has got a lot of low end. I end up filtering way down low, and even taking out some more at 30 HZ. I'll put a filter at 20 and then take out more at 30, and then I'm bumping up at 100 a little so I can get it to thump, but not blow the woofers right out. And I end up taking out a fair amount at 300, to try and get the "awnk" out of it. [Laughs] How are you going to spell "awnk?"

Are you a Pro Tools user?

User and owner. In fact, the last several albums I've mixed have been straight out of Pro Tools. I like to get the color on tape during recording, then I dump all the tracks right into the Pro Tools. It gives me more manipulative power later. I can stick Amp Farm on a mandolin and stuff like that. You can come up with a texture you might not otherwise have that's cool, or a little more modern sounding, or something wacky. Or you may decide that what somebody played in the second chorus is better than what they played in the first, and you can move it. It's great for doing mutes and things on toms so you can get control of the leakage. I do a volume graph and just turn the toms on when they're playing, so you can get it really tight but really smooth. It's not a linear off. You can do little fade-ups and outs so they don't sound so abrupt.

You still track to a Sony 3348.

Yes, and after the tracks, I go digital through the Euphonix 727, which is a wonderful box. It's a format converter, and it removes the need for having 888s, if you're working in the digital world. So I just plug my computer into the 727, and it spits a MADI word right out to the Sony console. I go "dig" straight from a Pro Tools rig, without 888s, to the 727 straight to the Oxford.

What's your favorite new piece of gear?

Right now, I'd have to say it's the new computer I got for my Pro Tools rig. I'd been nursing along this sorry old 9500 computer for way too long. Now I've got a G4 466. So, short term, that's my favorite new piece. Long term, I guess, it is the Oxford! I also switched to KRK E8 speakers and really love them. Chuck [Ainlay] turned us on to those, as well as the big ATC monitors at Loud. They rock!

I know you have to get back to work, but tell us what's up next on your schedule?

The big thing on my calendar is a trip to Disney World and the beach with my wife and children. They pay a high price so that I can do a job I love. I know a trip won't get all those late nights and weekends back, but we sure will have a blast in Orlando! As far as the studio schedule goes, I hope to be working on a new Faith Hill album before long. We've not scheduled anything with her yet, but recording with Faith is always great. I hate to take on too much more, but if the right production opportunity came along, I would likely take it!

Dave "Hard Drive" Pensado

Keeping It Fresh

SEPTEMBER, 2001

Overnight success almost never is. It's true that, suddenly, David Pensado's name seems to be everywhere, and those who haven't been paying attention might surmise that all his recent recognition has come out of the blue. The truth is, this talented mixer has labored in the trenches for years, turning out a steady stream of Top 10 records for the likes of Brian McKnight, K-Ci and Jo-Jo, Warren G, Sisqo, Bel Biv Devoe, and many others, along with soundtrack album cuts for films such as *White Men Can't Jump, Hurricane, Nutty Professor II: The Klumps,* and *Men of Honor.* It's just that lately Pensado's records have garnered new attention, thanks in part to the high profile mix he did for Christina Aguilera, Mya, Li'l Kim, and Pink, the four young divas who graced the hit remake of "Lady Marmalade." Featured on the *Moulin Rouge* soundtrack, "Lady Marmalade" charted Number 1 on *Billboard's* Hot 100, Top 40 Tracks, and Hot 100 Airplay.

Meanwhile, Pensado is hardly breaking stride in the six-or-seven-days a week studio schedule that he has maintained for many years. There's no doubt that this guy is a hard worker. He's also highly well read on subjects that range from geology, in which he has a degree, to painting, mathematics, and poetry. And, he's an accomplished photographer whose work has been purchased by the High Museum of Art in Atlanta.

For several years, this Renaissance man's mix room of choice has been Studio C at The Enterprise in Burbank, California. We met there early one June afternoon for a chat before he started the day's work: a mix for new RCA artist Mercy Street.

Where did your nickname "Hard Drive" come from?

Richard Wolf, who was part of the production team of Wolf & Epic, gave it to me. I like to work hard, and I tend to push real hard in the studio. Richard, who was always fascinated by my Southern accent, heard me say "hard drive" and liked the way it sounded. Then the guys from Bell Biv Devoe, who were always complaining that we were pushing them too hard on the sessions, picked up on it, and put "Hard Drive" in my album credits. In the hip-hop community, of

Photo: Edward Colver

course, everyone had a nickname, and since no one could remember Pensado, people started calling for that "hard drive engineer." And of course, from the day that they came out, I was heavily into computers for recording, so the name had a double meaning.

How long have you been engineering?

I started in the late '70s, in Atlanta.

How did that happen?

When I was really young, my mom taught me guitar, and I played with a lot of groups. After a while, I started looking around at the state that these musicians, who were fifteen years older than me, were in. They had less than I did — which was nothing. And I started thinking, "Man, I gotta figure out some other way to do this." Because I didn't want to be fifty years old with nothing, but I still wanted to do music.

And just by the hand of God, I met Paul Davis and Phil Benton, who had a studio in Atlanta called Monarch Sound. They'd heard some live stuff I'd done and really liked it. Phil was an engineer who had become a producer and was looking to get out of the engineering elements. Paul was a singer and

songwriter who'd had a lot of big records, like "I Go Crazy," and "Cool Night." The first project I worked on at their studio was a group called Brick, and we had a successful record.

They taught you how to be a recording engineer.

Yeah. As a musician, I was always the guy in my band to set up for the live stuff....

You mean the P.A. equipment?

Yes, and a big chunk of that translates over to recording. Particularly the need for speed, the need to avoid panic, the need to work well under pressure — those are all good assets to have when you start on this side of the recording world.

It's funny though; before that, it had never dawned on me that I could be an engineer. I always thought that was something for those revered, special geniuses I'd read about in magazines. I didn't realize that all it required was a little taste, a decent personality, and a willingness to learn. I was lucky; at Monarch, I had a one-on-one classroom. Phil was a great engineer, and he and Paul were both very patient with me.

We'd stay in the studios for days on end because we were having so much fun — to the point where we finally smelled bad and had to go home and take a shower. Paul was a pop and country artist, but he also loved technology. We had one of the first drum machines. We got the first Synclavier. We were always the first with new equipment.

How did you end up in L.A.?

If you want to be a sailor, you don't move to Kansas, you move someplace with an ocean. I think if you want to be a recording engineer, your options would be, in descending order: Los Angeles, New York, Nashville, and London.

Being originally from Tampa, Florida, the thought of snow didn't appeal to me. Country music didn't appeal to me, and the thought of gray skies didn't appeal to me. That left Los Angeles. But there was a fear factor in moving to Los Angeles, where I'd have to compete against guys who were legends to me—guys like Jon Gass. That quality of engineer. But I got frustrated, and felt I couldn't go any further in Atlanta. Finally, that frustration surpassed my fear.

I came out without knowing very many people. Although if it didn't work out, I would never have gone back to Atlanta, because my friends would never have let me live it down. I knew I was going to make it out here either as an engineer, a carpenter, a gardener—something!

Luckily, I met Herb Trawick, who introduced me to Kevin Fleming, the vice president at Island Records, and then Kevin introduced me to Wolf & Epic. Three months later, we had a Number 1 song, BBD's "Do Me Baby." It was pretty easy after that.

Wait a minute. That's too simple. It's not that easy for an engineer to keep getting work.

Well, you've got to remember that, at that time, there weren't a lot of engineers that stood up and proudly proclaimed that they wanted to do hip-hop. But that's where my head was at; it's what I wanted to do.

When we made "Do Me Baby," we made a record that didn't sound like anything else. It was a function of Wolf & Epic's vision. And it was a function of the fact that I had just come out of the club scene in Atlanta. I had ten years of hip-hop sensibility, making loops and stuff like that. Big bottom was everything there, even though at that time there was no bottom end on the radio. Also, I was a Quincy Jones and Earth, Wind, and Fire fanatic. I loved that sparkly kind of top end.

So "Do Me Baby" was the first song to hit radio that had this massive club bottom, hip-hop sensibility in the middle, and this real smoothed-out, classy, Quincy Jones-type top.

Where did you mix that?

I mixed that particular song at Alpha Studios. They had a Calrec console, but I am such a fan of SSL automation that I actually talked Denny, the owner, into installing SSL automation on that console.

SSL has treated me really well over the years. I can't say enough good things about them. I love other consoles, too, but I have to say that SSL has always been my favorite. Especially the 9000 J-series. I think it's the last great analog console.

Were you an instant convert to the J-series?

Yeah. I've got a mentality that likes new. I mean, I will use new things that don't work just because they're new!

You were also an instant convert to drum machines and sampling.

The first time that I heard a drum machine, it was "Wow, I like this!" I'd been doing live music, which I still enjoy to do, but there was something about the control that machines gave that was really appealing to me right from the start. And at that time, of course, drummers were not very humble. [Laughs] Since then, a lot of live players have become more humble.

I worked on my first rap record in the late '70s, and I'm not going to pretend that I could understand it. I'm from a different culture. But the music got me right away. It was an eye opener. The idea of taking a record, putting it on a turntable, and creating something new out of that was captivating to me.

I truly see no difference in the skill in doing that and the skill in sitting down on piano and playing Mozart. Of course, one requires a massive commitment and dedication to training and study. I respect anyone that can spend the bulk of their life mastering a craft. But in terms of the talent and creativity, I see no difference.

It's amazing what some of the producers I've worked with can create. And obviously, I'm not alone in liking it—look at how the general public responds. There was a time where I was the only guy doing hip-hop in Atlanta. No one else wanted to. I got work not necessarily because I was good, but because I was the only one willing to do it! Now, it's to the point where if you took r&b and hip-hop out of the recording business, there are not many studios that could sustain an income.

It takes a certain personality to successfully do hip-hop and rap sessions. For one thing, it requires a lot of patience. You have to be pretty relaxed, and you have to be comfortable with having a lot of people around you almost all the time.

I approach it somewhat like I do the live thing: the more the merrier. There's definitely something fun about doing something good and having a roomful of people get excited about it. Look at it this way: If I've got fifty people in my control room watching what I'm doing and one of those is my client, I've got forty-nine new clients next week.

I grew up in a Spanish family; there were always a lot of people around. The ability to concentrate in the face of all those people and all that Latin noise was something that I got as a child. It doesn't

bother me. In fact, I enjoy it. I hate working alone. I don't know about other mixers, but for me, if my clients don't show up, I mix a lot more conservatively. When they're there, I can try anything, look over at them, and say, "What do you think?" Nine times out of ten, they'll go, "That's cool, but what if . . . " and then take my idea to another level. Multiply that times a day's worth of ideas and you have a completely different mix than you would if you were working alone.

[Laughs] I've done sessions where I had people tagging the consoles. Or I'd look down at my feet and there's an albino python crawling across them. Let your imagine go. I have had everything happen in my control rooms.

At the end of the day, I think that we're making music for people. So, to try to make music in isolation is not a good concept. Unless you are the only person who is going to buy your record, it's probably better to have a little input.

I don't want to belabor the point but I will leave you with this thought: I've got engineer friends that consider the client a nuisance. I mean, would you go to a doctor that considered you a nuisance? Like you were only there to further his research?

In our profession, when you get so far on the technical side, it's sometimes easy to lose track of who is buying our records. I try every day to remember the things that got me going—the things that I liked, when I was a kid buying records.

I've always wondered how it is it that engineers, who traditionally don't dance, are able to make records that people want to dance to.

Actually, I do dance. And if more engineers would get out to a club and dance once in a while, maybe we would have some better records! Look, I am who I am. I don't try to dress like my clients. I don't try to talk like my clients. But, we're making records for fourteen- to twenty-four-year olds. At the end of the day, it's about some groove and hook. You used to be able to say groove and melody, but now it's groove and hook. That's what people buy. If you don't hit them over the head with a great groove and hooks, you are not doing your job. One of the reasons rap has been so successful is that it's reduced that concept to its barest minimum.

I think for popular music to work for kids you need to have something that strokes their hormones — something that gets them going. It needs to be kind of angry about something. Not politically angry, necessarily, but just pissed that your girlfriend left you, pissed that the police hassle you all the time, or pissed about this or that. When it's bitter angry, it doesn't really appeal to the masses, it appeals to a smaller group of people. That's okay, but we're talking in terms of appealing to a lot of people. And thirdly, I think it needs to be naughty without being vulgar. Naughty changes from generation to generation — what was considered vulgar in the '50s is considered not even naughty enough now. If you get those three elements, you've got good pop music. And rap music has done that brilliantly. It's reduced music to those three elements, the basic groove and hook.

Working as much as you do, when do you find time to check out other people's music?

I listen a lot to radio. I live about thirty minutes from the studio, so I get in about an hour a day listening to radio. And I leave MTV and MTV2 and BET on my TV screen while I'm working. If something catches my eye, I'll turn the sound up.

To be successful as a mixer, you have to be competitive. To sustain a career, you really have to grow and reinvent yourself. You have to love music so much that without knowing it, you search out the new things, and then you have to have an attitude that allows you turn loose of your old ideas very quickly and easily.

One of the many cool things about hip-hop is, we've got the only fans in the world where, if you use a snare sound that you used three months ago on some hit, they'll call you on it. They'll go, "That's the snare from OPP, man. Why couldn't you think of a better snare?" The only time our fans will give you any slack is if you use something that they recognize, but you use it in a more creative way. They'll go, "Man, I give you points for that."

Once sentence you'll never hear in a hip-hop session is, "You can't do that. This is hip hop!" If you pull out an MPC-3000 and go to program the drums on a rock session you're going to hear, "It's a rock band. You can't do that." Hip-hop, you can bring in Slash. You can bring in live drummers and dead drummers — whatever you want to do is fine. Not only is it fine, you are considered a genius for doing it!

You love computers but you still mix to half-inch analog tape on a Studer machine.

I love [Quantegy] GP9. What I do is, I listen to the output of the 2-track machine while I'm printing to tape. There is always a sweet spot somewhere between +6 and +20, where as you increase the level to tape, the signal saturates the tape, and it gives you this wonderful tape compression. It takes that digital Pro Tools sound and gives it another quality. So I take the master fader on my console and just crank it up, while I'm listening to the output of the 2-track, until I go, "That's it."

I mean, meters are useless if you've got ears. There were times that the guys who taught me wouldn't let me use meters. I'd go, How do I tell if it's too hot? Well, you hear distortion! How do I tell if the level is too low? You hear tape hiss! Anything in between is fine!

Do you have any tricks for coping with over-the-top numbers of tracks?

I study the rough mix, and then I visually try to locate the meat and potatoes of the mix.

I find the kick, snare, bass, the pads, lead vocal, background vocals ... and I try to construct a mix with that small number of elements.

My 9000 is so big, part of it is in another zip code, so I set it up with fifty channels on either side of me. I put my important tracks near the center of the console, because when I get off axis, my monitoring isn't as accurate. Drums and percussion go to the left and vocals to the right. Things that don't play very often end up out in the nether regions. Luckily, with Pro Tools, you can set up a lot of that visually, because you can look at a track and see that it only plays once in a song.

Do you use the board dynamics on the 9K much?

There are some things that you can't find any better compressor for. I don't like gating, so I rarely use the gates unless I am going for a special effect like getting a little tick on the kick drum. But I use the compressor on a lot of synthesizers and other instruments. Because I have so much outboard gear, I don't use it on vocals or drums.

Let's talk about vocals. What are some of your favorite vocal compressors?

I use my Gates Sta-Level on almost all my vocals. There are some singers I work with that it just loves: Brian McKnight, Christina Aguilera. . . .

Because it was designed to control the output of a mono radio station, it was more a "set it and forget it" type piece of gear, with lot of the controls on the inside. But my friend Kevin Mills, who owns Larrabee Studios, had one of his staff modify it for me. So the internal parameters, I don't need to change too much, and on the front, the controls are almost identical to an LA2A's.

I love the TubeTech on vocals. And I like the CompressorBank, a plug-in by McDsp—especially the 670 presets that emulate the Fairchild.

And I love the Waves C4 plug-in. It's a 4-band parametric with an incredible compressor on each band. So not only do I get to choose my frequency, my bandwidth on four different bands, and my level, but I get to choose all my compression parameters with a compressor that's designed to emulate not one, but all of the great classics.

The way I use it is, when a singer is singing kind of low, I'll have it take some of the mud out. But when they're singing harder in the vamp and it gets more midrangey, I'll set it to automatically dip out that 3K for me. It saves me time in mixing to have that compressor catch a lot of it.

You often split your vocal tracks as they come into the console, so that you can use both a vintage, tube processing chain and a high tech, modern processing chain. That probably explains why the vocals on your mixes avoid that unfortunate "rip your head off" sound and instead, seem to have more body to them.

Thank you for the compliment! Usually, I'll have anywhere from two to four faders—mults of the lead vocal—with each of those faders receiving the same vocal information. On one fader, I'll have my low tech analog chain. I'll use the Gates, or an LA2A, something with tube processing. I'll also maybe use a Neve 1073 on that fader. On the fader next to it, I'll go with a high tech chain, maybe FilterBank, maybe CompressorBank, or the C4 Waves. I might use an Avalon 2055 on that chain, or if we go to three faders, I might have an all-Avalon chain. As the song progresses, generally the verses are sung kind of low and breathy, so we'll go to the high tech chain a little more for that. In the parts where they're singing louder, and maybe getting a little screechy, then I'll go to the tube part of the chain for some nice rich harmonics. Or maybe not. You listen and see what you like best, because now you've got different options for different phrases.

I just sit there and move the faders. In some places, all the faders might be up on one phrase. You just try different combinations. The more you do it, the faster you'll get. The first time you try it, you'll add another two hours to your mix! But then it becomes almost like second nature, because as you are setting up each chain you're listening and thinking about it.

The same with drums. You can have the main kick drum fader, and another fader where you compress the dogsnot out of the kick, and add a lot of top end to it. Then, maybe in the chorus you add in a little bit of that second chain. It gives a tiny bit more attack to that programmed kick drum, as if the drummer was hitting it harder.

You can expand the concept into any piece of information. [Laughs] I'm lucky because I've got 104 inputs on my 9K. If you don't, you'll have to use that technique more judiciously.

What about the dilemma of level control vs. intelligibility of lyrics? There are a lot of hip-hop-type songs these days where lyrics seem to get lost in overcompression.

What you're hearing is not necessarily bad compression, but just overall bad engineering. I have to say that I think our profession is heading in a new direction. When I first started out, the stuff I was given to mix was pristine. Mixing was a different occupation, back then. You basically had 24 tracks—sometimes a little more—that were pretty much perfect, and you spent a few hours with a very small amount of gear to mix them. Nowadays, I would say that eighty percent of the producers I work with have a home studio. They engineer their songs themselves, and their skills vary, in terms of engineering, from horrible to incredibly amazing.

Mixing is now a different profession, in that we have to do a lot of repair work. We have to straighten out a lot of problems—from overcompression to where everybody and his mother went out and bought the Avalon 737, took that right-hand knob, and cranked it up 1800 dB. We get these incredibly bright vocals. Now, I happen to think that the 737 is one of the best pieces of equipment ever made, and it's one of my first recommendations when anybody asks me what to buy for a home studio.

But, the problem is that a lot of the young producers I work with don't have the monitoring capability to hear how much top end, or how much compression—or whatever—that they're adding. So a lot of the time, what you're hearing when vocals are unintelligible, is lack of skill on the mixer's part to straighten out problems they were given by an overzealous producer recording his own tracks.

As a mixer, you have to have a mindset now that says, "I can fix anything." Because with all the tools we have today, you really can.

You can fix overcompression?

Yes. I go into Pro Tools, and I type in the level on every syllable. I uncompress what the compressor did. And I automate the EQ on every syllable. I've got FilterBank sitting there, and I automate the top end back into just that syllable. On a four-minute song, to fix a lead vocal with just the most horrible compression, takes me about two hours. The average is about forty-five minutes.

I think any engineer who complains about having to do that will probably be an engineer who is not working in a few years. Because that's the future. If you develop that skill set, of being able to fix anything and then mixing it, you'll be working a lot.

The upside about all this is that these are the best times for creative people, because you can just turn on a computer and get your ideas down.

I encourage my producers not to worry about the sonics. Just bring me anything that's creative, and I'll fix it

You're a brave man.

I would rather have a great song and poor engineering than the best engineered crappy song any day.

Okay, enough of fixing, and back to mixing. What are some of your favorite vocal effects?

I love the Eventide Orville. I used the Orville on all of the vocals on "Lady Marmalade."

I like to chain a lot of effects together—a harmonizer with a delay, with a reverb unit. I almost always have effects on my effects. With the Orville, I can do it all within the unit. And their harmonizing presets are the best ever for vocals.

What's that Roland Dimension D in your rack for?

I use it on bass and on rap vocals. It's one of my favorite pieces of gear. I loved "C'est La Vie," by Robbie Nevil, and what I got from that record is a hundred ways to use the Dimension D.

What about background vocals? Any tricks there?

I've got this little box: a Boss EH 50, that an engineer named Ed Seay hipped me to. I paid fifty dollars for it, and I use it on my backgrounds. It's like an enhancer. It gives you just the top end, like

an Aphex Aural Exciter. So, rather than put a chorus on the whole vocal, I just chorus the EH50 signal, so my chorus isn't getting all the mud. There's only one setting to use though. You can't use any of the other buttons.

And that would be?

The last button on the right: Expander 2. Super glue it in, and make sure that nobody hits any other button.

What are some things you use to get all those big bass sounds?

I use the Moog parametric, which you don't see too much on bass. Also I use API 550s, the Pultec [EQP1A], and a plug-in made by Waves called MaxxBass, which saves my butt a lot of times. If you get a pure sine wave sound, you can create enough upper harmonics to actually hear it on a 3-inch speaker. And if you get a sound that's all upper frequency range, the MaxxBass will give you the sub stuff. For the sub stuff, I also like to use a dbx 120XDS, a boom box we used to use in the clubs.

What are some of your current favorite reverbs and effects?

I use the Eventide 2016, like Mick Gazauski does. The "Stereo Room." On toms, I use the "Room" program, but there's something about the stereo room that's great on some vocalists.

I use the DP4 Plus a lot. The presets I like are called "Big Acoustic Guitar" and "Electric Tines."

The Korg A1 is great for guitar effects. It's a chained effect, not unlike the Roland DEP5, where on a particular preset you've got distortion, an EQ, a compressor, a delay, and a spring reverb, and you have control over all of them. I use a setting called "Blues Vibe," and I also love "Wankadelic."

I use the Roland SDE 330 a lot; Dexter Simmons turned me on to it. Dexter also gave me a Spatializer, which is incredible. I love putting things outside the speaker plane. I've got several pieces of gear that will let me do that. One of them is the Beringer Edison stereo image processor — the best $200 you'll ever spend. Also the Ultrafex II, an enhancer/exciter that also has the spatial component.

And the Forat F16 is my little secret weapon. Ben and Bruce at Forat are two of the brightest guys on earth.

As hard as you work, and as long as you've been doing it, do you still feel lucky to be an engineer?

The profession of engineering is unique in that you have to be technical and creative at the same time. It's hard to imagine Picasso designing the first computer. It's also hard to imagine Bill Gates painting "Guernica." And as a mixer, you have to be Bill Gates for thirty seconds, then Picasso for thirty seconds. You're constantly shifting back and forth.

That's why there are not that many really great mixers. God didn't create too many people with that particular ability. In another culture, in another time, people who have it would be doomed to be freaks! The gift of equal left brain/right brain power in any other time would probably be an undesirable quality. But, at this point in time and place, it's a good freak of nature to be. Because, luckily, there's a profession called mixing....

Tony Maserati

DECEMBER, 2001 ## Driven to Mix

Any definition of the "New York sound" that's front and center on so many of today's hits has to credit Tony Maserati with being one of its main authors. He's been seminal in the creation of a style sometimes described as "outhouse on the bottom, penthouse on the top." Big, powerful bass paired with smooth, classy high end is Maserati's trademark. You've heard variations on cuts by R. Kelly, Mary J. Blige, Lil' Kim, and Faith Evans, as well as by more mainstream chart-toppers Mariah Carey, Destiny's Child, Brian McKnight, Jennifer Lopez, Ricky Martin, and Alicia Keys.

Maserati started on the New York scene in the mid '80s working with artist/producers Full Force, churning out records for the likes of Lisa Lisa and Cheryl "Pepsi" Reily. These days, he continues to be busy as ever. Even in a field notoriously populated with dedicated workaholics, Maserati's especially focused and detail-oriented style attracts notice. His targeted approach to the job is evident in such hits as Ricky Martin's "She Bangs," Mark Anthony's "I Need To Know," and R. Kelly's "I Wish." Given his organized work habits and rather studious attitude toward technology, it's not too surprising to discover that, before left-turning into the studio world, the friendly and soft-spoken Maserati had decided to become a lawyer.

I spoke with him one Sunday afternoon in mid September as he relaxed at his East Village apartment. He'd been up late the previous night mixing a new Alicia Keys release at Hit Factory's Studio 3, but after he made a quick run to the corner coffee shop for a cappuccino, we settled in for a chat.

I have to ask. Is Maserati your real name?

[Laughs] Well, it's not the original spelling, but it's phonetically correct. It's how my Italian family name, Masciarotte, gets pronounced in English.

Selected Credits

Christina Aguilera
"Get Mine, Get Yours,"
"Can't Hold Us Down,"
"Fighter"

Amarie
All I Have

Marc Anthony
"I Need To Know,"
"When I Dream At Night,"
"You Sang To Me"

Mary J Blige
What's the 411?
My Life,
Share My World,
Ballads,
No More Drama

Mariah Carey
"Fantasy,"
"Honey,"
"The Roof,"
"Breakdown"

Destiny's Child
Survivor,
Eight Days Of Christmas

Faith Evans
Faith,
Keep The Faith

R. Kelly
R, TP2.com

Jennifer Lopez
"If You Had My Love,"
J.Lo

Maxwell
"Fortunate,"
"Got To Get To Know You"

Let's go back to the beginning for a minute. You studied at Northeastern University in Boston, heading toward a law career, when you made a switch into music.

Yes. I was playing guitar and singing in a band while at school. When I realized I didn't want to be a lawyer, I switched to the Berklee College of Music and studied what was called "composition," which was, to me, just songwriting. At the same time, for money, I started doing live sound. I ended up doing sound and lights for a ten-piece r&b revue: three singers, horns, two guitars—a totally wild show. We traveled with a P.A., and we'd do three different venues a week.

So, early on you had a feel for r&b.

I was always into it. I grew up listening to it because my sister was a big r&b head—Marvin Gaye, Diana Ross.... When Berklee started their program for production and engineering, I signed up. I loved it, and that's when I started listening to guys like Bob Clearmountain, Neil Dorfsman, Roger Nichols, Steve Hodge, and Jimmy [Jam] and Terry [Lewis].

When I finished school, I went right to New York, to the Power Station, trying to get a job. They didn't need anybody, but it turned out there was a guy working there that I'd played hockey against when I was a kid. He suggested that I try Sigma, which, at the time, had a studio in Manhattan upstairs from the Ed Sullivan Theater.

Another r&b connection, considering Sigma's Philly history.

It was totally luck for me. A lot of the other studios were doing the '80s rock thing, and that was all cool, but it doesn't exist anymore. Sigma was doing a lot of machine stuff, and a lot of remix stuff— Robert Palmer, Talking Heads, Steely Dan, Madonna—a lot of really cool music. We also did jingles in the morning. I got to work on everything from horns to strings, to vocals and mixing. Joe Tarsia was the owner and a great engineer from way back in the Philly days, so we all got really great training. And it was fun. Hank Meyer, the studio manager, would come up, on a whim, with things like "Margarita Day," and all the clients would participate.

How'd you move up to the engineer's seat?

Glen Rosenstein, who is now a good friend of mine, was engineering for the production team of Full Force. He'd started a Ziggy Marley record with Chris and Tina from the Talking Heads, and Full Force needed some work done, so he was nice enough to recommend me. One of the things we worked on was a Samantha Fox single, which I somehow also ended up mixing, that went to like Number 3. And when Glen continued to be busy with other things, I continued to work with Full Force.

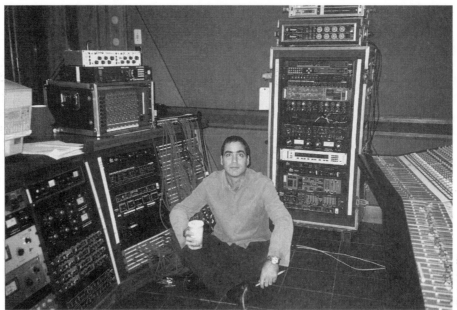

Photo: Duffy

What happened after Sigma closed?

One thing I did was to immediately get into the role of coordinator for the Full Force guys. And doing that, I started booking all my favorite studios, so I got to work at them. We went to Skyline and to Hit Factory and all over town, and I got to know all the studios and to become friends with the people who ran them. That saved me, because when Full Force created their own facility in Brooklyn, and started using the guy who built it for them to engineer, I called up all the managers I'd become friends with and said, "I need work."

And they all came through. Barbara Moutenot at Skyline, Laura King at Chun King, Troy and Danielle at Hit Factory—they'd call me with gigs. That's how I got hooked up with people like Heavy D, Brand Nubian, and Poke & Tone, who became some of my biggest clients.

It's an art: the way a talented studio manager can "cast" a session, pairing up clients with an engineer who will make the session go well and the studio look good.

That's absolutely right. Relationships are a lot of what this business is about.

Of course, you've also got to be good. I trained and worked the traditional 90-hour week, and I also studied very, very hard.

Studied how?

I would be on the subway every morning with my SSL manual, or whatever manual, reading it and marking it. I tell my assistants now: It's great to record your friends' bands, but don't just do that. Take a tape or a file and the manuals and work through a room's gear—the reverbs, the plug-ins. Keep working it over and over. I'd sit there with the gear for hours. I think that helped me become a mixer, and to be able to come up with things that were creative and new.

Where a lot of my counterparts were into getting a big "Power Station" drum sound, I was into looking for my own sounds. One of the conclusions I came to was that I couldn't do what Bob Clearmountain or Mick Guzauski does. To this day, if a client brings me something that I think someone else could do better, I'll tell them so. I'll say, "That sounds like a Mick Guzauski song; I think you should call him." I don't do the lush, beautiful thing.

Okay, then, describe what you do?

My stuff is harder, it's edgier, it's fat—more in line with the hip-hop r&b thing. I worked with guys like Heavy and Puffy and D'vante and Poke & Tone. And because of what I had to do, I played a role in creating the modern r&b hip-hop sound. My clients wanted a lot of bottom; they wanted it really heavy-sounding. And I wanted it to sound crystal-clear. The compromise is what I sound like now.

I got a lot of my ideas from others, of course, like Bruce Swedien and his Michael Jackson and Quincy Jones records. Bruce had the great top, and also some nice punch. He didn't have the crazy, heavy bottom that I needed for the hip-hop stuff, but he knew how to make it pop. And Steve Hodge had a real ethereal spectrum and soundscape that I could never get but always tried to. And Mick [Guzauski] had [laughs]—I don't know what.... Mick is a Martian, a genius from outer space. I cannot figure out what he does, and he's always using something that nobody else has.

Do you always work on SSL consoles?

Well, I used to say I could mix on a Mackie console in a bathroom. I think that's true of any good mixer. But now the competition is really stiff and I use everything I can get, so I mix on an SSL J Series. I used to do a lot of work on the [Neve] VR —the Mary J. Blige stuff was on a VR—because I wasn't into the [SSL] G console with VCAs. I would gravitate toward anything that didn't have VCAs.

So the SSL J-Series was a natural fit for you.

I jumped on it immediately because of its sonic difference and its flexibility. And its software worked really well. The automated EQ and dynamics in/out switching are especially useful when you've got a "difficult" vocal. I'll automate it to filter out low end on a talking part in the bridge, or to put a telephone sound in the intro. The insert in/out I'll use for the same thing, or maybe to add a different sound to an instrument to make it rise a bit in the hook.

I also have racks of Neve EQ. I own an old Neve 5316 console, a broadcast board that has 33114 EQs in it that I've rack-mounted. A 33114 is a mic pre, line amp, and EQ, similar to a 1081 as far as frequencies. It has switchable top between 15 and 6k, plenty of frequencies in the mids—although there's no Q control—and a low and high shelf as well. It's got a lot of flexibility for a Neve, and typically I have a rack of eight of them with me. Or, like last night on the Alicia Keys session, they wanted an old sound, so I had all three of my racks.

Are you always mixing off of Pro Tools now?

Yes, and it works great with the J, because I can clock the console to an Aardvark Aardsync and clock the Pro Tools as well. They're both getting the same clock source, which means I'm frame-accurate. You can change the SSL to read 29.97 and, of course, Pro Tools will read anything. I run the console as my master, which is great, and which you can't do that with other consoles.

What do you mix to?

I still mix to half-inch. I prefer a Studer 820, but I'll mix to an ATR, and even an MCI.

I've been using BASF 900 [tape]. It seems to stand up well. I don't hit tape that hard; I record at +6 over 185. When the new formulas came out, there was this whole thing about +9, +12, but I'm not into it. I recently got a tape that was recorded at +12, and I called the engineer and yelled at him. It was flat, mushy, and there were no dynamics. It was like, "What the hell were you thinking?" I understand the effort to reduce tape hiss, but I've got a gate on every channel here! Give me a break—you're supposed to be capturing the dynamic of a performance.

Actually, I do that a lot—call up engineers. [Laughs] Mostly I give compliments, but sometimes it's, "Whataya doin' here?"

What are some of the techniques you use to get your bottom end the way you like it?

Early on, when I was working with Full Force, I started splitting things up. It's a way to compress the low frequency differently than the highs. I'll split the signal and EQ and shelf them each differently. I'll do that on kick drum, on bass and on vocals, and other things as well.

So, you'll do that on your main tracks, the ones in the center of the mix?

It doesn't matter where the sound is in the spectrum; it only matters what its job is. I'll take guitars and just nick bottom and top, or I'll nick all the bottom up to 2k—just to fit something in. I learned from listening to Roger Nichols and Steve Hodge. These guys place stuff, not just with level or pan, but with frequencies and phase. They would use EQ to move things front and back. Obviously, the brighter something is, the closer it is; the duller it is, the farther away. A bright reverb is present; a dull one takes you farther back in the hall.

Some of my clients bring in drums that just need a little tweaking; some of them need more work. Obviously, with a kick, I need tons of bottom, so after I split it, I might filter out all the top on one [split], pump the bottom with a Pultec or Neve, and compress it a little less. Then, on another kick, I'll nick off everything at the bottom, find the spot that ticks or knocks, and compress that differently. And all the while, I'm checking phase. That's the most important thing whenever you're combining two of the same signal that's been EQ'd and compressed differently.

What compressors might you use for your top split vs. the bottom?

On the top, I'll often use something that has less of a full frequency response but gives me a quick release. Mostly, the dbx 160, 160x, the [SSL] console compressor, Drawmer or Aphex—stuff I normally consider to be effects dynamics, because of the tendency to add a sound of its own to the signal. On the bottom, I'll generally use very little —with an 1176 or compression from the board, or nothing at all.

What EQs besides Neves and Pultecs do you like for bottom?

I also use a lot of Tube-Techs and Langs. And plug-ins work quite well for filtering. I use a lot of Focusrite, Renaissance, and Filter Bank.

What about on vocals?

On vocals, I'll use two EQs: one before it hits the console and another on the insert point. I want the one that I use to hit the console to come with more of a sound of its own, like a Neve.

So, you tailor your first EQ to the sound of the vocal, and use others to fine-tune?

Yes, like I'll use GML to notch things out or to add a little bit of top. I don't want to hear the GML, just the effect of it. Whereas, with the Neve, I want to hear that sound that it adds and I'll choose the particular Neve model that I want. I have a set of 1066s that I just love. I'll often use those across the stereo bus, where they aren't doing much.

You just want the unique sound of the unit itself.

Yeah, there's just that color. That goes for compressors, as well. Depending on the frequency content of a signal, and what I want the outcome to be, I'll use everything from LA2As and LA3As—the optical stuff, which I like a lot—to a dbx 160X.

I used a dbx 160X on a Toni Braxton vocal once, just because in that instance I needed the control. Normally, I'd never do that, but it worked—it did the right thing. Today, I probably would have used an Empirical Labs Distressor for that.

I think quite a lot about how a piece of outboard gear works with the frequencies, and whether it's a transient sound or perhaps a bass, which is less transient. I wouldn't put a kick drum through a 160X and expect to retain a lot of the frequency spectrum that went in. I know that I would lose some of the brilliant top and a lot of my bottom, as well, because of the way the unit is made.

Obviously, this goes one step deeper when you start talking about the kinds of splits you're doing on an instrument.

I'm thinking about the kinds of compressors and EQs that work well for that frequency content that I'm splitting. I'm also very particular, especially with things like LA3As and 2As, about which actual unit I'm using. I'll spend time on that. When I find a good one, I'll write the serial number down and make sure I rent that one all the time. It's the same with Fairchilds. I call the rental company, and I want a specific one or I don't want any. You have to, because they can sound totally different.

The first question I ask of the assistant when I plug in an LA2A is "Which one is the best?" A lot of times, they don't know. There's one room I work in that has two LA2As. One does the job it was meant to—works perfectly, sounds great—and I'll use it on vocals quite often or I'll use it on bass. The other one sounds like crap, so when I want something to sound like crap, I'll put it in there.

[Laughs] It's not necessarily a bad thing; it's just another thing.

It doesn't really matter if you're using newer gear. A Distressor is going to pretty much sound the same, as do plug-ins, of course. Which I do. I use the Renaissance compressor on vocals all the time. It just depends on what I get. If something sounds terrific already, like with the Alicia Keys stuff I was working on yesterday, where you just need a little control, the Renaissance is good. Whereas, with something that's really bad, I'll have the Neve EQ, the Distressor, a GML, a de-esser, the board EQ, an old Dolby, an 1176 offline that I'm busing, too…anything. I'll throw every trick in the book at a bad vocal. You don't stop until you've got something, because the vocal is the magic. If the vocal isn't doing its job then you've not done yours.

A lot of mixers lately have commented on the poor quality of material that they often receive. What's your opinion on the subject?

It's not that everything is bad. I get lot of tracks that sound terrific. But it is a major issue. I'm used to getting tracks that are horribly recorded, whether it be analog or digital. Vocals that are punched terribly, with a mic choice that wasn't even thought about, a preamp choice that wasn't thought about—obviously not right for the vocalist. Everything, down to poor recording level. It's just something that we all deal with.

What monitors do you use?

I go through a million. I spent quite a long time with Tannoy DMT12s. Mine are actually broken, and they buzz when you turn them up, but I still cart them around. I also own a pair of ProAc Studio 100s, and a pair of Dynaudio System 1s. I even have a pair of AR18s that I drag around.

I almost always have Yamaha NS10s set up. My clients are used to them, and so am I. Then, most of the rooms I work in have George Augspurger mains. I'll change the smaller set, depending on the music style.

Which ones for which styles?

If I'm doing a straight up, hip-hop, heavy-duty bottom kind of thing, I'll use the DMT12s. They give me clarity as well as bottom end. If I'm doing a more pop kind of song, I'll use the ProAcs. If I'm doing something more pop/rock, with a little more guitars, I'll use the Dynaudios or the AR18s. I play with the effect on my brain.

Back at Sigma, we had something called Big Reds. They were the worst-sounding speaker on earth. But there was an engineer named Jim "Doc" Dougherty who used to do a lot of dance mixes, and he made them sound really good. I learned from that, that if you could get those Big Reds to sound good, the mix was amazing. I never did, but it made me realize that you could use the speaker to force your brain to do something it didn't want to.

I don't use something like Genelecs that make everything sound good, because I'll stop way before the mix is right, thinking, "Oh, that sounds nice." I want something that makes me work really hard. That's why I use Dynaudios for guitars. You can't hear guitars on them, so you push guitars.

Do you listen at high levels?

I listen at quite a lot of different levels. I also listen a lot in mono on the Studer speaker, or, if I don't have an 820, I'll listen on a single Auratone. I do most of my EQ'ing on the ProAcs, Tannoys or Dynaudios, listening quite low. Then I'll do rough leveling on the NS10s a bit louder. Then I'll go to the mono speaker and do the more intricate vocal levels, and background levels. Then I'll go back to, say, the ProAcs and listen louder for fine EQ'ing, then I'll go to the NS-10s and listen lower for my fine leveling.

Sounds like science. What do you listen on at home?

I have pair of Snells: big, tall orchestral speakers that go down to 20 Hz, with a Perreaux amplifier and a preamp that I think everyone should own, by a company in Norway called Electrocompaniet. I found it at the Stereo Exchange.

What's the ballpark time it takes you to do an average mix? Do you leave it up overnight?

If things are put together well, I don't necessarily leave things up overnight. But, if I've spent most of my energy fixing things all day long, then I definitely want to leave it up overnight. If I've spent all my time fixing problems, my creativity will be gone. I'll want to come back in the next day and say, "Okay, now what does this need to become a record?"

What motivates you and keeps you coming to work every day to make those records?

I've thought about how the projects that we do tend to blend into each other from day to day, and I've realized that really, it's about a day's work, and how you put yourself into it. I'm not a visual artist, but when you're doing several songs for an artist, it's almost like you're doing studies of that artist—studies in a particular emotion or sonic development. It really becomes your art, as well, and you go somewhere within yourself to create it.

There's always a lot going on—dealing with the phone, legal stuff, political issues. Sometimes, you'll have an artist who's unhappy with the producer, or a producer who's unhappy with the A&R person. There's always that stuff happening around you. I find that those who excel in mixing are able to put all that aside and concentrate on going inside themselves, finding what their feelings about the music are, and presenting that.

I got a wonderful, inadvertent compliment from a production team called the Matrix. I'd done a mix for them on a new Warners artist. Although we'd worked together once or twice before, I'd been brought in by management and by A&R, which is always a little weird for a production team or a producer—to work with a mixer that wasn't of their choosing. My approach was dramatically different from their rough mix. I was in New York and they were in L.A., and we sent them an Ednet. Usually, when we do that, I hear back in a few minutes: "I hate that vocal thing," or "I love it," or "It's banging, but you need to change one thing." But this time, a couple of hours went by, and we didn't hear anything. So, of course, I thought they were hating every note. And, actually, I think they were—at first. But they were respectful enough to listen, and listen again, and they eventually heard what I was trying to do. They finally called and said, "We were a little shocked when we first got it, but you know, it works! We love it!"

I appreciated so much that they really listened and came back with some great comments, and we worked together on it. What I'm trying to say is that, as a mixer, there are so many things swirling around you, but the song has to get by you first. You learn to make decisions and to trust your decisions. It can be difficult to verbalize, but you're trying to crystalize the magic that the artist is creating—to bring it to the forefront. And you're always learning about that, and about communicating with the artists that you're working with. That's part of what makes our art so special.

There are some days when I wonder what prompted me to become a mixer, or a recording engineer, but when you come right down to it, the answer is obvious. I may not be the one everybody is cheering for, but it's quite a lot of fun to listen to your music on the radio or on TV. That's something that's still thrilling for me.

Brian "Big Bass" Gardner

MARCH, 2002

"Big Bass" and Other Secrets From One of Mastering's Best

Just how long is Brian Gardner's discography? Well, pulling up his AllMusic.com page results in a list of over 750 credits. It was hip-hop heavy Dr. Dre who gifted Gardner with the handle "Big Bass," so people tend to think of him as purely a hip-hop/r&b expert. While there's no question that he is expert in these genres, those in the know seek him out for mastering expertise on all styles of projects, from alternative to classic jazz. And among those 750-plus credits are such monster hits as Janet Jackson's *Velvet Rope*, Blink 182's *Enema of the State*, Eminem's *Slim Shady*, En Vogue's *Funky Divas*, Fastball's *All the Pain Money Can Buy*, Smashmouth's *Astro Lounge*, and Tupac Shakur's *All Eyez on Me*.

And the hits just keep coming. On the day we spoke, Gardner had six cuts in the Top 10 o*f Billboard's* Hot 100: Mary J. Blige's "Family Affair," Nelly Furtado's "Turn Off the Light," "Hero" by Enrique Iglesias, "Get the Party Started" by Pink, and two by Jah Rule: "Livin' It Up" and "Always On Time." How's that for a hot week?

Because, in person, his vibe is so energetic and youthful, it's a surprise to discover just how long Gardner has been tweaking knobs in the mastering business. He got his start cutting vinyl, and early on worked in the studio with such notoriously challenging artists as Credence Clearwater Revival and the Jefferson Airplane.

Maybe it was those early psychedelic experiences that resulted in Gardner's unflappable demeanor. I've personally seen him sit calm and collected, a lightning rod in the kind of violent storm that sometimes strikes when creative artists hit mastering—that last chance saloon for changes.

We sat down for this interview in Gardner's suite at Bernie Grundman Mastering in Hollywood. That unpretentious room is where, five days a week, he gets down with DATs, CDs, hard drives, and analog tapes of every stripe, turning confusion into cohesion, and individual songs into the complete statement that's an album.

Selected Credits

Beck
Midnite Vultures

Blink 182
*The Mark, Tom and Travis Show
(The Enema Strikes Back),
Enema of the State, Dude Ranch*

Bone Thugs-N-Harmony
*E. 1999 Eternal, The Art of War,
Creepin on Ah Come Up*

Destiny's Child
Destiny's Child

Easy-E
*Str8 off Tha Streetz of
Mutha-Phukkin Compton,
Eternal E, It's On (Dr. Dre),
187 um Killa*

Emperor's New Groove
soundtrack

Fastball
*The Harsh Light of Day,
All the Pain Money Can Buy*

Herb Alpert
*Colors, Passion Dance
North on South Street*

Ice Cube
*Greatest Hits, War & Peace
Vol. 2 (The Peace Disc)*

The Isley Brothers
*Tracks of Life, Spend the Night,
Smooth Sailin'*

No Doubt
Rock Steady

Smash Mouth
*Smash Mouth, Astro Lounge,
Fush Yu Mang*

Suicidal Tendencies
*Freedumb, Prime Cuts:
The Best of Suicidal Tendencies,
Friends & Family*

You actually began your career in the mastering room.

Yes, I started in mastering first, then did some recording. I had always had a desire to get into the industry in some form or another. I was trying to get jobs when I was, like, twelve! I didn't realize that I couldn't because I was too young! I always enjoyed tweaking—EQing music at home. I always knew you could improve it by adding certain frequencies.

Were you into electronics and building stuff?

No, I just had a basic interest. I played piano when I was young, of course. That's actually something I regret: not having pursued the piano. But I still have the basic skills, and I have all this MIDI equipment at home. I work on it and think I've come up with something good, [laughs] then I come to work and a client comes in with something they've done... and I just put my track aside.

What was your first break?

Bill Robertson at Capitol helped get me get my foot in the door and land a job at RCA Records, where my professional career started. I started out in mastering but when I wasn't busy, I got to go down and second engineer for a lot of big dates. Harry Nillson, the Guess Who, Jefferson Airplane.... I was a teenager, and it was the late '60s, so it was quite an experience. Huge, mega dates with big artists—Henry Mancini, Vic Damone, the Monkees....

How did you learn to use a lathe?

It was at Century Records, my very first job. It was a custom kind of place, and they cut records for schools and the armed forces. I don't remember the first session I did. I understood the concept—the transfer of mechanical energy to electronic energy through the cutting head—so it wasn't any big surprise to me. I learned from watching it and reading about it; just knowing the process.

Of course, at that time, I wasn't allowed to EQ. Back then, you were forbidden to touch what the engineers had done. Your job was just to put it on the disc. It was: "Do not touch this tape; it is perfect!"

And then Credence Clearwater came along. We kept cutting refs for them over and over, thinking there might be something off on the frequency response. And it still wasn't right. So, I broke out the Fairchild limiters and the Pultecs, and I tweaked it, and that kind of changed the whole thing—being able to doctor up tapes.

They liked it better.

Oh yeah. It was a radical difference. And that's really where my career changed. Because, after a few years of mastering Credence hits, they [Credence] plucked me out of RCA, and I went up to Fantasy for four years.

Fantasy Studios, in Berkeley: The house that Credence built.

I was the first employee there. They wanted mastering in there first, before anybody else moved in. It was '69 or '70. That was another fun part in my career. Living in Berkeley, hanging out, having the Grateful Dead around. It was a great time—going over to Record Plant in Sausalito for the live KSAN broadcasts, hanging out at Wally Heiders Studios with Jack Cassidy and the Airplane.

And that led to the next phase, because after my four years there, I went to Allen Zentz Mastering, where we ruled in the disco department. We did all the Donna Summer records, all the Casablanca catalog. That was really something.

Was doing all that disco music the beginning of Brian "Big Bass" Gardner?

Well, kind of. Donna Summer, the Village People, and all of the George Clinton stuff. Really, the thing that struck me most at the time was the different levels of stardom that I was working with. I remember doing the Jackson Five's first record and having Berry Gordy in the room. Having Ike and Tina Turner there, in the room alone with me in the evening. And the Jefferson Airplane memories . . . seeing Jimi Hendrix loan speakers to them . . . .

So you learned to "go with the flow" from some very talented and eccentric artists.

Yeah, people say that I find a groove. And that is how I try to approach a lot of the stuff we do today. You can go in almost any direction with a project: you can make it real crunched and bright, you can make it hurt, or you can make it warm, mellow, and wide. Usually, I just go with what I feel. Most of the time it ends up being what my initial EQ was. [Laughs] But sometimes, we go on a big trip—a big circle—trying different things. And then, we end up with the original.

To a lot of people, the mastering process is very mysterious.

Well, a lot can be done here. Today, we have projects where recording goes on for months and months, sometimes in different studios, with different producers and engineers. What we have to do is put it all together and make it come up the same.

I do miss sequenced albums. And one mix, one version. The projects we get now are in so many different formats. There are a lot of different things you have to know how to use.

It takes a lot more outlay to equip a mastering room today.

It's just my opinion, but I do think our technology has gone too far, sometimes. I mean, who really cares about 26K? Take the Beatles. I don't think there's anything above 10 or 12K on all those great-sounding records of theirs. There's nothing wrong with having the capabilities of capturing that 26K, but it brings in all kinds of other problems. And with our levels today—with having to deal with always operating on the threshold of distortion —well, that's always fun.

Do you mean that people are sending you stuff cut hotter than ever?

No, not necessarily how it comes in. It's just that they want the end product to jump. They always wonder, "Can't you make this a little louder?" It keeps moving up, and it's got to stop somewhere. [Laughs] I'd like to put out a record sometime that's the lowest out there: "Oh, did you hear that new record? It's so low. It's so cool." But that's not going to happen. Although Steely Dan put out a record that sounded good, and it wasn't loud. It didn't have to just slam the levels.

You're talking about losing dynamic range.

Of course. But a lot of today's music is enhanced by taking some of those things out—punching it up and giving it less dynamics. That's the nature of much of the music that's popular. It's just more intense.

It seems like the great mastering engineers all started with vinyl. It gave them an understanding of what's important.

Yes, with vinyl there are certain parameters you have to really be careful of. And sonically, well, sibilance can still be aggravating on CDs, even though it doesn't splatter like it used to on vinyl. Some of the phase things are still important today, even though there are less restrictions on CDs.

You still cut vinyl yourself, right?

All the time. Nelly Furtado, Pink, Jah Rule, Dre—they all have vinyl. Even the soundtracks get put out on it. All the majors will usually release a vinyl. Because of the time factor, with albums running 70 minutes, we have to split them up to four sides just to keep the level competitive.

Really, vinyl is a lost art that wants to go away but can't. There are too many vinyl lovers out there. People who are into it miss the sound. And although digital is getting a lot better, I'm still an analog guy, basically. In general, I think bringing in some analog somewhere in a project really makes a difference. Preferably, on the basic tracks.

Although, I've had full digital projects in here lately that amaze me with how good they sound. But then, I've also seen groups come in here with really funky setups that sound fabulous. And then, they become stars. Money rolls in, they upgrade everything, and they lose it—they lose the sound. So, you never know.

For a long time, all of you at Grundman avoided using computers.

Our basic philosophy is to stick with the original source. Whatever it is. Now, though, we're using the German [computer] system called Audio Q, which is really amazing. Actually [laughs], it's one of our secret weapons, so I don't think you should print that!

Nothing is stock here, everything has been modified. And we've always been very particular and careful. We listen to blanks and hear the difference.

Blanks?

CD blanks. We'll throw away thousands of them, if they're not right. We get samples from manufacturers and make tests and A/B. We listen very carefully before we pick the lot that we're going to buy. A lot of people think once you're going D to D, it doesn't matter because it's all numbers. But you can hear it. Every step makes a difference, and when you add all the subtleties up, the result is dramatic.

So yes, we're in the computer age. But there's so much more to it than just the technical part. You can't just sit there at a computer and think you'll make it right. The person sitting there, operating the equipment, has to be able to feel it to turn the right knobs.

You're also very particular about the consoles here.

Yes, it's all discrete. There are no transformers, and all the equalizers are hand-made by Karl Bischof and Beno [Thomas "Beno" May]. In some instances, they've avoided switches. We'll actually change the patches, say, to the 1630, or to the computer, to avoid switching and to make the signal path better. It's a pain, but it's worth it.

And, of course, we went through great expense to make sure that, even for the shortest runs, the wire is the best possible. It really is surprising the difference a cable can make.

What do you monitor on?

Our main speakers are Tannoys, of course. And then I have an array of different ones, from NS10s to KRKs to the new little Yamahas, which DJ Quik just gave me. Those are kind of interesting; they have a switch on them that makes them sound like NS10s. And they also have adjusters to give you a little more bottom and make them sound better.

They're all just another reference point, and for clients to listen on. Really, I depend on the main Tannoys. But I also use KRK 7000s. And little Radio Shack Minima 7s.

Those little things? Why are they on the floor?

I like them there. A lot of people have copied me on that. They don't serve any purpose sitting there in your face. It's an in-the-next-room, on-the-radio kind of thing. Sometimes, they're turned the other way; I don't care. It's a good reference. I usually listen to them low level and you can tell a lot. Unfortunately, they don't make that particular model anymore.

Do people hear things in your room they haven't heard before?

All the time. And most of the time, for the good: "Well, I never heard that before; it's great!"

Do you listen at home or in the car?

I do still listen to my projects in the car once in a while, if I'm really trying to discern certain things —like long fades. And then, I'll try to talk the client into not letting them go so long! Things like that. But you also have to consider the environment of listening at home; the long fade might work there. Noise and traffic are factors, and sometimes I'll listen in the car for balances. [Laughs] I have a Jeep and a sports car ... so it's, "Let's see, who am I working with today? Oh, yeah, I'll bring the Jeep."

Do you listen to radio stations?

That's another thing that I've had the luxury of. Over the years, I've often been able to hear stuff on the radio almost instantly, and to experiment with limiting parameters, and with EQ and how it translates. Especially with rap stuff, we'll pick a ref and it'll be on the air in an hour. Some of the big guys can do that. We can hear it right away, and that's been really valuable.

I don't really need to do that anymore. Now, I pretty much know what goes on and how they limit it to death on the radio. So I've learned what kind of limiting you can get away with without it being ruined on the air. I've heard some records—good records—but they end up horrible because there are vocals in your face, and all of a sudden the band comes in and they're gone. You've got to know how to work with it so it doesn't do that.

What converters are you currently using?

We have the DBs, and we also still use Apogees, occasionally. Of course, how you hit them and how you hit all the different variables—the EQs, etc.—is very important.

But everything goes through an analog process in your room.

Yes. And that's where we adjust it and try to make everything fit together, even though they are from different formats.

You can fix a lot ... but what things are unfixable?

If a machine was set up wrong. Or if something's been saturated. In either the analog or digital domain, if they just slammed it—if it's just crunched and really distorted, there's nothing to be done about it. You can try and adjust the sonics a bit, but those crunches are always going to be there. Or sometimes, I get projects where it's almost distorting, but not quite, and the mastering process will bring that out. We have to deal with it,

and that can be difficult. Sometimes, EQ and level adjusting will work, but sometimes, it will really need to be remixed.

The most common problem is too much level, so that the tape is saturated. Not only is distortion the result, but that kind of saturation takes away the attack. It flattens things out. A kick drum, for instance, becomes all mush, so you don't feel the real solid slap to it.

Do you prefer to get multiple mixes of a song?

Occasionally, when they want a vocal up, that's a help. But to have a lot of mixes of guitar up a quarter dB ... I haven't found that useful.

Okay, you're mastering some really hard core stuff. How do you relate to the lyrics?

You have to appreciate all forms of music. There are good elements to all of it, even hardcore rap. But actually, when I hear a mix initially, I don't even hear the lyrics. I just hear the whole thing. The lyrics are like another instrument. You've got to place them in the right spot.

Speaking of placing things in the right spot, what compressors do you use?

Well, we've modified most things; they're not stock. But we have Dominators, and an SSL-style limiter that was handmade by Beno in our shop. Really, I use limiting very little. I don't like to do it. As opposed to what you might think by hearing some of the things I've done! I really don't like to take away attack—I just love that punch. But that SSL is a good one, when I do limit. And I bought a Wave L2 when I was over in Germany last year—an Israeli electronic piece of gear. Once in a while, I'll fire that thing in, and it works wonders.

You just have to know by feel what to put in when. Some limiters will deceive you, and you won't hear them suck, but they will still be holding back desirable transients. You always have to A/B to the original and make sure you're improving it.

Photo: David Goggin ©1999

Mastering for Eminem's Slim Shady *sessions: L to R Gardner, Engineer Richard Hureida, Larry Chapman, Eminem, Producer Dr Dre, Co-Producer Mark Bass*

I see a Spatializer among your gear. What do you use that for?

It's a modified Spatializer, which I will use when the mix is kind of dead. I've almost been able to create a miracle with it, on occasion, playing with space and width and then re-EQing. It's a fun tool to have.

Do you have an overall philosophy for the work that you do?

Let's see ... that would be: "Compress 'til it sucks then back off a quarter dB." [Laughs] I'm not necessarily a technical person. I go by my ears. To me, the most important thing is what's coming out of those monitors. That should also be the most important thing to the mixers—what they're listening to. Some people get caught up in the technical aspects of a mix. They may have a great sounding mix in their studio, but their monitors are screwed. And that's where we have to come in to fix it. To them, it was probably great. But sometimes, it's hard to explain that to people.

Do artists and producers generally come to your sessions?

It's a mixture. Once they've done a project with me, they will often just send the masters in. But usually, the bigger groups will come. They care. And I like it when they care. No Doubt was just in here—the whole group. That's kind of neat, when they're interested in having a part in even the segues and spaces between songs.

It's the last chance.

It is, and I've had to do percussion, and keyboards, bass ... all sorts of things in the mastering room. It's fun, actually. Sometimes, creative people have an idea at the last minute, and we'll do it. What the heck.

Sometimes, there are songs or mixes that just have this magic to them, and that's what I love, that's what I reach for. And I'm probably more of an experimenter. I've never been afraid to break the rules—in fact, I enjoy breaking the rules.

What kind of rules?

[Laughs] Well, level, for instance. I guess I have to admit that I've been responsible for a lot of what I complain about. Because I always went for loud. Not meaning to destroy anything, but.... And a lot of the stuff I may have been judged for sounding too crunched is not necessarily my fault; it may have been the mix that I was working with. Because, as I've said, we are at the mercy of what the engineer has done. It's just our job to make it better.

Sometimes, you go too far and you have to back off. I don't mind going too far—try it! If somebody has an idea, I'll go for it. I remember cutting a Donna Summer song with Bruce Swedien, and we kept blowing circuit breakers. "Well, that's too much—we'd better back it of a half dB." That's when we were doing the club records. We had a lot of fun doing that stuff.

So, why do people come to you to master their records?

I hope those who chose me like me! And I guess they like the end result. Maybe, they also enjoy working here—which they should; it's fun working here. And those who haven't been here owe it to themselves to come here. There's a plug! [Laughs] There are a lot of people I haven't worked with yet that I'd like to.

For the last few years, r&b and hip-hop have been predominant for me, but, liking all forms of music, I want to do it all. [Laughs] I'm looking forward to compressing the heck out of a classical piece one of these days. Just kidding! But I do like my work. It's always fun to make things better.

Neil Dorfsman

APRIL, 2002 ## Award-Winning Engineering and Production

Just a few minutes into a conversation with Neil Dorfsman, you get the feeling that he'd be a great guy to hang with. A lot of fine musicians have felt the same way. Dorfsman's unique array of engineering, production, and people skills has put him with such artists as Sting, Mark Knopfler, Dire Straits, Paul McCartney, Tina Turner, Bruce Hornsby, and Bob Dylan, to name a few. Unlike most in the business, he's equally adept at production and engineering, and has taken home Grammy and TEC awards in both categories. Among them: a Best Engineered Album Grammy for Dire Straits' *Brothers In Arms* with its ultracool single "Money for Nothin,'" two Grammys for Producer of the Year (Sting's *Nothing Like the Sun* and Bruce Hornsby's *Scenes from the South Side*), two additional Best Engineered Album Grammy nominations (Dire Straits' *Love Over Gold* and Paul McCartney's *Flowers in the Dirt*), and an Engineer of the Year TEC award—interestingly, in the same year, he was also nominated for the Producer of the Year TEC. Most recently, in 1999, he was one of the engineers on the Grammy's Best Pop Album, Sting's *Brand New Day.*

I spoke with the amiable Dorfsman by phone as he was holed up in his Westchester County home one bitter cold winter day. He was spending time with his family after wrapping up a project that he'd produced, recorded, and mixed: *The Edge of Silence*, by the critically acclaimed Solas, an Irish-American band with deep Celtic music roots.

Um Neil, I'm kind of thrown off by your accent. I'd always assumed you were English.

[Laughs] Most people do. They're always shocked when they meet me. It's probably the name. Everybody thinks I'm some furry little British guy, as opposed to a tall, balding New Yorker, but I was born in Manhattan and grew up on Long Island.

Selected Credits

Laurie Anderson
Strange Angels (three tracks)

Crowded House
"World Where You Live"

Dire Straits
Brothers in Arms

Bob Dylan
Infidels

Bryan Ferry
Boys and Girls

Bruce Hornsby
Scenes From the Southside

Billy Idol
Whiplash Smile

Kiss
Kiss Alive II,
Love Gun

Paul McCartney
Flowers in the Dirt

Bobby McFerrin
Beyond Words

Solas
The Edge of Silence

Bruce Springsteen
Tracks,
The River

Sting
Nothing Like the Sun,
Brand New Day

And you started your engineering career in New York.

Actually, I first went out to California to try to be an engineer. I was one of those guys with a massive record collection, and I always listened from a producer's point of view. So I went out to L.A. in the mid '70s trying to get a job at a studio. I didn't know anything or anybody; I just figured that was the place. And I had absolutely no luck. An example: There was an ad in the newspaper to interview for a job with the Beach Boys. And there I was in L.A., dead broke, with no car! I took a bus all the way to Santa Monica from Hollywood, which took about two hours, and the first question of the interview was "What's your sign?" I didn't have a clue and I didn't get the job. I also realized at that point that maybe heading west was the wrong direction for me.

Eventually, I went back to New York and got a job at a voiceover studio, recording radio commercials. We had no multitracks. We'd use two 2-track machines—one for stock music, one for the voiceover—and we'd mix and bounce down to a third machine. I was learning, but I was still frustrated. But I kept at it. I sent out about a hundred résumés and finally got a job as an assistant at Electric Lady.

I was there about a year when I did a project with Eddie Kramer that ended up getting mixed at what was then the Power Station. I went to help on the mixing and Bob Walters, the owner, asked me if I would stay on.

A lucky break; Power Station was legendary then.

It was great. Everyone had heard about the place but few people had really seen it—it was like "They've got a Pultec on every channel! They've got this giant room, and they've got a parking lot inside the building!" All of which was true. I was completely over the moon just to visit there, never thinking they'd actually ask me to stay. I guess Bob must have liked my completely subservient attitude! I was there for several years, then went freelance and have done that ever since.

Let's talk about the Solas CD, that you've just finished up for Shanachie Records. It has a very warm, un-Pro Tools kind of sound.

Funny you should say that; actually it's a total Pro Tools record.

Oops. There goes my "golden ears" rep.

It's my first project recorded start-to-finish into Pro Tools. Which was pretty daunting because I had my doubts about both sonics and operation.

I'm a huge fan of digital; I have been from day one. I loved the fact that what you heard was what you got, in the sense that every day

Photo: Petra Dorfsman

your tape would sound the same. One of my big frustrations recording with analog is that every day, while you're overdubbing, your mix sounds different. I don't know if it's humidity or temperature or particles on the tape—whatever—it drives me crazy. I don't get the whole reverence of analog tape at all. Once I used a Sony 3348, that was it for me. And there are even better quality machines out today, like the Euphonix R1, which I think sounds incredible.

Having said that, I was still very worried about the sonics of Pro Tools. Of course, I'll never know what it would have sounded like in another format, because my motto has now become "Don't A/B." Because there's always going to be something out there that you think might sound better technically than what you're currently using. But, considering the small budgets of most projects these days, you have to make the best of what you've got. I'm very curious about gear, and I always like to try new stuff, but for my own sanity, I just put blinders on and go.

Take what you've got to work with and make that great. Isn't that kind of the engineer/producer job description?

What you're working on at the moment has to become your world. You're given a certain set of tools, and that's the way it is. Hence my motto, "Never A/B."

How was it working at Bearsville, up in Woodstock, New York?

It was great. It's a really nice place, and you can completely focus on the work because there's not much else going on. We had two weeks in the barn for rehearsal, which was great. It's all acoustic music and the sound of the instruments in this big wooden barn was lovely. It allowed us to hear everything very clearly. Also, the console in Studio A, where we recorded, is an old Neve, which I would rather work on than anything. It's an early 80-Series that used to be at the Who's old Ramport Studio, a beautiful sounding console. We also mixed there, in Studio B, the SSL room.

You definitely achieved that sought after, "larger than the speakers" sound.

That's great to hear, because I'm still not sure. We had a heck of a time mixing because we had syncing problems between Pro Tools and the SSL. I found that when I changed whatever clock I was using, the sound of the record suffered drastically. Which was disconcerting because I was running on Apogee clocks for the whole of recording, and I thought it was one of the better recordings I'd done. Then when it came to mixing, the clocking was set up a little differently and the sonics really suffered.

What went wrong?

At first, I didn't have a video card for my Apogee converters. We had to use an analog multitrack tape machine as the interface between Pro Tools and the SSL 4000 computer, and Apogees are not happy when the word-clock and the positional reference are even the slightest bit off, which invariably, they are with analog tape machines. The video card allowed both the Apogee and the Studer to clock to house-sync via a Lynx, so my positional reference from the tape machine was identical to my word-clock reference.

What was your approach to recording this very acoustic band to a computer?

I took what is, for me, a completely different approach in recording this album; that is, I hardly EQ'd anything during the entire record. Usually when I'm tracking, I pretty much go for it. I try to make things as punchy as I can so that I start building the structure of the thing sonically. I use that as a production tool because, if you get the mix sounding strong, you can tell right away whether an overdub is competing sonically and musically, or whether you have enough performance energy. It's funny, I think I have this reputation as being this audio purist, and I'm not at all. I've never been hesitant to heavily process stuff while I'm recording. But on this record, I took a pretty pure approach.

You made nice use of ambience.

A lot of that was thanks to Seamus Egan, the bandleader. We worked really hard on arranging the songs, which left space for ambience, much of which came from the room at Bearsville. It's a beautiful room, really large. I generally recorded with some room ambience, although we cut it down in size quite a bit. They also have EMT plates up there, which sound really good. And I used TC stuff, which I'm a big fan of: the 3000 and M5000. I like very clear reverb, something you can make really long without it starting to sound grainy. I tend to set up a lot of different reverbs at the start of my mix—maybe eight or nine, then I play with things as I go.

Do you set them up any special way?

I'll use a tone burst or a click to get them nice and balanced, then listen to a voice—something natural and acoustic—to see if they sound too dark. I like to have it all set before I start putting up faders, so I don't have to spend any time between thinking of something and trying it. I used to work at one studio and had the luxury of assistants who knew what I liked and had it ready when I came in. Now, I'm working everywhere, so I usually spend a half-day before we start getting all that set.

Speaking of working everywhere, what's in the rack you bring with you?

Actually, I'm "Mr. Rackless." I own an Aguilar bass preamp, an Eventide H3000, and an SSL stereo compressor, which I use on drums. I have a LittleLabs guitar splitter box, which I love because it makes re-amping stuff so easy—and I have a SansAmp . . . [Laughs] Really, I've got nothing. I used to be so into gear. Now, I just try to make do with what I've got.

What was the instrumentation on the basic tracks, and what was your setup like?

It was one of the more live records I've done. They band is incredible on stage, and I thought if I could capture 60 percent of that, we would be in great shape. I still don't know if we got it as great as they are live.

For most tracks, the instruments were an accordion or concertina—some sort of squeezebox—a fiddle, an acoustic rhythm guitar, an acoustic or electric melody guitar, electric bass, and some sort of drums.

We had homemade booths in the room in kind of a circle, and we built a baffled house for Mick McAuley's accordions. I was more worried about him leaking onto other things than stuff leaking onto him because he was close miked with two TLM 170s.

For drums, I used the normal assortment of stuff: [Sennheiser] 421s, AKG 451s, [Shure SM]56s and 57s—each song was different. We had an amazing drummer, Ben Wittman, for the record. He brought forty or fifty percussion devices and built all these hybrid drum kits.

I relied a lot on the overheads, which were two, sometimes three, 451s (with –20 pads), which were about five feet above him. I miked everything very closely, as well, to get some impact. During overdubs, I often miked him with Neumann 254s —about eight feet back and pretty widespread— along with a close mic, generally a Neumann 149.

We had seventeen or eighteen mics on the drums, which is not unusual for me because I tend to top and bottom mic drums.

Phase reversed?

I always reverse the phase on the bottom mic and often find that the kick drum also needs to be reversed relative to the overheads. That's something you've got to play with that can totally change the sound of the kit.

What about those really low frequency drums? There were some tones that sounded like they'd be pinning meters.

Those are Irish Bodhrans and Brazilian hand drums. They were squashed pretty hard while I tracked them and again a little in the mix with the channel compressors on the SSL.

Were you compressing the overall drums and percussion?

Only in the mix. I generally create a "sub-squeeze" where the natural sounding drums are also split out to a pretty radical squasher—usually an SSL stereo compressor. The percussion I usually leave untouched, unless I compress it for an effect, like a "sloshy" tambourine.

How did you treat guitars?

I compressed the acoustics a bit, usually with an LA2A or 3A. The same with clean electrics. On heavier stuff, I'll often use an 1176. Again, I mult signals a lot so as to get a natural sound mixed in with a "smashed" one. With all the tracks available in Pro Tools, I'll usually record a DI as well as the amped tracks, keeping them separate so I can re-amp the DI in the mix if something's not fitting in. No Amp Farm!!!

Between all the polyrhythms and all the instruments, there's a lot going on. How did you keep the bass present?

I took it through two different DIs: my Aguilar and the Avalon 737. The Avalon, which has a preamp, compressor, and EQ, sounds really good flat. And I really like the tone controls on the Aguilar. I use it when necessary to make the bass more "poky," or more nasal, or more "bassy." I also used my modified LA3A.

The famous "Clearmountain" mod! What is that, anyway?

[Laughs] It's supposedly just a 75-cent modification—a different capacitor, I think, that somehow makes it sound much better. Ed Evans, back at Power Station, came up with it.

Winifred Horan's fiddle never sounded harsh, as that instrument sometimes can.

More than with a lot of things, that seems to almost completely depend upon the instrument and the player. I have found that a Telefunken or Soundelux 251 can sound really great on solo violin, but this time, we used an M149 as a center mic and two Neumann 254s as a stereo pair. The 254s are vintage, cigar-shaped tube mics, which are incredible. You can have them six feet away from the sound source, and it will sound close miked.

Did you use any outboard preamps?

My secret weapons were a Trowbridge, all tube preamp and compressor. They're hand made in Ohio by Jack Trowbridge, and they're incredible—super transparent, with tons of headroom. We used them on most of the overdubs—vocals, percussion, woodwinds.... The Neumann 149 was a particularly great combination with the compressor.

The attack and release on the Trowbridge compressor are really independent, which is unusual. Usually, you change one, and the other changes. It also has an amazing range of attack and release times. You can squash the heck out of something and not really hear it as compression—

just more impact. The mic pre has three amplification stages; if you need more gain you change stages. It's got amazing amounts of headroom and it's very clear sounding.

Did you stereo compress the mix?

I almost always use the bus compressor on the SSL, usually at 4:1. I'll change the attack and release to suit the material. To me, that thing is the sound of SSL.

Is your Pro Tools system pretty stock?

Yes, except I have my Apogee SE converters, which I think are noticeably better sounding than most of the ones out there.

Did you mix in Pro Tools as well?

I hopefully will never have to mix in Pro Tools. We mixed to DAT with an Apogee PSX100 converter. But I mixed through a half-inch analog machine in record and repro, because I wanted to make sure it didn't sound too "Pro Toolian." The stereo bus fed the half-inch, and while it was recording, it was playing back into the DAT. I'm not really a fan of how tape changes the sound of your mix, like a lot of guys are, but I wanted to hedge my bet and smooth some of the edges and give it some fatness.

Clarity must have been especially challenging on this project with so many midrange instruments: tons of percussion, rhythm squeezeboxes....

You've got to choose carefully while you're recording, because you get used to parts, and you build your arrangement around what's already on tape. The track can fall apart musically if you start to take that stuff out just because it seems busy.

We made sure things worked acoustically before we started to record, which made my job a whole lot easier. It was totally great that we got to rehearse in the barn where we were playing unamplified. You could really tell if something was going to speak in a song, or carry enough weight. I recorded the rehearsals with one mic direct to DAT, which was really telling.

I generally try to get by with as few parts as are necessary to get the job done. Even if I hear another part, I'd almost rather you hear it in your head when you listen, rather than recording it. That's a hard trick to pull off; only the really masterful records achieve that sense of being a little understated.

What monitors did you use?

I've been through every speaker out there, buying stuff and hating it two months later! The ones I've stuck with are ProAc Studio 100s; I switch between them and Auratones. I know that they're a little bit flattering, so I work around that. The philosophy I learned at Power Station was, "Use the least flattering speaker you can, and it will make you work harder." I appreciate that, but at a certain point when you're mixing, you really need to get some pleasure from the speakers and also to be able to listen for a long time without fatigue. The ProAcs do that for me. They do need a lot of power. For this project, Richard Rose from Hothouse Amplifiers was kind enough to loan me a really great Hothouse amp: a Model 500 Mosfet.

You've gotten awards for both engineering and production, and you seem to move easily between those roles.

Actually, it's more like I crawl between the two! [Laughs] It's very difficult to do both. If in doubt, I'll always sacrifice the engineering for the producing, making sure the performance is right rather than that the sound is "perfect."

I was trained to work very fast. When I first started at Power Station, I used to do a lot of jingles, and that's served me well. Sounds shouldn't take a lot of time. But it's still demanding. And these days, of course, you're expected to be an engineer, a producer, *and* a Pro Tools guy!

But when it's all happening, there really isn't a better job. I've been very lucky to work with some amazing guys who have very strong points of view, and who are really looking for a sounding board— a partner to help push things along. Sometimes, I'm a little embarrassed for getting accolades for producing and engineering things that probably would have sounded just as good if I weren't there! Of course, there are also those projects where you really get in there and get a workout!

Not everyone has the personality to be able to do both kinds of projects.

I try to be what you might call "proactive" and to give an honest appraisal of what's going on. I've also tried to develop a better bedside manner over the years! I'm still very excited about the opportunity to be doing this for a living, and hopefully, when I'm doing a record, I bring good energy to it. I've also learned not to get too picky, and to stay positive.

Jeff Balding

JULY, 2002

Mixing It Up in Nashville: Renting Talent to Music's Best

Selected Credits

Faith Hill
Breathe

Jewel
This Way

Lonestar
I'm Already There,
Lonely Grill

Reba McEntire
So Good Together

Megadeth
Cryptic Writings,
Risk

Owsley
Owsley

SHeDAISY
Brand New Year,
Whole Shebang

Chely Wright
Never Love You Enough

Lee Ann Womack
I Hope You Dance

Trisha Yearwood
Real Live Woman,
Where Your Road Leads

Nashville can be deceiving. With all that low key style and relaxed attitude, people from the rest of the country can sometimes get fooled into thinking there's not much going on. But in reality, Music City's people know how to get a lot of quality music on tape without wasting a moment. Take the session players: those guys have three tunes learned, played, and recorded in the time it takes the L.A. cats to finish their first lattes! (Okay, maybe I'm exaggerating just a little....) Same thing with engineers. Jeff Balding, for example. After a bunch of cell phone tag, I hooked up with Balding one Saturday morning and found he'd spent the previous week working—with producer Dann Huff—on projects for Keith Urban, Faith Hill, Deana Carter, and Wynonna Judd. Yeah, that's right, all in one week. See what I mean?

Balding, who has received several Grammy nominations—including one for Best Engineered Album on *Owsley*, 1999's eponymous release by Alabama-born instrumentalist Will Owsley—plies his trade in studios all around the country on all kinds of music. These days, however, he makes his home in Nashville. Recently, you've heard his work on recordings for Jewel, Trisha Yearwood, Lonestar, Shania Twain, and SHeDAISY, among others, as well as on Megadeth's latest onslaughts. Talk about versatile. Did I mention he's also president and co-founder of Underground Sound, one of Nashville's top audio rental, sales, and cartage companies?

Obviously this is a guy at home with the concept of multitasking. Here, he shares some tips on how he gets so much accomplished.

Four projects in one week; that's a lot of bytes.

Well, I have a fiber channel drive setup on my Pro Tools HD system, so there's plenty of reliable storage. It gives me lots of room and flexibility.

Photo: Nicole Cochran

Are you doing more tracking or mixing?

Mainly mixing, but I do enjoy tracking. I also enjoy doing an entire record, which is how I work with Dann Huff. He likes to split things up and get two or three rooms going.

So, you'll cover whatever is necessary.

Yeah, it just depends. You want to spend a lot of time on the project to get the best product you can, within the budget. But in country music, that budget is often slimmer than in pop. So sometimes, that means running one hard-drive system in the control room, another one out in the lounge for comping and editing, and yet another one in a second studio where we can get another set of overdubs going.

It's not just country. Most budgets are slimmer these days.

There's a lot going on in the industry right now that's causing things to be tight—for example, all the pirating of music through downloads from the Internet. But I also think the introduction of computer-based recording and editing systems has made the thought process change within the industry as well. With one of these systems, you can basically make a record anywhere, even in your bedroom—which we actually did on the sides I co-produced and engineered on the Owsley record. And this kind of technology has, in some cases, encouraged the belief that a lower budget can be justified. Personally, I think the savings the technology creates should be reinvested to develop a better product. In other words, that translates into spending more time creating the product.

Tell us about your optical-fiber drive system.

It's a fiber-channel hard-drive setup from Studio Network Solutions. The system allows two or more computers to work on the same song at the same time, on the same drive. I got it mainly because I was tired of having FireWire and SCSI problems, and DAE errors when my sessions were packed with a lot of tracks. With the old setup, I also had to do a lot of file management. Now, it's much easier to put it on one drive, and rock! And it's fast—something like ten times faster than my other drives. You can easily do 128 tracks on one drive without having the system freak. I don't see DAE errors any more, and I can run a backup at the same time, on the same computer. I keep the backup running all day at the same time as I'm doing quick, intensive editing, and the system never hangs me up.

SNS put the package together. In appearance, it probably doesn't look much different than a SCSI setup. It consists of a PCI card and a cable into the drive chassis, which holds four drives—either 36 or 72 Gig, so you can get a lot of desktop space to work on. The big difference is in performance and in the multi-user aspect.

You don't mix inside of Pro Tools though, do you?

No, I use individual outs, usually 48 into the console, and I feel like I get the best of both worlds. With some of the pop stuff, I may have eighty or ninety tracks to mix. The old Pro Tool systems were 64 voice, and sometimes you had to get real creative with drive management and sharing voices.

But you still have to combine tracks to end up with only 48 out.

Yeah, and I actually prefer having some things combined down. In general, I would rather have 2 to 6 tracks of backgrounds than 18 to 25 coming up on the console. Actually, I think if I could get away with a stereo track of drums, I would do that! The less I have to worry about eight hi-hats and four snares, the more I can focus on mixing.

What consoles do you like?

It depends on what I'm mixing. I remixed "Break Me," the new Jewel single, on the API console at Sound Kitchen, which sounds really good; I like it for tracking as well. I also mixed SHeDAISY there. I thought it would be a good match for them, and it really turned out great. They have a lot of vocal work on the record and to have a little more openness in the overall console sound really made a big difference. I also like the SSL 9Ks and 4Ks. There are a couple of 4Ks in town that I've mixed a lot of records on. In fact, the album mixes on Jewel's record were done at Emerald's Studio A on a 4K with a G-series computer.

So, you consider the overall sound of the project and try to choose a console that's complimentary.

Definitely! The right tool for the right job. To me,

that's part of being versatile and adapting to a record's style. The same with recording: a lot of times, I'll use a totally different chain to record digitally than I would with analog. I know I need to adapt to the sound of the converters, and also to take into account that the sound won't change after I put it to a digital medium—unlike recording to analog, where it sounds different a week later.

What's an example of what you do differently?

For instance, I'm a fan of vintage gear and tube gear. So if I'm recording to digital and I use a Pultec EQ to put an edge on a vocal, I'll use the Pultec before the converter to avoid also bringing out the top edge of the converter. Generally, when you add 10 or 12K on a vocal, you'll get extra out of it before it gets converted to digital. Whereas with analog, it might be better to use the EQ coming back, after you've got that analog tape compression.

What processing do you prefer to use after your digital conversion?

If I'm recording vocals to digital, I'll usually compress them after they're recorded. If I was recording a real rangy vocal to analog, I always felt like I had to compress on the way in, because with all the hiss, etc., there's no way to put that wide of a dynamic on analog tape. But then . . . that one, over-the-top vocal blast might get swallowed or distorted from the compression. And if that's the magic take the producer wants, I'm up the creek. I'd rather have the note clear and deal with it later in the mix.

Doesn't that mean you have to record at very conservative levels to avoid any digital distortion?

Not really. I cut a lot of my vocals at –12 or –14dB, as far as the input level going to the converters. That way I can pack it on as hard as I want, but when it gets low, it's not a big deal. The thing that you really have to watch, regarding input level and older gear that may not have much headroom, is overdriving the preamps and compressors, etc., trying to put a hot level to digital.

Say you're doing drums through a Neve. If you don't pay attention to whether you're cutting at –20 or –12, you may overdrive the preamp so hard that you get compression or distortion out of it (unless you want that sort of effect!), while on your digital meter, it still looks like your levels are low. I usually cut at –14 or –16. You don't see a lot of VU meters anymore, and that way, I'm sure I'm within the headroom of my gear—especially the older gear.

What preamps do you like for vocals?

[Laughs] Actually, I sometimes feel like I'm in the preamp of the month club.

Yes, I've heard that you like to change things up a lot on your sessions. What's this month's favorite?

For vocals, right now I'm a tube preamp fan, and there are a couple that are sounding good to me. The Telefunken V76m—the one without the roll off—and the Martec, which I'm using on Faith right now. It has a nice open top.

How about microphones?

Lately, I'm a Neumann fan; the old ones just have a certain air and "core" to their vocal sound.

There's a vintage Neumann U269 that I like a lot. It looks exactly like a U67, but it has a little bit more air on the top.

What's this month's drum mic setup?

[Laughs] I use what everybody else does! Right now, I like an Audio-Technica AT25 on the kick, a Shure SM 57 on the snare, with an AKG 451 on the bottom. For toms, it varies depending on the room, the drummer, and of course the drums, but it can be anything from AKG 414s to TLM 170s, if you want a nice warm fat sound.

For overheads, it varies. I use Audio-Technica 4051s sometimes, or C12s. There's also an old Neumann tube mic I like—a 582. It's a small-diaphragm mic. You can't get them too close or they will snap from the sound pressure, but they sound great. They're also great on acoustic instruments. It's definitely one of the best sounding mics nobody's ever heard of.

Wait a minute. I just remembered you're an owner of a rental company! That's why you get to try so many different things all the time! You do R&D for your customers.

[Laughs] Yeah, I'm one of the owners of Underground Sound, Inc. In fact, the Neumann 582 was one of the pieces [co-owners] Bill Whittington, Brown Bannister, and I found a few years back. They've been a big hit in Nashville.

What preamps do you like on drums?

Neve1081s and 1073s. Although when I cut at Sound Kitchen's Big Boy room, I use the API preamps in the console. They sound great too.

Are you also likely to use your compression after recording the drums?

It depends on the style of record I'm doing—the room, the drum setup—but I usually don't put the kick and snare down compressed. I like having whatever options I might need open later. From the tracking standpoint, I'm probably a little more old school. I like to get a good fat sound down. But I don't shy away from compression, if it's what the project needs, and the rooms usually get a little compression.

What's your favorite room mic compressor?

A few that sound great are the Urei 1178 and the Neve 33609s or 33264s. Another compressor that has a cool character for a lot of things is the Empirical Labs Fatso Jr.

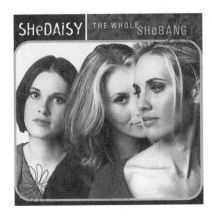

You like character in a compressor.

Yeah, a lot of times, I look to the compressor to add color. I can really vary in the sound of what I'm looking for, from hi-fi to totally quirky, but I can't say there are a lot of times I grab for that compressor you can't hear.

Well, with Pro Tools, you've either got to add color on the way in, or the way out.

If you're talking tonal coloration, I like adding as much as possible on the way in, because when you're recording, you're compensating for the sound of whatever you're recording to *and* whatever you're recording through. If those devices have a sound to them, which everything does, you're trying to find what works in that setup that gets you what you want to hear in the monitors.

And the monitors you'd most likely be using are?

There are a few I'll use. Mainly Tannoy SRM10s with Mastering Lab crossovers. They're a workhorse that I've had for years and a lot of producers like to listen on them. I've got an amp that matches them real well: a Yamaha 2200 that's been modified by Mastering Lab as well.

Also, Mackie 824s can be a great reference. You're not going to get anything muddy by mixing on them. I still listen to NS10s; there's stuff that you hear on them that you don't catch on the others. And I mix a lot at Emerald, where I like the Hidley rooms and use the big monitors.

Are you originally from the South?

[Laughs] No. I'm from a small town in Illinois; I came to Nashville to go to Belmont University. I'd been heading into electrical engineering and started thinking "I don't want to do this." So, what *did* I want to do? Like everybody else I'd played guitar in rock bands through high school, so the music business sounded like the obvious choice. I wanted to make records. I really didn't think about the possible downfalls on the income side; I just wanted to do it. I think a lot of people head into engineering thinking they're the next hot thing. But when they get into the studio and see what's actually involved—the hard work, the long hours, and the "no problem" attitude required—they go, "On second thought, this really isn't what I want!" But I loved it. I just lived and breathed it.

I was fortunate enough to have a roommate at Belmont who was a senior, Steve Fralick. He was studying recording engineering as well, and he took me under his wing. My last year in college I took a job as chief engineer at a small Christian studio in Brentwood, TN. I met Keith Thomas there and started working with him, and while I worked there I also recorded a band named Whiteheart—the band that Dann and David Huff were in back then.

I guess my last question for the day is what do you do in your spare time?

What spare time? [Laughs] Well, I'm married, and I've got two kids, and what little spare time there is, I try to spend with the family—watching the kids' sports and doing outdoor stuff. And something else, for a few years now, I always put aside the first couple hours of the day for me. That usually involves going to work out. I owe my good friend Dave Mustaine for getting me into working out. I try to keep that part of my life together, because sitting in a studio all day... you can get pretty out of shape. I go to the gym, do the routine, and have a healthy breakfast. It's made a real difference, in how I feel in general and also in how I feel at the studio.

DENNIS SANDS

SEPTEMBER, 2002

Capturing the Orchestra, Harnessing the Synths

Selected Credits

American Beauty

Back to the Future

Erin Brockovich

Forrest Gump

Independence Day

The Last of the Mohicans

Men in Black II

Planet of the Apes

Pleasantville

Romancing the Stone

Spider-Man

Who Framed Roger Rabbit?

Dennis Sands loves his work, and it shows. A three-time Oscar nominee for Best Sound (*Cast Away, Contact,* and *Forrest Gump*), a TEC award nominee, and a winner of two Golden Reel Awards for Best Sound Editing: Music, he's achieved a career momentum that puts him in an enviable place—working daily with the best composers and the best musicians on the best stages. Sands has over a hundred feature film scores to his credit, and he's adding more all the time. As either music, scoring, and/or re-recording mixer, he's worked on such high profile films as *Erin Brockovitch, American Beauty, Pleasantville,* and *Good Will Hunting.* He's also accumulated an impressive album discography with projects for such luminaries as Joe Pass, Sarah Vaughan, Ella Fitzgerald, and the Count Basie Orchestra, along with numerous soundtrack albums.

Yes, life is good for Mr. Sands. It's also good for the people who get to work with him. His years of experience and relaxed style make for smooth, and even—dare we say—fun sessions, a talent that's prized in the high-pressure world of feature films.

I first sat down with Sands on the Warner Bros. scoring stage after he'd spent a day mixing music with composer Alan Silvestri for *Showtime,* the Tom Dey-directed buddy cop spoof starring Robert DeNiro and Eddie Murphy. The huge control room was filled: a big synth setup in one corner, a wall of converters, signal processing, and computers in another, and behind that, a jam-packed machine room. Every fader of the 96-input SSL 9000J was in use. Outside the control room, the stage was set for the next day's session, a 98-piece orchestra. As we wandered among the maze of microphone booms, baffles, music stands, and chairs, I got clued in on some Sands-style philosophy and techniques.

It looks like you're doing pretty much back-to-back sessions.

We finish here Saturday night, then I start *Spider-Man* with Danny Elfman on Sunday at Sony. Two quite massive projects. But it seems

Photo: Maureen Droney

like most projects are massive now. Even this [100-input] board is sometimes too small.

There do seem to be a lot of machines in here.

We're recording to a 48-track digital—a Sony HR machine. There's usually an additional analog machine for synthesizers, and I also record orchestra to analog. Then we'll probably have another machine for choir. So, we're using at least three analog 24s and a digital 48...and even that....

Isn't enough?

There's a lot going on: a hundred and some odd tracks. And it can be more. When we did *Planet of the Apes*, I had to have three additional DA88s running. We did that at Fox, which has the same board as here, and they had every single fader filled, plus I had to bring in sidecars. Projects are just expanding

Why is that?

Some of it's my choice, because I like to have flexibility and control—not so much with the orchestra but certainly with synths. And if I'm working with Danny, he uses a lot of stereo samples, so every sound requires two channels.

Also, mixes are expanding, and I like to have the ability to create surrounds. Then, of course, they'll want elements separate for the dub: percussive elements separate from pads, which are separate from orchestra. And if you have choir, that's separate. It's more and more complex. Here's a board that's relatively new in design, and it's right on the edge of being obsolete. It's not the manufacturer's fault. It's just so hard to keep up with the demands. Then you add in the fact that the typical post-production schedule has shrunk down a lot. Directors are continually editing and changing. That affects us, and we have to allow for it.

It's just part of the job these days.

It's the way the business is now. There's so much money involved, and there can be so much tension.... But when you understand everybody's issues and problems, you can't really get angry with anyone. Everybody's under the same time pressure, and everybody's trying to do the right thing. You have creative people who want to maximize what they do, and there are time constraints. It's a frustration that everybody has to deal with.

I've heard it suggested that things will improve when everybody is on the same computer system, getting the changes at the same time.

[Laughs] Actually, I have this great fear. I was thinking about digital distribution of movies, whether over the Internet or whatever, when it dawned on me what could happen: A movie would not necessarily have to be completed by the release date! The director will be able to say, "Okay, the movie's done but there's a cue in reel two that really bothers me, and I want to replace it...." The release print was always the cutoff, but that doesn't mean anything, if you're downloading digitally. You can have endless new versions.

You could spend your whole life on just one movie.

[Laughs] Actually, sometimes it seems like I've done that already.

You're all set up for tomorrow, except for the mics. I guess you take them down every night.

If mics are left up, there literally has to be a guard in the room with them all night. A lot of the mics are irreplacable; you can't even put a dollar amount on them. Like my four M50s. I use them on every orchestral project. If anything happened to them, I would be heartbroken.

The M50s are your main overhead mics?

Yes, for the orchestra. They're wonderful microphones, and they only made 600, of which there are probably 400 left in the world. They were the first purchase I made as a mixer, and I treat them better than I do my children.

Can you describe your setup of the musicians?

There are two basic setups I use. This is a traditional one: [audience left to right] first violins, second violins, violas towards the center, cellos with bass behind them, piano to the right. Or sometimes, I'll pull a piano out of the orchestra so it's right in front. Harp is in front also. French horns in back, woodwinds in the middle, brass and trombones over to the right, percussion in the back.

You have the percussion more baffled.

There are two Latin percussionists, and I kind of isolated them. If percussion is too much out in the room, it gets washed out, and also, you hear a bit of delay. It just doesn't sound good, so I try to contain it as much as possible.

The rest of the setup is very open.

I don't use many baffles for orchestra. I prefer to control the dynamics out in the room. And I don't use a lot of microphones. I have a fair amount set up, but most of them, I use just for spot, if I want to reach for something here or there. Mostly, for orchestra, I use about a dozen. Usually five room mics: the three M50s and two Klaus Heyne-modified Brauner VM1s. Dirk Brauner, who's German, makes a contemporary tube mic that Klaus modifies fairly extensively. I've had them less than a year, and I think it's the best sounding contemporary tube microphone. It's also very expensive.

You can buy it stock, but modified is much richer sounding. Klaus handpicks them. Dirk sends him twenty or thirty mics, and, for example, if he has a client who wants a great vocal mic, he'll go through them and find the one that's best for that. In my case, he found two mics that matched as closely as possible, and in his opinion, were best suited for scoring, left and right wide.

Where else do you put overheads?

I like percussion overheads. I'm not big on percussion in your face, and if it was a classical recording, I probably wouldn't use the overheads. But for film, where you're dealing with sound effects and dialog, you want a little more presence to help it cut through. You still want to keep it in the room, in the same perspective with some nice depth to it, but a little more presence and texture helps. It's subtle, but it makes a difference. So I'll use B&K 4006s on left and right; in the center, I have a U47 over the timpani.

I like to put the timpani in the middle, particularly with Alan Silvestri. He often writes a lot of it, like in last year's *The Mummy Returns*. It was in everything, very rhythmic, almost like a drum kit, and I love the sound of it in the middle. Some classical composers have it set off to the side; it's personal taste. To me, in the center, it gives a nice power, both in the room and coming off the screen.

So your setups change depending on the style of the composer.

To a degree. The other setup, which Danny Elfman likes, is we'll split the violins: firsts on the left, seconds on the right. Violas go mid-left, cellos mid-right, and basses in the middle. Danny's orchestrator Steve Bartek orchestrates for this setup, giving it a beautiful quality where the violins answer one another. Sometimes, it's harder on the musicians, because typically, violin players want to sit next to one another. It helps their intonation. But they've been great, and it's really worked on the last few movies. Also, having the basses in the middle, there's something nice about having that low stuff right in the center.

What are your other mic preferences?

I love the Schoeps CMC54, and use it on harp and woodwinds. I'll use the Sennheiser MKH40s, Neumann KM84s, or B&K 4011s for the violas. I use two Stephen Paul-modified U87s for the celli, and on basses, I use Soundelux U96s. I am fortunate enough to own a matched pair of Neumann KM54s, and always use them for the piano. I mic the brass two ways: M-149 overall, and Coles 4038s [trombones], and Royer M-121s [trumpets] for solos.

You work regularly at several different studios.

As far as scoring, there are really five facilities in Los Angeles: Warners, Sony, Fox, Todd-AO, and Paramount. I move around. We're fortunate here to have these five really excellent facilities. And also what comes with them: excellent crews that understand film work. It's really very different from record work.

What are some of those differences?

Cue systems, for one. For example, string players typically like to hear only clicks, but percussion players want to hear the whole mix, plus click. If we have pre-records and we want to hear just the piano part, or just the percussion part, these facilities are set up for a number of different cue systems, and they have someone to operate them. If you go to a facility accustomed to doing record work, and they're running to rent the video machines, it's very hard on a mixer. I just don't have time to train people and also to do my job.

A film is a world unto itself, and a big part of my job is dealing with the politics. There are more people involved, and everybody needs to have an understanding of who's who, and when to say something and when not to. It's all part of the job. And it's a great job; there's always something to learn, something to get excited about.

Do you listen in 5.1 surround while you're recording?

Yes. My three main monitors are PMCs, tri-amped, with a built in X-curve—the film equalization curve. I always use them for mixing. There are subwoofers, and the surrounds here—a JBL system—are actually built in the side and back walls.

You don't switch between systems while you're working?

No, I use this system for mixing. When I'm scoring, I use another set that are full range, ATC Model 100s with Entec subwoofers. They have built in power amps. Although, for this project, we'll continue on with these that are specifically for film mixing [for the scoring], because it's too much to move them in and out.

How many channels are you mixing to?

This is a 16-channel mix. There are four stems: percussion, orchestra, a stereo extra, and five channels of synthesizers. We usually mix to two machines and also Tascam MX24. Essentially, we're mixing Pro Tools files; the drive goes out to the Pro Tool system. This has been a wonderful addition because you don't have to deal with Pro Tools here, which often falls offline and can slow you down. They're also a pain to set up and interface. So this works great. I use Genexes for backup. The studio takes them and has the mixes archived automatically.

What else is in the racks here?

I have Neve 1081 mic preamps for scoring. Then there are converters, sixteen channels. I like the dB Technologies 122s. And I use an outboard folddown mixer. We're always having to do two tracks for soundtrack albums, but there's rarely an opportunity to do a separate 2-track mix, so I use an outboard mixer to take the sixteen stems and create a 2-track.

Sorry, but the only word for all this routing is "awesome."

That's this man here: Greg Dennen. It does take few minutes to set up. [Laughs] Just to transition to the mix from scoring is a good eight or nine hours. It wouldn't take that long if it were just an orchestral score, but we have all the electronics, and they need a lot of reverbs to create ambience. Then to split it all out means there's more tracks, so there are more things to patch.

These guys have to check everything out and make sure everything's patched right, that it's a clean signal, on and on. There's no quick way to do it. Again, as mixes and complexity grow, the time required to get it together grows.

What else is in your rack? I see a lot of Millennia logos.

I like Millennia a lot. We have some Avalons. Manleys, some GMLs which are great. The nice thing about it is, they all have a little bit of a sound to them. The Millennia probably are the least colored. It's nice to have a selection to get the right combination of sounds.

Obviously, you're using the [SSL 9000J-series] console preamps also.

We are. The 9000 is a great-sounding board. The preamps are really good. I was never an SSL fan, but this console has completely changed my perspective on it, in terms of sonics.

Can we back up for a little history? How did you get into scoring?

My first studio job was for MGM's record company when I was twenty-two. A friend of my brother's who worked there called me because they had a huge tape library and they needed someone to administrate it.

You were looking to get into film?

I just wanted to get into music; I didn't really know that much about film or television. Working there taught me a lot. The studio had three rooms, and I got to know the mixers. It wasn't a rock 'n' roll studio; the mixers were more traditional, very experienced guys who were mixing a lot of Steve Lawrence and Eydie Gorme, Sammy Davis Jr., Frank Sinatra.... I just loved it. I loved pop and rock but the orchestra got me. When I wasn't working, I'd just hang out. I lived at the studio; I didn't want to leave. One night, we scored a film, and it was the most thrilling thing I'd ever done.

After I was there about six months, they taught me record mastering because the mixers didn't want to do it. Then at night, if there were nothing going on in the studio, I'd take a tape into a room and started learning on my own.

One Friday night, there was a session booked with Joe Pass, and the mixer showed up so wasted he couldn't even stand. Every other mixer was gone; I was the only guy there who knew how to work the equipment. It was me or the guard, and the guard didn't want do the take! I was nervous at first, and then I was fine. It was just so great.

The producer liked me, so he started asking for me, and I did more and more of his records. After a while, I'm doing Count Basie and Ella Fitzgerald ... Oscar Peterson. Amazing things. I couldn't even believe I was sitting there engineering.

Eventually, MGM sold the studio. I stayed with them and did administrative stuff, but it wasn't what I wanted to do. I'd hit it off with another mixer at MGM; we formed a partnership and started doing record dates. Our business grew, we started doing television shows, and we got the idea to build our own studio, and to focus on television work. No one else was doing it. So in 1977, we opened Group IV, in Hollywood. It was the first really modern recording facility available to the television and film world.

The great thing was, I really learned how to mix there, because at that time, TV used live musicians and it was all mixed live. Not only that, I'd be doing two different shows a day, one in the morning, one in the afternoon. Different composers, completely different styles. I worked on *Dallas*, I did the show where J.R. got shot! *Hill Street Blues, St. Elsewhere....* I met Alan Silvestri doing *Chips*. And we also started doing some film work

The studios at Group IV weren't that big; it must have been cozy doing orchestras!

For *Romancing the Stone*, which was a pivotal movie for me and a lot of other folks, we had fifty-six musicians, and they were absolutely jam-packed. I had four musicians in the control room: the electronic drum kit and three keyboard players behind me. Then the director, Bob Zemeckis, Michael Douglas, and whoever else was hanging out. It was too cozy! We had one iso booth that had two guitars and bass, then strings and brass and percussion. But it was a hit movie, and it was such an innovative score. It was Bob Zemeckis' first hit movie, the same for Danny DeVito and for Alan Silvestri. Prior to it, Michael Douglas had been doing the *Streets of San Francisco*. It was a real special project. People saw it and liked it, and I got phone calls and started to get more and more into film work.

Do you read music?

I taught myself. I do better mixes because I can follow it, understand it, see what the concept is. It helps me adjust the dynamics in a room, which I much prefer to do rather than reach for the fader. If I feel bar 23 would be great if we heard more trombones, I'd rather say, "Let's do another take and have the trombones play louder."

Do you get the score beforehand?

No. But I try to get the movie with its work track and temp music, particularly if I'm going to dub it also. I do about two movies a year where I'll also dub. Not too many people do that, but Bob Zemeckis gave me the opportunity, starting with *Back to the Future III*.

How else do you prepare for a session?

I do a fair amount of homework. I'll have a number of conversations with the composer about what approach we're looking for. And I can tell a lot of things just by looking at how many, and what types of musicians.

If it's a straight orchestral score, I don't need to ask much. But when there's a lot of electronics, there's more planning involved. Then I do the right kind of setup and the right kind of preparation in the control room, with the right machinery.

Are you a hard taskmaster on people who work for you?

They're not scared of me! I think it's important to be easygoing. We're all human beings, we all make mistakes. If people are diligent, trying hard, that's all you can ever ask of them. I think it's important not to freak out, because the mixer sets the tone. If the mixer is obviously tense and nervous and seems concerned, everyone else is going to be the same way. There will be tension, and you don't want that; there's enough tension on a film. The last thing in the world that you want is for there to be a sense that you're nervous or concerned.

Sometimes, people are scared when they walk into a control room. It's not their world, and it's got to be frightening when you know you're dependent on this, but it looks so unbelievably complex. If you sense the operator is tense and nervous, and you know there's a big meter running, you're going to be really uncomfortable. So I go out of my way to stay very calm.

Was that always your style or did that develop over time?

Certainly experience relaxes you a lot. There just aren't many things that can happen that I can't fix. But I think I've always been calm and good with people. As I say, I understand that people walk in and they're nervous. Directors have a lot of pressure on them. Studios have a lot of pressure on them. There's a lot of money on the line, and I understand that.

I have great respect for the business; I really do. I'm very appreciative to be here, and I want people to have a good time. It's all an experience. You want the technology invisible. It doesn't have to be a miserable experience, a tension filled experience. You can do good work and still have fun doing it.

I love what I do, and I think of myself as an artist. I don't think of myself as a technician at all. I don't care why something works. To me these are all tools to create the sonic experience. And I feel very fortunate to be able to work in this environment and this kind of job. I've had a real job before, and this is way better!

GEOFF EMERICK

Selected Credits

America
Nine albums, including:
Holidays, Hearts, Hideaway, Highway, 30 Years of America

Badfinger
No Dice

The Beatles
Revolver, Sgt. Pepper's Lonely Heart's Club Band, Magical Mystery Tour, Abbey Road, Anthology 1, 2, 3, "Strawberry Fields Forever," "Penny Lane"

Jeff Beck
Wired

Elvis Costello
Imperial Bedroom, All This Useless Beauty

Art Garfunkel
Lefty, The Animals' Christmas (with Amy Grant)

Paul McCartney
Tug of War, Flaming Pie, Run Devil Run

Paul McCartney (& Wings)
Band on the Run

Carl Perkins
Go Cat Go

Split Enz
Dizrhythmia, Spellbound

Supertramp
Even in the Quietest Moments

The Zombies
Odessey & Oracle

The Beatles, the '60s Sound Revolution, the Hall of Fame

OCTOBER, 2001

The most revered and respected pop music of all time is, indisputably, that made by the Beatles. Almost forty years after they were recorded, their words and melodies are still heard all over the world. Even today, producers and musicians speak of Beatles' records with awe as they strive for some modicum of the artistic and commercial success achieved by those records. And while many much more recent albums have quickly become dated, the Beatles' records still sound fresh, current, and desirable—as evidenced recently by the chart-topping success of Beatles 1, 2000's Apple/Capitol Records compilation.

Now, think of the greatest Beatles' works: "Strawberry Fields Forever," "Penny Lane," *Revolver, Sgt. Pepper, Abbey Road.* Behind the console for all these milestones was Geoff Emerick, an engineer who truly, has never been accorded his due respect. The superb songwriting of Lennon and McCartney and the brilliant polish of producer George Martin were, of course, essential elements, but without the courage, vision, and determination of Emerick, these recordings would have been lesser accomplishments. He pushed the boundaries of recording, doing things that others had either never thought of, or never dared to try. He challenged hidebound traditions and rigid administrators, and created perfect sounds, along the way developing groundbreaking techniques that today's engineers invariably take for granted.

It's almost impossible for those currently in the field, who work in a world with limitless access to specialized equipment—and limitless numbers of tracks—to imagine the skill and creativity required to make those records. Emerick was a maverick—one who saw music in colors and engineering as artistic expression. Not only was he unafraid of new ideas, he embraced them. Simply put, Geoff Emerick brought record engineering into the modern era.

Since those long ago Beatles' days, Emerick has amassed, as both a producer and an engineer, a lengthy roster of credits. He's worked with the Zombies, Badfinger, Supertramp, Tim Hardin, America, Robin Trower, Jeff Beck, and Split Enz, as well as on numerous albums for Elvis Costello, including Costello's classic *Imperial Bedroom* and 1996's *All This Useless Beauty*. He has also continued to work with Paul McCartney, and with Wings, on records including *Band on the Run, Tug of War*, and *Flaming Pie*. But in our interview the summer before Emerick's 2002 TEC Hall of Fame induction, the talk was mostly Beatles. I met with him one sunny afternoon as he was taking a break from production rehearsals with a new young band he was readying to record at Capitol Studios in Los Angeles.

I guess my first question has to be, "Why you?" How did it happen that you became the Beatles' engineer at that particular place and time?

Well, I'd started at EMI as a second engineer when I was 16, right out of school. It was, actually, the same month that the Beatles went in for their artist test. I used to get on well with George Martin, so when I was an assistant, I used to do most of his sessions. Norman Smith, who was the Beatles' original engineer, used to like working with me as well, and we had a great relationship. He taught me some priceless fundamentals that I've never forgotten.

From assisting, I was promoted to mastering—disc cutting. The reason for that was, in those days, to know mastering was to know what you could get on the tape that could actually be transferred to the master. Because, of course, if you overdid the bass end, or didn't get the phasing right when you were recording, there were problems.

Learning mastering was a part of your training.

Yes. At that time, you were never going to be a recording engineer and producer until you were forty years old. That was just the system. When the

Beatles started, of course, things began to move at a different pace. And then Norman, their engineer, wanted to become a producer. He also wanted to carry on engineering the Beatles, but EMI said, "No way." So suddenly, the situation arose where Norman had to be replaced. EMI knew that was coming, and as I'd been second engineer on some of the Beatles' sessions, and got on well with George Martin, it was decided to promote me to engineer.

I was not quite twenty, so everyone was aghast at this. Because, you see, in the studios, there were the second engineers and the tape ops who were youngsters, and there were the engineers, who were all over forty. The age bracket of twenty to forty were all in mastering, away from the recording scene. But EMI knew that Norman was going to leave, and they had to have someone, so I was made an engineer.

How did that go?

Well, I was terrified. For one thing, multitrack wasn't on every session at that time. You had to record straight to stereo—huge orchestras and a singer—the whole bit. And the mixing console had only eight ins and four outs, so you had to know what you were doing. Because no one's going to spend a fortune putting an orchestra in the studio with you, if you don't. The responsibility was absolutely enormous. I was doing Matt Munro, Cilla Black, Manfred Mann—all EMI artists. My first hit was Manfred Mann's "Pretty Flamingo." And then George Martin approached the Beatles and said, "Here's the situation: Norman's going to leave, and I'm going to suggest that Geoff take over." And I was called up to the manager's office.

You hadn't realized what was in the works.

I was shocked at being asked to do it. I was playing this little game in my head—eenie meenie, back and forth. If it stopped on this, I was going to do it; if it stopped on that, I wasn't. And it stopped on yes.

At the time you got the position with the Beatles, had you already shown signs of being a bit of a maverick?

Really, it all started when I was mastering. We used to get American records in and wonder how they got the sounds they did. We, of course, were limited to EMI equipment. There was no outside equipment allowed in, apart from a few Altec compressors. If they did bring a piece of equipment in, they took it apart and rebuilt it … just to find out how it worked, I guess.

So we were listening to these records, like the ones from Tamla, and there was all that extra bass end. And we were always talking about how did they get that sound? Now, a lot of it was the musicianship, of course. But there was no one to tell us these things; we had to find out by our own methods.

It was the amount of bass and also the level—the loudness—that fascinated us. You see, there were certain things that we weren't allowed to do. There were limitations on how much bass we were allowed to have on, because in the early days, there had been one particular Beatles single that was mastered and it jumped [skipped]. They'd pressed about a quarter million of them, and they had to redo them all. After that, for any Beatles single that was cut in England, everyone was instructed to cut all bass below 50 cycles.

You just had to roll it all off.

Yes, and it also had to be 2 to 2 ½ dBs quieter than any other records. It was ridiculous, but they were selling in those huge quantities, which, of course, had never been done before, and they were afraid the records would jump. Later on, when I was the Beatles' engineer, we had a discussion—which became quite heated—with the manager, myself, the Beatles, and George Martin, and it was decided that we would be allowed to cut them louder.

The first record you did with the Beatles was *Revolver.*

Yes, and "Tomorrow Never Knows" was the first track.

Photo: Courtesy Geoff Emerick

Of course. They would start with what was to become the most complicated track. Can you describe a bit of what the equipment was like?

The 4-track was remote, in those days; it was never in the control room. We had two 4-track rooms where the tape machines were, and there were three studios, so they had to patch them through. But because of the difficulties of recording "Tomorrow Never Knows" with the backwards things and so forth, where you had to communicate with an intercom to tell the tape op to drop in—which was ridiculous—we requested that the 4-track machines be brought into the control room.

Well, that was just a "no go" area, but eventually they relented. And they sent out six technical staff from the main EMI technical department to supervise the moving of the 4-track machine up the corridor.

There goes the azimuth!

Yes, they were sure the azimuth would go out, it wasn't going to work, all sorts of things . . . really, it was unbelievable. And the sheer look of horror on their faces as it was lifted over the door threshold!

Let's step back a minute. How would management know if you put too much bass on something?

Well, the mastering engineers would complain to the manager of the mastering department, "Geoff's put too much bass on his tape, and we can't transfer it." And I used to get reprimanded.

At that time, the producer and engineer weren't allowed in the mastering room.

No. In fact, when I did *Sgt. Pepper*, I put on the box "Please transfer flat," and it just caused chaos. Now, I knew, having gone through the mastering stage, what could be done and what couldn't. There was no need to touch the tape, and I wanted just to transfer flat. And also, I wanted to go in there while it was being done. Eventually, I did get special permission to sit in on the mastering. Over time, of course, things gradually changed, and it became the norm to go in with the mastering engineer.

But you really did have to do battle over certain things.

Yes. For example, on Ringo's drum sound, I wanted to move the mic closer to the bass drum. Well, we weren't allowed. I was caught putting the mic about three inches from the bass drum, and I was reprimanded. I said "Look, this is the bass drum sound we've got, and we don't want to touch it." And so, I was sent a letter, from one of the guys in the office down the corridor, giving permission—only on Beatles sessions—to put the microphone three inches from the drum. They were worried, you see, about the air pressure—that it would damage the mic. There were a lot of things like that.

But what made you think to break the rules?

It was the fact that I was looking for something new and different all the time. The only way that I could do that was to change the way things were done. In fact, one of the first sessions I ever did, with Force West, we did in Number 2 studio, where the strings always went on the hardwood end and the rhythm and brass up on the carpeted end. But I was after a more live rhythm sound, and a different string sound, so I put the strings up on the carpeted end and the rhythm and brass on the hardwood. And it caused all manner of problems. When the next day, some of the older engineers found out what I'd done, they said, "You can't do that; we've been doing it this way for all these years." Other people would set the session up, you see, and they used to just walk in and know where to put everything. Then the engineer would just sit down, and away they went. So it was, "If someone else wants to do this, we'll have to do such and such . . . and we can't have that." Because, really, they'd had it easy for ten or fifteen years, and if things were changed, people might expect more from them.

I've heard that there was, at that time, a sort of adversarial relationship between engineers and artists.

Well, there were certain rules and regulations. It was very regimented. You weren't allowed to get too close to the artist; you were only supposed to speak to them if they spoke to you. That was very hard. We had to wear collars and ties and make sure our shoes were polished, and we had to get permission to take our jackets off on a session. And to be seen without a tie—forget it. Of course, you were working with classical people, remember, who expected a certain amount of respect.

Then it's back to my question of, "Why you?" I mean, the Beatles could have been stuck with someone who said, "It can't be done" when they asked for something new.

That's right.

So, what was different about you?

It's just something that I hear, I guess. I've always leaned more toward the artistic side. I didn't get into the recording business for the technical side.

You have said that you hear in "colors."

Oh, I do, definitely. The way I approach it is I use what I'm given by the studio like a palette of paints. It's very hard to explain, but I hear visually. I hear certain sounds in different colors. It's really an art form to me. If you start asking me technical stuff, I'm not really that interested.

Yet you're quite a technical engineer, especially in the techniques that you developed—close miking, preamp distortion, backwards sounds, automatic double tracking, tape loops....

It was only out of frustration. Because the Beatles were quite demanding on the sessions. That's what gave me the fuel to do what I was doing. I couldn't just sit there and leave it; you had to do something different every track—like "Geoff, we're going to use the piano, but we don't want it to sound like a piano; we're blending the guitar, but we don't want it to sound like a guitar." So, what do you do?

Did you usually have a sound in your head that you were going for?

No, I just built the picture from the textures and colors of what the other instruments were doing: what Ringo was playing on the drums, or the way the other guitar or keyboard sounded, trying to get something from that. Obviously, it was still going to sound like a guitar. But I knew what they were saying. They just wanted that extra little bit of magic to make it sound like a *different* guitar. So I was just applying what we could apply.

I was given the equipment and have used it. Basically, that's what happened. Like triple compressing a bass, or going from one compressor into another compressor and out of that compressor into a limiter and out of that limiter into another limiter and seeing what happens.

Speaking of compressors, in other interviews you've mentioned Fairchilds quite a bit. What is it about them you like so much?

The Fairchild 660s; it's just a sound they've got that I loved. It's good for specific drum sounds. It's great on electric guitars, and it's great on vocals. That's about it, really.

Do you think there's something to the notion that bigger is better in terms of recording equipment?

[Laughs] Well, that's because it was all tube equipment. All the albums up until *Abbey Road* were recorded through a tube desk. *Abbey Road* was the first album that was recorded through an EMI transistorized desk, and I couldn't get the same sounds at all.... There was presence and depth that the transistors just wouldn't give me that the tubes did.

That must have been frustrating.

Oh, it was. But, of course, it gave a texture to the *Abbey Road* album, after all, which is quite pleasant. But at first, being used to the tube desk and being confronted with the transistorized desk, it was like chalk and cheese. It was hard. And there was nothing I could do about it except craft the music around it. It was a much softer sort of texture.

When Studer came out with their transistorized multitrack tape machines, we were A/B-ing with an MCI 8-track, and the same thing happened. The tape machine just wouldn't produce the same snare or bass drum sound. And, of course, they could never give you an answer. You could only hear it and say to the people from Studer, "Why does it sound this way?"

And they'd run test tones through it and say it was all to spec.

Exactly.

You say you're not technical, but you did have a lot of technical training at EMI.

Yes, and it was superb technical training; it really was. Referring to what I said earlier, to be able to record in straight stereo, with no multitrack backup....

And the quality of EMI's equipment, even to the tape, was excellent.

Oh yes, it was extremely high. When I went to do the Beatles' *Anthology*, I took some of the tapes out of boxes that hadn't been out for thirty years, and they didn't shed or show much sign of wear at all. Even the tones went straight to zero. It was quite unbelievable. But then, we never had a problem with the tape. Of course, we were never allowed to go back over it.

You used fresh tape for every take?

Oh yes. That was another one of the rules: we always had to record on virgin tape. Because the technical people at the research department said — due to the flux or something — we shouldn't record over.

"Paperback Writer," which you recorded, had a rather unprecedented amount of bass on it.

Yes, and the bass drum also. It was one of the younger mastering guys — Tony Clark, who was a pal of mine — so there was some rapport between us. Whereas before, it would have been "No." I also remember the buzz that quickly went around *Abbey Road* when it became apparent what we had achieved with the sound of a record. People were standing outside the door and listening.... It was so different; really, it was like seeing the first screening of *2001*.

Do you recall the setup for those sessions?

We did it [ed: "Paperback Writer" and also "Tomorrow Never Knows"] in Number 3 at Abbey Road — although most of the Beatles songs were done in Number 2. I think I was miking the toms from underneath as well as on top. And I think

I was experimenting with 4038s — which were originally BBC design, and are now made by Coles — on overheads. They're big ribbons; you have to boost the high end. But there was a certain relationship, for some reason, on the 4038s, between mixing them in with the close mics, that really worked. Something to do with the phasing, I suppose. When you reversed the phase on the snare mic, it always came as a much bigger, fatter snare sound when you used the 4038s. It had to do with the bottom end on them. And they were also figure of eight, of course, so it was kicking back.

What mic would have been on the bass drum?

I think D20s. But whatever can take the impact of the bass drum. We always used to keep the front skin off of the bass drum and put in cushions and a big weight. That sounds better to me than with the head on and a hole cut in it.

What other mics do you recall using on drums?

There were D19s, which were AKGs, I think — just a cheap talkback mic. AKG always said they were the "throwout" capsules for D20s. Then they came out with the D19C, which had a little vent in the back to help the bass end, or something, which never sounded the same, of course. Like Neumanns — the way they progressed up the chain from the 47s and 48s to the 67, which never sounded as good as the 47, and the 87, which didn't sound as good as the 67. They were always trying to prove to you that it did, but it didn't.

Overall, your favorite microphone for vocals was a 47.

Yes, and also for guitars.

And you liked using a microphone in figure-8 pattern on bass.

I used to try to pull the bass out of the track to get its own space, and hear it more defined. And one way I tried to do it was to put a tiny bit of chamber echo — well, actually, I should say "reverberation" — on it. I started to do that on *Revolver*, but Paul could always detect even the slightest amount, and he wouldn't accept it. So I had to be careful.

But when we were doing *Pepper*, Paul would often overdub his bass after everyone had gone home. It would be just Paul and I and Richard Lush, the second engineer. We'd spend a couple or three hours doing bass parts, and I started using a C12 on figure of 8 about 8 or 10 feet away from his cabinet, which I would bring into the middle of Number 2 studio. I'd bring it out into the open from the corner area, where it was baffled off because I wanted a bit of the room sound.

Did you ever take the bass direct?

Maybe once. I didn't like the texture; especially, not on Paul. I guess I never have liked anything that went straight from electrics to electrics. There's something missing for me if it hasn't any natural acoustic sound.

For a while, you were monitoring in mono, even for stereo releases.

Stereo was late being introduced in England; we were quite behind the times. Up until *Abbey Road*, everything was monitored in mono through one loudspeaker. Which was hard, but it also helped. Because it's easy to get distinctive sounds between guitars if you've got them left and right. But if they're coming from one sound speaker, they merge together, and it's a fight to find a place and a tone and an echo for each guitar. And then, of course, when you got it and you switched to stereo, it was wonderful. It's still a good way of putting sounds together.

You have to work harder on it.

Yes, it would take, on the average, two and a half to three hours to work on each sound. We had the luxury; we weren't holding up the session. Most of the tracks were started in the studio, and they would go on for many hours working on the basic rhythm track, which gave us time to work on the sounds.

Of course, we were recording and mixing at the same time because we were still 4-track. So we were putting the real sounds on the instruments. They weren't going on separate tracks; they were all mixed on to one. That was the finished sound. It wasn't a question of doing it in the mix. That was it, and the rest of the track was built around that sound.

Well, that's pretty much a lost art. It's certainly apt that your job description was "balance engineer."

Actually, originally in EMI terminology it was called "balance and control" engineer; you balanced the sections of the orchestra. And our overdubs used to be called "superimpositions." In my second week at EMI, as a second engineer, I had to do a superimposition with a classical orchestra: Elizabeth Schwartzkopf doing "Cosi Fan Tutte," singing over a recorded orchestra. On classical sessions, you had to record in quadruple stereo—four machines running, and of course, sending the music tape for her to hear—on the speakers, not headphones, we didn't have headphones for foldback. So you had to play back, while recording on all four machines! [Laughs] And you never recorded over a take, you had to keep track of numbers with a mechanical clock on the tape machine, and you had to write out all the boxes.... [Laughs] It was horrendous. I'll never forget it. I actually had nightmares.

Is it true that the kind of slap you used on John Lennon's voice couldn't be duplicated anywhere else because the EMI tape machines had a different kind of head gap?

You could work it out now, I'm sure. But the head gap between play and record isn't the same on EMI's machines, that's all.

I'm confused about how you were doing ADT—Automatic Double Tracking—back then.

It's funny you should say that, because not long ago, when I saw Jack Douglas who had worked with John, he said to me, in a humorous kind of way, "How did you do that ADT? I could never get the copy tape to go fast enough to actually lie on top of the original voice like it was double tracked."

From his question, I got the feeling the tape was going so fast it was about to go up in smoke. John must have told him you could do it while you were recording, but actually, you could only do it when you were remixing. You have to take the signal of the vocal from the sync head. So you're mixing off the replay head. The sync is in advance, and you put it into another quarter-inch tape machine, then you put that on frequency control, and you slow it down. You're not trying to advance it. It's already advanced. You're just slowing it down. The trick is taking it off the sync head.

You were having to devise all this crazy stuff on the spot: backwards bits, phasing with tape machines, loops—were you having fun?

Looking back, it was great fun, for the most part. There were some moments that weren't, of course — there was a sort of bad period during the *White Album*. I actually walked out halfway through. It was something like the eighth attempt at "Oh Bla Di, Oh Bla Dah"...they were arguing, and I could see the whole thing disintegrating. I just couldn't handle it anymore. I said to George Martin, "Can I have a word?" and told him I wanted to leave the sessions. We went to the manager of the studio; it was a Tuesday, and he said, "Well, can you stay 'til Friday?" And I said "No." We went back to the studio and had a discussion with the band, who tried to make me stay. But I said, "No, I've had enough."

Your mind was made up.

Yes. Because if someone had twisted my arm, to stay 'till Friday, when Friday came I wouldn't have gone. I would have been there the next week and the next week, and felt worse and worse. I had to leave there and then.

You stayed on at EMI for a while after that, then what happened? How was it that you came back to make *Abbey Road*?

Being so young, I felt I couldn't further myself at EMI. I'd gone as far as I could, and was desperate, really, to leave. Apple [Records] had formed, and Paul asked, "Will you join Apple and do the studio?" I did, and built the studio, and during that time Paul phoned up and said, "We're going to go in and do a new album, would you like to do it?" So I said, "Of course." And that's how it all worked out. I just went back.

If you were teaching someone how to record vocals, what would you tell them?

You normally know which microphone will suit the artist's voice; talking to them and listening to them sing in the room gives you insight into their tonal quality. Limiting and compressing depends on what kind of track it is. On "Because," for instance, I didn't use any compressors or limiters on anything. I just rode the faders. It's not about grabbing the nearest bit of outboard gear when there seems to be a problem; you don't want to over-react.

If there's a problem, you want to rectify it with the person and work from there. If you're working with a true artist, it's not really a lot of what you do, it's what the vocalist does. Of course, you can now, with Pro Tools, do a lot of pitch shifting and fixing, which seems to be the norm, no matter whether or not someone has done a great performance. But a great performance can get lost that way. When everything is made perfect, it can become insignificant.

I like to hear [drummer Steve] Gadd make a personal statement [with timing]. One of the magic things with Ringo, he'd be hesitant, sometimes, on his drum fills, and then you'd hear them really pick up, and you'd realize it's a human being, playing. When something is so rigidly in time, it's like listening to a clock ticking in the bedroom. After a few minutes, your ear just doesn't hear it ticking anymore. It's unnoticeable.

Many drummers have said they were inspired by the way the drums you recorded sounded on Beatles records.

It was the presence, I think. No one had heard a bass drum up in your face, sounding as solid as it did. Maybe my approach to recording was magnifying them. I don't know. Getting back to this visual aspect, it was a question of putting into focus various instruments. Whereas before, everything had been sort of a blur. We just pulled everything back into focus.

There'd been very little close miking done before.

I used to put my ears near to things to hear what the makeup of the particular tone was. I would go out and have a good listen, and see if there were any places where things sounded slightly different. It's like miking a cymbal on the edge. Have you done that? I put a little condenser on the very edge, and it vibrates and you get this enormous big bottom end—things like that.

Were you puzzled the first time you had to record a sitar?

[Laughs] No, because I'd worked with other instruments on sessions, and had been listening to the tones and where the sounds came from. The sound of the sitar was so quiet and complex. I think I used Neumann 54s or 56s, which are really nice condenser mics—little tubes you could get right close onto the strings or the soundboard, then probably through a Fairchild, to get this amazing big wall of huge sound.

After that, Ravi Shankar came in and was doing a classical recording in Number 3. And George Harrison, who was friends with him, said to me, "Do you want to come in and see Ravi? Because something's not quite right." Well, they had him wired up on a wooden rostrum, and they had a ribbon mic, a 4038, about twenty feet up in the air. And of course, you couldn't hear anything; he was getting more room than sitar, which was just kind of mush in the background. I was just the young kid and the engineer had been there years and years, so I had to be a bit diplomatic.

Considering that you were using loops as far back as 1966 [on *Revolver*], it must amuse you that they are now so prevalent.

A lot of it was that Paul had a couple of Brenell tape recorders at home. You could disconnect the erase head on them, and he used them to make tape loops, putting new recordings over the first. He'd come in with a bag full of them—some long, some very small—all labeled with a grease pencil. We'd lace them up on our tape machine, and people would have to hold them out with pencils. I recall that on "Tomorrow Never Knows," there weren't enough people in the control room to handle holding them, so we got some of the maintenance department down to help. I think we put five loops up on faders, and then just played it as an instrument.

Of course, now, it's endless, you can do anything. But often, all that doesn't mean anything. If you just press a button and it's there, you haven't really created anything, have you? Going back to the artistic side of it, it's the difference between painting by numbers or being a Rembrandt and painting a picture. Anyone can apply this technology to recorded music. But there's that certain something that you can't put your finger on, something that you can actually give to that piece of recording that the equipment can't. It's something that's in your heart, that's in you, that doesn't come from any equipment whatever. It comes from what you hear.

Being pushed to come up with all sorts of new sounds, to try all sorts of things, did you ever think, "Oh, this will never work."

Oh no. Never. Everything was always possible. Nothing is impossible. That was always my theory.

CHRIS FOGEL

OCTOBER, 2002 ## From Albums with Alanis Morissette and Seal to Film Soundtracks

In our sometimes overinflated, overhyped technological world, where audio addicts frenzy over the latest, the greatest, the oldest, and the coolest, Chris Fogel is a refreshing breath of fresh air. The emperor better not try wearing any new clothes around this guy—a brisk engineer who works with streamlined gear, Fogel espouses a totally no-nonsense approach to his art.

The results of his engineering style are the pudding's proof. It was Fogel's mixes that scorched the airwaves the summer of '95 on Alanis Morissette's *Jagged Little Pill*. He's continued to work with Morissette on almost all of her music, as well as with U2, Seal, Aaliyah, Sheryl Crow, John Hiatt, and Robbie Robertson, among others, garnering a Grammy nomination in 1998 for Best Engineered Album for his mixes on Robertson's *Contact from the Underworld of Redboy*. Since 1998, he's also been mixing for film and 5.1 surround, working with composer Edward Shearmur on the scores for such features as *Charlie's Angels, Cruel Intentions, K-Pax*, and *Miss Congeniality*.

Reno, Nevada-born and currently bicoastal, Fogel recently constructed a ground-up studio for himself at his Glendale, California home, where we sat down for this interview. Meet Chris Fogel: You oughta know....

You got your start as a DJ, commuting from the Reno area to San Francisco to work weekend clubs. What kind of music were you spinning?

Industrial, mostly. Ministry and Wax Trax bands and everything around them. Also Depeche Mode, New Order, that kind of '80s Euro dance music. Song-based stuff with guitars and melodies and a good driving beat—that's what got me into it. DJs weren't the sort of rock stars they are now, making $10,000 an appearance. I couldn't afford to get a place in San Francisco, so I'd commute for two nights, staying with friends and sleeping on the floor. I also ran my own clubs in

Reno — Underground and Red Square — when I was only nineteen. I leased space, promoted them myself, and got over a thousand kids a night.

So recording school came after you were already a DJ.

In fact, it was a total accident. I was at a party up in Tahoe, and I saw a brochure for Full Sail on the back of a toilet.

It was a sign.

Yeah. Why the hell was there a Full Sail brochure on the back of a toilet in that house in Tahoe?

I went, graduated number one in my class, and got a job a Westlake [Studios in Los Angeles] right after that.

I remember hearing that Westlake only hired people if they'd graduated from a recording school.

Actually, for a time, they were against it. There were areas of knowledge students were definitely lacking in, but they came out kind of cocky like they knew everything. And I'm here to tell ya,' nobody knows everything. I'm nowhere near the engineer I potentially could be. I'm learning every day. I go through periods — like, now I'm in one of my "Van Gogh" dark periods. That's where everything that I listen to that I've done, I don't really like. I think I could have done it better. I'll come out of it, but the point is, you don't come out of school knowing anything except how to wipe your nose.

You started you as an intern?

I started as the night runner at Westlake's Beverly location. I remember what got Steve Burdick, the manager, to give me a shot at assisting. It was Christmas, and all the regular assistants were out of town. Because I was the night guy and he was the first one in every morning, he'd see what kind of cleanup job I'd done. And he noticed that I would line up all the coffee mugs on the shelf so that the handles were facing the same way.

Very impressive. Like when you open the fridge in a studio kitchen and all the labels on the drinks are facing the same way.

That's what got me moved up. Now, when I see someone who's doing the same thing, I think, "An ambitious runner, we've got here — just like I was." But back then, I didn't know. I was just doing it. But Steve gave me a shot, and my first gig was a Pontiac commercial.

Photo: Edward Colver

That's a speedy start.

Yeah! With a hard core jingle engineer whose license plate said "Mix4Bux." I remember, I was terrified.

Was it at Westlake that you hooked up with [producer] Glen Ballard?

I actually hooked up with Francis Buckley, his engineer at the time, on a project he was doing with someone else. And then we did a Curtis Steigers record—a great singer and sax player from New York—with Glen. And when they did the second Wilson Phillips record at Westlake, I was the technical director.

Technical director?

That was Francis Buckley's neat way of giving me more credit. We did that record on Mitsubishi X880, and I was in charge of everything—come in on Sundays . . . you know. After we finished that

record, Glen decided to build a studio at home. He bought a Euphonix, and he took me from Westlake to run his show. I learned the Euphonix, and we did a lot of demos together. If there were albums, Francis would come in. But Francis happened to get hired by Quincy Jones to do *Q's Jook Joynt* right at the time that Alanis showed up on Glen's door saying, "Let's work together." And that was it.

So you've been working on Euphonix since 1992.

Euphonix may correct me, but I think Glen's was the second install. It was a CS2, a tiny little frame. It was Francis' idea. They didn't want to do a big battleship console because the studio was upstairs above the garage. They wanted something fairly light, that didn't give off a lot of heat, had a small footprint, and still sounded really good.

I learned from Francis not to fear new technology. He sat me in front of the Euphonix, and for one whole day, I went "What is this?" I didn't get it.

Midway through the second day, I got one little section and the light went on for the whole console. I understood it, and now—if I don't have to—I won't work on anything else.

You like a more transparent sound.

I prefer a much less colored sound. A lot of other engineers don't like the EQs. Well, I love them. I like having the visual "Q" curve, like in Pro Tools. I like Euphonix's tactile and visual interface that allows you to see what you're doing in addition to hearing it. Plus, the instant recall.... [Laughs] That's really important because we recall everything. I don't think there's been a single song —on any of the three records that I've done with Alanis—that I didn't have to recall at least twice. Because of the way she's worked, she understands that a recall is not that big a deal. Of course, when we're getting towards crunch time, it is.

With recalls so easy, how do you know when a mix is finished?

I'm satisfied much earlier than a lot of people. I think if you've gotten the point of a song across, you've done your job. Alanis—I don't know what her process is. We'd do recalls, I'd send her home with them, she'd drive around in her car and call me and say, "Yeah, this one's done." What's strange to me is that on the more important songs, she's usually willing to let go earlier. Like the first single from this album, "Hands Clean" was the mix we finished earliest. It was finished, and she never revisited it. But everything else, right up until nine hours before mastering, we're doing recalls.

This time around, Rob Jacobs did most of the recording.

I recorded almost everything in her rock genre up to this; that's because I worked with Glen. He and I had a falling out. I think Alanis and Glen also had a falling out, and she started with Rob. And there couldn't have been a better choice. He's perfect for her—an organic-based engineer. Frankly, I wouldn't have revisited much of what he did.

But to her ears, something was missing, and I think it was just that she was used to the process that I give her. She wasn't looking for just mixing; she was looking for what we could do to make the songs better. So she said, "Why don't you try mixing a few songs?" We had to do it in New York because she was doing videos and photo shoots, and because there are no other commercial Euphonix studios left in New York, except for System 5s, we ended up in a tiny overdub room at Battery Studios.

A programmer, Carmen Rizzo, and I tag teamed, he in one room and I in the next. I flew tracks around and kind of rearranged with some of the additional elements Carmen added. She loved it, and wanted to do the whole album, so we did it in chunks. We did the first four in New York and the rest here at [Glendale's] Front Page Studios. The only song we didn't look at was "Flinch." I listened and didn't want to touch it. Actually, I felt that way about a lot of the mixes that Rob did. But that goes back to my point; I'm willing to let things go a lot earlier than other people are. If I'm getting the song and the point of what she's trying to say and the emotion she's trying to convey, then to me it's done. I don't have to get a perfect kick drum or bass sound, or the perfect overall texture.

I think people can spend way too much time trying for perfection and get perilously close to sterilizing a song. I'm more into the immediacy of it. I think that's what Alanis is into also—getting your gut reaction and maintaining it without going too far, but her process is different.

Not many mixers do both CDs and film work.

I love being able to have my hand in both. I like having five speakers set up and digging into the technology and the art. On the other hand, I think mixing for stereo is more of an art than mixing for surround. Mixing for surround is more of a science—more color-by-numbers. When you're mixing for stereo, you take the speakers out of the equation and create the image. For 5.1, the speakers are every bit a part of the equation. I actually think it's more limiting to mix in 5.1 than in stereo.

Seal brought it up. He said that when mixing in 5.1, he tends to lose the emotion because he's thinking about the technology too much. He's thinking about how cool it is that something's coming from behind, rather than what the point of the piece of music is.

That's a problem that plagues a lot of surround projects.

Most titles sound sterile—due to no fault of anybody. It's just the technology. "Yeah, that's cool, but do I want to listen to it again?" No.

What about for film?

If I had my choice for film, I'd do it in stereo stems. When I'm given a mandate by the stage that I have to deliver in 5.1, I have to think about placement, rather than the entire picture. When the stage doesn't have a preference, I'm happier. I can create a stereo mix that totally kicks butt, then break out stems for them. If they need to extract surround, or the center, they can do it.

Mixing film for 5.1 is, of course, totally different than mixing albums for 5.1 because you have to clear the center for dialog. For 5.1 albums, that center is discrete, it's got its own life and you can put whatever you want in there.

How do you work with [composer] Edward Shearmur?

He'll write at home, and I've got mirror equipment for his writing setup—which is mostly [Nemesis, now Tascam] Gigastudio, so he can just come in with his files. I start building mixes early in the process, and we overdub where needed. Keeping cues in a near mixed state, we always know what they are. When they're done, I just print. Also, it's important to have cues in good shape for that day the director decides to pop in for a listen. Sequencing is on Digital Performer, and I have a Pro Tools rig as well. I'm not a huge fan of Pro Tools; I use it because I have to. You can do most of what you do with Pro Tools in a Euphonix R1, and it sounds so much better!

Do you generally do a lot of rearranging in mixes?

Not usually. If an artist has gotten to the point where they're ready for me to mix, I'm assuming that they've already put thought into having what they want on tape. If there's something that's really bugging me, I'll call them up and say, "Hey, can I do a little rearranging?" I'm not into the school of replacing every kick and snare just for the sake of retriggering. If they were getting a vibe off of what they had on tape, there's a reason why they put it there. Unless they tell me to go through and do whatever I need to, I'll mix what I'm given.

I just mixed two singles for a band called Custom. They brought in some mixes that had been done, then played the original track and said, "We never gave the guy the right to do this. He never asked us. He just did it, and it really pissed us off." This is a band that's like a New York version of Beck. They've already put all the thought into the way they want the songs to be put together. Why should some yahoo mixer presume to come in and screw it up to his heart's content?

You're really from Reno? You've got some pretty New York style attitude.

No, I'm from Reno. I have a place in New Jersey though, and if I had my druthers, I'd live there full time.

Let's do some tech talk. What format do you mix to?

The Alesis Masterlink, through an Apogee PSX 100 SE, in and out at 96K. I used to dislike Apogee sound, but I've grown to really like it, in the past few months. I just bought Apogee's DA-16 converters for my Pro Tools rig, and I love them.

If it's a big project, I'll wheel in a half-inch Ampex ATR 102. Seal and Alanis were done to half-inch. Sometimes I can't tell the difference, anymore, and sometimes I like the Masterlink better.

What about for 5.1?

If it's for film, I mix back into—usually—six channels of Pro Tools. Because they don't care if it's 96K; film is usually 44.1. If it's for DVD-A, where they do care about sample rate, I'll mix to another Digital Performer 3.0 because I get twelve channels of audio at 96K. That sounds really good—117 dB of S/N ratio. I could get a Genex or a DA98, but Performer has the same resolution, and this way, I get to see what's going on so I can clean up tails, etc. Just like the old Pro Tools, but it's 96K.

Not much analog shows up here.

If it does, I'll take it over to Front Page and transfer to Pro Tools using Euphonix converters.

What's in your racks?

My GML 8200 stereo EQ, which I always use across the stereo bus. An Avalon [AD-2022] mic pre that I use for vocals. I also have a rack of API mic pre's. But I've got seventy-two mic pre's in the Euphonix that sound great. I don't have to go outboard much. I love the Manley [Variable MU]. I use it for everything. The 1176, I use on bass all the time.

This particular Euphonix has 24 channels of built-in dynamics. There's nothing else out there, all in one, that's as good as this, as far as dynamics are concerned. And it's totally recallable. The console is a CS2000 with the latest F-series towers where all the audio is processed. So it's identical to a 3000, except it doesn't have machined knobs and it doesn't have moving faders. I don't use moving faders anyway. If I'm on a desk that has them, I turn them off.

Because Euphonix is modular, you could retrofit to your specs.

You can add dynamics to any of the CS series. You can add later or earlier revisions of hardware to anything and make it work. I bought the desk from John Tesh, some other things from Seal, and the Cube—the device that allows you to break out into surround-sound or to multiple stems, giving you up to forty-eight different auxes on each fader—from a guy in Milwaukee.

Euphonix has been that modular from day one. If I was doing a mix that had three more sets of dynamics on it, I could bring in the dynamics units and just plug them in. The desk instantly sees them and puts them into the template as part of the console.

Do you use your NHT Pro speakers for both stereo and surround?

Yes. The only thing I like better is the ATC50, but they're $12,000 a pair. The NHTs are self powered, but the amp isn't built into the unit, they're down below. They have their own proprietary cable. They get plenty loud, and they're completely linear from top to bottom, very open on the top and at all volume levels. Every time I put up a new pair of speakers, I think I like them, and then I put the NHTs back up and go, "These are so much better." My only complaint is I wish they had a little more "boom," which is why I'm trying out some bigger speakers like Questeds.

With speakers, like with the console, you're into linear and uncolored.

Yes, and I think my mixes tend to show that. They're not real hype-y on the top. My vocals tend to get a bit zingy, but, for example, if you listen to Alanis in a room talking to you, it's very zingy. That's the way she sounds.

What about those little Fostex 6301 B personal monitors?

I use them for leveling vocals and checking overall balances at really quiet level. And if we're doing a film and Ed is sitting here writing, I flip one around and give him dialog in it so he can set his own levels.

I don't see much vintage equipment. I guess you're not one of those collectors of Eastern European broadcast gear.

I went through that stage, but now my main question is "Why?" The Lexicon 960, for example, my main-axe reverb, has all the sounds that the 480 had, and I get a ton more DSP. The only things that I've kept since the beginning are my Yamaha SPX 990s. I have to have a pair of those.

There are a couple of drum rooms that I really like. And without fail, when I mix Alanis' vocals, they're processed through the wood room for the reverb and the vocal doubler for a little bit of spread. Except on the current record, where I strayed away from that, and now I kind of regret it.

Overall, I'm into tried and true stuff. I'm not into collecting. The bottom line is [that the older gear] doesn't sound any better to me. To me, it's a waste of money from a maintenance standpoint. I work all the time; I can't afford to be in the middle of a mix and have a problem. I had two vintage, black face 1176s, and I got rid of them. Either the barrier strip would fall off or the resistance would get funny.... I bought one of the reissues, and it sounds—I won't say better, but it doesn't sound worse. And I know it's going to remain stable. It's got XLR outputs, a discrete transformer....

For me, I like a transparent mic pre, and then let me go after the sound I want via filtering or whatever. I am into microphones. The Coles ribbon mics are cool, and there are times to use real crappy old Shures or weird, vintage mics.

Who built your studio?

I built the room myself, including acoustics, which I designed along with Ty Moyer at ASC—Acoustic Sciences Corp.—in Connecticut. I just e-mailed them out of the blue and said, "Hey, I'm building a room in my backyard." I gave him dimensions, and he came up with the coefficients of where the [treatments] should be placed. ASC also has a wall construction that I used. They recommend multiple layers of drywall.

Charlie Bolois and Kevin Kaiser of Vertigo did the wiring. They had wired the console for Tesh also, so they were familiar with the system.

I patterned it after Seal's room; I used matching specifications. He has a CS3000, and he built his studio in his gym without really doing any acoustic treatment to it. I got some of my best mixes out of there, and it made me realize I could build my own room. I'm very happy with the results.

What's up next for you?

I just finished recording and mixing the score for Cameron Diaz' *The Sweetest Thing*, and I'm currently remixing *Under Rug Swept* in 5.1, with Alanis' previous two albums to follow. I'm also recording and mixing the score for Spyglass' *Reign of Fire* with Matthew McConaughey and Christian Bale. After that, I'm doing the score for *A View From the Top*, composed by Theodore Shapiro, starring Gwyneth Paltrow and Mike Meyers. And I've got a bunch of unsigned bands in development that I'm working with on and off, until winter, when we should be starting the *Charlie's Angels* sequel. I guess you could say it's a multi-channel year for me!

ELLIOT SCHEINER

Selected Credits

Jimmy Buffett
Feeding Frenzy (live),
Off to See the Lizard,
Bring Back the Magic,
You Had To Be There

Natalie Cole
Stardust

The Eagles
Hell Freezes Over,
The Eagles MTV Special

Donald Fagan
Nightfly, Heavy Metal,
Nightfly surround mixes

Fleetwood Mac
The Dance

Glenn Frey
Soul Searchin',
Strange Weather,
"You Belong to the City"

Dave Grusin
Two for the Road

Bruce Hornsby
The Way It Is

Van Morrison
Moondance,
Moondance surround mixes

Queen
Night at the Opera
surround mixes

Steely Dan
AJA, Gaucho, Royal Scam,
Two Against Nature

Toto
Tambu,
Mindfields

Master Craftsman

JANUARY, 2003

I once heard a group of established engineers debate who was the best all around engineer. It should have been a difficult question, given the opinionated nature of the average audio professional. Yet, in a few minutes they were in agreement: Elliot Scheiner.

Another story: Not long ago, three producer/engineer owners of a studio that had just completed installation of a new 5.1 surround mix suite were giving me a tour. As we walked into the new room, the maintenance technician and assistant were setting up for the day's mix session. To check the positioning and balances of the multiple speakers, they were playing back a DVD of *Hell Freezes Over,* the Eagles' live video recording. There were six people in the room, all long time recording studio veterans, with the requisite jaded tastes, yet, when the first notes of "Hotel California" rang out, we all stopped what we were doing, jostled for a place in the sweet spot and settled in to listen. Everyone in the room was rapt, listening for the pure enjoyment of it. It was one of those memorable moments. Y'all should have been there, because the only word to describe the sound of that recording is "gorgeous."

The man behind the board for those sessions was, of course, producer/engineer Elliot Scheiner, someone long known for making recordings that are, somehow, both pristine and soulful. Since his early days with Van Morrison and notorious taskmasters Steely Dan, he's worked with Toto, Jimmy Buffet, Bruce Hornsby, Ricky Lee Jones, Smokey Robinson, David Sanborn, and many others, garnering five Grammy awards and ten additional nominations. He's also been the recipient of two Emmy nominations for Outstanding Achievement in Sound Mixing and three TEC Award nominations. His recent pioneering work in 5.1 surround mixing has made him in-demand in the genre, and, besides the Eagles, he has done projects for Faith Hill, Sting, Beck, Steely Dan, Donald Fagan, and the current surround pièce de résistance, Queen's *Night At the Opera.*

Scheiner started his career in New York at A&R Studios, working under legendary producer/engineer Phil Ramone. For many years, he's done much of his work in Los Angeles, but his heart remains on the East Coast. He makes his home in Connecticut, choosing to work in Manhattan whenever possible. I spoke with him by phone one autumn morning as he was preparing REM's *Document* for a 5.1 surround mix.

Just a few questions about your career beginnings, please. How did you know that you wanted to be an engineer?

I didn't. I was a musician, a drummer. I beat around in a lot of rock 'n' roll bands, nobody that really made it. And I realized, after being on the road on a bus and doing these horrible tours, that it wasn't what I wanted to do.

At the time, my uncle, Chauncey Welsch, was a studio musician in New York, an "A" player. I said, "I can't do this. But I want to be in the music business; I want to to make records." He invited me for lunch, then took me over to A&R Studios, because he was doing a date there. He introduced me to Phil Ramone. We talked for about five minutes and Phil said, "When can you start?" I said "Now." And that was it. I was on the payroll.

Just being in a control room and watching Phil work was so awe inspiring. I was just so taken by all that was happening. It was only a jingle, but seeing what was going on, the interaction of Phil with the musicians, and the arranger, and the composer, and the agency people, even. It was so electric. I knew right then and there, that's what I wanted to do.

Did you spend some years at A&R working your way up?

You've got to remember, this was 1967. So the technology wasn't archaic, but it was minimal. Phil taught me the same way he was taught by Tom Dowd and Bill Schwartau. You were given a room to work in, and you had to know what the room was about. You had to understand the acoustics of it, where to put certain instruments, what mics to use on them, and how to place a microphone.

Given all these variables, sometimes you put up a mic, and when you listened in the control room, you'd say, "This doesn't sound right." We were taught that, when that happened, something was different in the room. There were more people, or less people, or whatever, and that made it sound different. So you went and moved the mic until you got it right. Because there was no EQ in the console; there was no compression in the console. The room that we worked in had two Pultec EQs and two Fairchilds, and that was that. You were very selective about what you used.

So there really wasn't that much trouble you could get into.

[Laughs] That is absolutely true. You had to know how to mic an instrument, and where to place it. That was all there was to recording. You had to be able to mix because it was pretty much live. It was only 4-track, so if you were doing a big orchestra in the room, you pretty much had to put your rhythm section on one track. You put the strings and horns on the other track, and then you left two tracks open for lead vocal and background. Since you had to mix [all the instruments] to two tracks, you had to be able to hear what it should sound like. You had to have some kind of instinct about what it was going to be.

For a long time there has been a trend toward "fix it in the mix." But I think it's becoming important again to people to get things sounding right when they're recorded. Because then, it's easier to just mix inside your workstation.

It depends on who's recording it. For the guys from my era, that's always been the case. We always made sure that we recorded it correctly going in because we felt there was no going back. So we're still of that mind, whereas the younger guys, you know, "We'll just get it in there, I can fix it once it's in. We can move it, we can slide it, we can take out any distortion, we can add distortion, we can put amps on it. We can do anything."

So, I'm not sure that everyone is getting on the page where they think that they have to record it

Photo: ©2002 Ebet Roberts

better going in. I've seen too many files lately that have no care put into them. Actually, the tracks that I get on analog are often better. For instance, I just mixed Beck's latest record [*Sea Change*] in 5.1. It's with a band, and most of the vocals are live, and it was very well recorded. Not only did Nigel Godrich record it beautifully, but he also put the effects on tape. He totally committed to it, and it was just awesome to put up the faders and mix it like that.

Didn't it used to be a goal to have a "straight line mix?"

You knew that you were a good engineer if you recorded it, and whoever was mixing could put all the faders at zero and it was a mix. [Laughs] I don't ever think that I got that.

In your career, you've worked with many people who were very sonically conscious.

Well, that was primarily Steely. I've never worked with anyone else who was into it to that degree.

Here's a quote about Steely Dan and *Aja*: "It was the record that took their obsession with sonic detail to new heights."

That would probably be pretty accurate.

Were you that obsessive also?

No. They just liked what I did on certain things. Like, I would end up doing the tracking and mixing and nothing in between. They liked the way that I record a track. It had the sonic structure that they liked, that's all.

Have you consistently used the same microphones throughout your career, or are you using completely different ones now than you did in the beginning?

The funny thing is that a lot of it has come full circle. When I started, all we had were really great tube microphones, and obviously, the classic list of dynamics. But as the newer microphones started to come in, everything was about "Let's try this new thing." It seems like that's how it was right up until about ten years ago. Now, people are looking back and going "Wait a second, these records that were made thirty, forty, fifty, years ago really sound better than anything today."

I use a lot of the old tube mics, but I use a lot of new mics as well. The one thing that has maintained a constant for me over the years, that I have never changed, is the snare drum mic. I've used the same one since the first day I recorded, right up 'til now.

And that would be?

A [Shure] SM57. And I don't use a bottom mic, I only use the one mic on top.

If you were tracking today, what other drum mics would you be likely to use?

I'm pretty consistent about the drums. For the toms, I always use [Audio-Technica] ATM-25s. I love those mics for toms. They take a beating, they really do. You can slam those mics and they're fine. They sound great flat; I never have to EQ them. So, not only do they take an enormous amount of sound pressure level, they're just great sounding.

How about bass drum?

Through the years, it's changed. That was flavor of the day. We were always searching for the best bass drum sound. When I started with Phil, as an assistant, he used the [AKG] D-12 on the kick. Most guys used either the D-12 or the [EV] 666. I used those for quite a long time, and then the [Sennheiser] RE-20 showed up. After the RE-20 was the Sennheiser 421, and I used that for a long time. Now, I never touch that mic. The only mic that I really use for kick right now is the [AKG] D-112. I will sometimes use an RE-20 as well, but most of the time, it's a D-112.

Where do you tend to put the mic on the kick drum?

Assuming there's a hole in the skin, I put it just a little bit past the hole, just ever so slightly inside. There have been so many trends. I remember when they wanted to take the whole head off. When I started, you basically put a mic on the beater side, or on the other side. Most guys put it on the front side of the drum. At A&R, we put it on the beater side. But you know, if you listen to earlier records, the bass drum sounds weren't that great.

So, once there was a hole in the front head, or no front head, you didn't continue to mic the beater side.

No, you didn't need to. And the bass drum sounded infinitely better that way. Then, of course, we started stuffing things in them.

Sure, blankets, bricks, sandbags....

We did all sorts of stuff. Shelly Yakus worked at A&R also; he and I started on the same day. And I remember walking into his session one day, and he'd rigged this thing on the house bass drum, where he took the head off, but left the screws on. Then he took bungie-style cords and a tape reel hub, attached the bungies to the hub, and hung it right in the middle of the drum.

Suspended it.

Right. Then he put eyebolts in, to secure an SM57 to the middle of the hub. It was the best looking thing. You know, a lot of times we do things because they look great.

Really?

In this case, the idea was, how loud can you be? So Shelly did this thing, and it sounded pretty good. I tried it, but I could never get it to sound good.

What's something you did because it looked great?

I did a date once with an Australian artist. We were working in a smaller room, and it was two guitars, bass, and drums. They were using an enormous amount of amps, and they were worried about the leakage. I knew it would be a problem no matter what, so I figured I'd do something a little weird. I set up scaffolding in the studio, and I put all the amps at the top of the room.

You had to carry them up on a ladder?

Actually, we had guys who could do that. They set up ladders and carried them up to the scaffolding. We put the mics up there, and we did the whole record that way. I don't know if it made any difference or not, because we'd never heard the amps down on the floor. But I've got to tell you, when the band walked in, they were frantic with excitement. It was definitely a vibe.

Right then, back to drums. Overhead mics?

I try to stay with tubes most of the time. I would use AKG C12s, I'd use [Neumann] U67's, or [Telefunken] 250's.

You prefer warmer rather than brighter for overheads.

Well the C-12's are pretty bright. I've used those and the C-12A, I've even used—as far as new mics go—I've used these AT-4060's. Those are tubes, and they're pretty nice-sounding as well.

C-12's are bright, but they're not crispy bright like some people choose.

Well, at this point, you never know, because they're so old, and you don't know who has been inside of them. It's hard to say what any of them really sound like and whether any of them sound right anymore.

Do you generally use room mics?

I have always put up room mics, but I never used them all that much. Actually, I'm using them more now then I have in the past.

Because of surround?

Yes, and also even for stereo. Like with Steely, we recorded room mics on the new album, and in the mix, I'm using a fair amount of them, which is different for us.

Where did you record that project.

Sear Sound, in New York. All analog.

That's a change for you.

No, that's a change for them. I always try to record analog. That's my primary choice. I talked them into it. It was funny, the way that it worked. They did one song there, [at Sear] that was for a tribute to Joni Mitchell. They have unbelievable mics there, and when you walk in the door, all of the sudden, it's 1974. It's wild. There are even beads on the entryway. So there's this vibe. And when we got into the studio, I looked at Walter [Becker] and said, "Can we do this analog?"

You just kind of casually slipped that in, because you were in that vintage environment?

Yeah. And he said, "This is a tribute, let's do it." So we did it analog, and they were amazed; they'd forgotten how good analog sounds. Because of that, when we started the new record, about two months later, they said, "Let's do it analog." And we did. The basic tracks are all analog; all the overdubs were done in a workstation.

How about mixing?

Analog and digital. Just last week, we finished off a couple of mixes, and Walter said, "Maybe it's time to A/B the analog and digital and see what we're going to use." So I set it up to A/B, almost perfectly, and the analog killed it. And we were using the 24-bit, 96 kHz digital.

I'm surprised.

It killed the digital. And it was so far beyond it that they weren't convinced. They said, "Let's take it to a mastering room." So we did and did the same process, and the analog still killed the digital on a completely different machine.

You know, very few people have actually had the opportunity to do that kind of accurate A/B comparison, listening to the same program material, in the different multitrack formats, side by side.

I've found that when I do a seminar at Berklee, the kids want to know, how can we get our hands on analog? They want it, but it's not around. That's becoming a problem. And I think this is so cyclical, that eventually it will come back. I'm thinking about buying the two-inch 8-track machine because when I mix surround, that's what I use.

But you also use a digital workstation.

If I'm working with old product, and obviously the old tape can't be used. You bake them and you make a transfer and that's that. I dump them into [Steinberg] Nuendo, and I work off of that. Nuendo is my multitrack. I use a lot of the EQ and processing in there. When I'm working at home, I have the Yamaha DM2000 digital console, and Nuendo, and I make full use of it.

I'm a big fan of how the guitars on your records sound. Do you still use a Shure SM81 for strumming rhythm parts?

I don't stray much from that. For strumming rhythm parts on guitars the SM81 is the best as far as I'm concerned. It's so impacting, so powerful and it doesn't distort. It's great for that. I've never used it for anything else.

If you're going to compress a rhythm guitar what would you use?

Well, I was using the Summit, the TLA-100 because it would really slam down on the acoustic and sound great. I've recently been using the 160-SL, the new dbx—the blue-faced one. It's an incredible sounding compressor. But like the TLAs, if you don't really slam it hard, it will eat up the top end. When I hit it a little harder, it sounds more even to me.

You like a tube U47 for picking guitar parts. What else might you use on them?

Nothing.

Nothing, just leave it alone, no compression?

No, the only time I put compression on a guitar is on the acoustic strum part. I don't use much compression at all. Like I said earlier, I grew up not having compressors, so with Phil, I'd say, "What do you do here?" then, he'd say, "You use your hand on the fader."

You used your hand, you rode a fader, and you acted as a compressor. I've gotten used to doing that. I watch guys come in, throw on a compressor, throw on an EQ, and then never touch the fader again. Everything is predetermined.

For me, part of it is that I feel, as an engineer, you are as much a part of the performance, especially when you are doing a live band, as any member of the band. And you're interpreting what they're doing, and your hand rides dictate that. It's not a constant compression where everything is safe, everything is slammed, and everything is at a certain level. A lot of times, the dynamics are totally missing when people do that. It's like when some guys are digitizing stuff, they maximize it, and there are no dynamics. A lot of the problem with the music today is the lack of dynamics.

You use an SM57 for electric guitars, and you've said you put it on the best speaker in the stack. How do you find the best one?

Usually the guitar player can tell you.

I guess I should have known that.

I always rely on guitar players, "Where on this bottom?" And they will point out, right here. They know exactly where. For the guys that don't know, you just mess with it.

In your career you seem to have been very flexible in going with the changes in technology. You're very adamant about certain things, but it's more about how the finished product should be rather than about what you use to get the finished product.

That's true. Like having a home studio. That's something I thought I would never do. I'm a big proponent of commercial studios, and I think everyone should make records in commercial studios, and not in their home. But, right now, there are certain projects that wouldn't be done at all—smaller records, that just don't have the budget to do that. The attitude is, if we can't do it for a certain amount, we can't do it. And especially for 5.1, for an emerging format, there needs to be more selection, more titles.

So, I'm glad to do it. But I still definitely try to work in major studios for almost everything.

What advice would you offer to someone starting out?

There is no one way right now because of all the different technology, but I would say that finding a mentor, like I did with Phil Ramone, can be very important. Find someone you really respect, and apprentice. Try to gain as much knowledge as you can from that person, and also from all of the other people in the industry that you come in contact with.

You have to be respectful of everyone in the industry. Every day is a learning experience, and everybody has something important to offer.

MAUREEN DRONEY

Afterword: An Interview with the Interviewer

Jonathan Feist, Editor

Photo: Ken Kessie

Author Maureen Droney has worked in the music recording industry for over twenty years, during that time engineering for such artists as John Hiatt, Kenny G., George Benson, Aretha Franklin, Tower of Power, and Carlos Santana, including Santana's Grammy-winning *Blues for Salvador*. She lives in Woodland Hills, CA and is the Los Angeles editor for *Mix* magazine, as well as a frequent contributor to numerous other performing arts publications.

As an engineer, studio manager, production coordinator, and writer/editor for *Mix*, she has examined an extraordinary number of the world's best recording studios and talked shop with many of the top names in the business. This gives her a unique perspective on the modern world of audio recording.

After editing this set of interviews, I realized that there was an important omission: an interview with Ms. Droney herself. So, I caught up with her via Internet chat one morning before she headed off to work.

How did the idea for this series of interviews come about?

For a long time, I'd felt that most engineers are, in many ways, under-appreciated. They fill so many roles on a recording, but most people have no idea what the job encompasses. My first interview was with Don Murray, a wonderful engineer who works constantly and is greatly admired by his peers. He had innumerable Grammy nominations, but got very little press. I felt he deserved more attention.

I found that I really enjoyed doing the interviews. I was still an engineer, when I started writing them, so you can imagine — I was learning so much, and having fun too! While I have total respect for the people who do this job, I've also seen the humorous side of it. There's certainly plenty of that! So maybe I tend to be a little more irreverent than some people might be.

Generally, did you seek out your personal recording heroes or were they assigned to you by *Mix*?

The editors at *Mix* suggested a few, but mostly, they trusted my instincts. There are people in the recording business who got very successful just because they were in the right place at the right time; that's all they did. None of the people in my interviews are like that. All of them are people who have paid plenty of dues, and have truly earned their success.

Do you still do engineering work?

No, and when people ask me if I miss engineering, the answer is always "yes and no." Yes, I miss those special moments. The ones that give you chills. Like being behind the board, or even just in the room, while Carlos Santana comes up with some incredible, emotional solo, or when Johnny Mathis starts singing in that inimitable voice, or the Tower of Power rhythm section hits on a great groove. You feel lucky to be there. I don't miss long hours (all nighters!), the job insecurity, recording bad musicians, trying to fix the unfixable, or working with people who don't know what they want.

You seem well informed and well researched—up on all the details about what kind of gear the engineers are known for. Are there good information resources that engineers should know about, in order to find out this kind of information?

Mix magazine, of course!

I also manage a small studio, and help out with a couple of larger ones, so I pretty much keep up. As much as anybody can with everything changing so fast.

Do the people you interview sometimes keep secrets from you? Withholding information that they don't want anyone to know?

My interviews are collaborations. They all know I will not print something they are uncomfortable with. That allows them to talk freely. Although I have occasionally saved them from themselves, in terms of things they should not say in print!

The people who have lasted a long time in this business are usually generous with their knowledge. Like I said, it's an art, and an individual one, and I think the best engineers know that. Two people can play the same piano, and it sounds completely different. Same with engineering. Tips and equipment are great. The more you know about that end of it, the better craftsman you are. But everyone hears things differently, so you use them differently.

What makes a great engineer?

An engineer has to be a psychologist, technically proficient, have musical talent, be artistic....As Dave Pensado said in his interview, the job requires a unique combination of right and left brain.

Also, they have to be very personable. Especially when making a whole album, you're spending twelve or so hours a day, six or sometimes seven days a week, in a small room, with the same people. You have to be easy to get along with. And you have to subtly—or not—be able to move the session along in a timely fashion.

An engineer is a hybrid of an artist and technician. A craftsman. Like a jeweler.

What advice do you have for beginning sound engineers? Or for advanced ones?

For beginning engineers, it's something I heard Jimmy Douglass say once. The most important quality for working in a recording studio, and getting ahead, is "willingness." If you have that kind of helpful, do anything to get the job done, always say yes attitude, you've got a good chance at success. Oh, and keep your mouth shut. Speak when you're spoken to! Nobody cares about your opinion of the part that's being recorded, or your theories on the music business. At least not yet.

For experienced engineers, take care of your health and your ears, and stay humble. If you do you might get to be as lucky as Al Schmitt, with a long and rewarding career, the respect of your peers, a lot of Grammys, and a lot of good friends.

More Fine Publications from Berklee Press

![berklee press logo]

As Serious About Music As You Are.

GUITAR

BERKLEE BASIC GUITAR ▸ by William Leavitt
Phase 1
50449460 Book $7.95
Phase 2
50449470 Book $7.95

CLASSICAL STUDIES FOR PICK-STYLE GUITAR ▸ by William Leavitt
50449440 Book $9.95

COUNTRY GUITAR STYLES ▸ by Mike Ihde
50449480 Book/Cassette $14.95

A MODERN METHOD FOR GUITAR 123 COMPLETE ▸ by William Leavitt
50449468 Book $29.95
Also available in separate volumes:
Volume 1: Beginner
50449404 Book/CD $22.95
50449400 Book $14.95
Volume 2: Intermediate
50449410 Book $14.95
Volume 3: Advanced
50449420 Book $14.95

MELODIC RHYTHMS FOR GUITAR ▸ by William Leavitt
50449450 Book $14.95

READING STUDIES FOR GUITAR ▸ by William Leavitt
50449490 Book $14.95

ADVANCED READING STUDIES FOR GUITAR ▸ by William Leavitt
50449500 Book $14.95

VOICE LEADING FOR GUITAR ▸ by John Thomas
50449498 Book/CD $24.95

THE GUITARIST'S GUIDE TO COMPOSING AND IMPROVISING ▸
by Jon Damian
50449497 Book/CD $24.95

GUITAR WORKSHOP SERIES

JIM KELLY'S GUITAR WORKSHOP
00695230 Book/CD $14.95
00320144 Video/booklet $19.95
00320168 DVD/booklet $29.95

MORE GUITAR WORKSHOP ▸ by Jim Kelly
00695306 Book/CD $14.95
00320158 Video/booklet $19.95

Berklee Press Publications feature material developed at the Berklee College of Music.
To browse the Berklee Press Catalog, go to www.berkleepress.com

BASS

THE BASS PLAYER'S HANDBOOK ▸ by Greg Mooter
50449511 Book $24.95

CHORD STUDIES FOR ELECTRIC BASS ▸ by Rich Appleman
50449750 Book $14.95

READING CONTEMPORARY ELECTRIC BASS ▸ by Rich Appleman
50449770 Book $14.95

ROCK BASS LINES ▸ by Joe Santerre
50449478 Book/CD $19.95

SLAP BASS LINES ▸ by Joe Santerre
50449508 Book/CD $19.95

KEYBOARD

HAMMOND ORGAN COMPLETE ▸ by Dave Limina
50449479 Book/CD $24.95

A MODERN METHOD FOR KEYBOARD ▸ by James Progris
50449620 Vol. 1: Beginner $14.95
50449630 Vol. 2: Intermediate $14.95
50449640 Vol. 3: Advanced $14.95

DRUM SET

BEYOND THE BACKBEAT ▸ by Larry Finn
50449447 Book/CD $19.95

DRUM SET WARM-UPS ▸ by Rod Morgenstein
50449465 Book $12.95

MASTERING THE ART OF BRUSHES ▸ by Jon Hazilla
50449459 Book/CD $19.95

THE READING DRUMMER ▸ by Dave Vose
50449458 Book $9.95

SAXOPHONE

CREATIVE READING STUDIES FOR SAXOPHONE ▸ by Joseph Viola
50449870 Book $14.95

TECHNIQUE OF THE SAXOPHONE ▸ by Joseph Viola
50449820 Volume 1: Scale Studies..$14.95
50449830 Volume 2: Chord Studies $14.95
50449840 Volume 3: Rhythm Studies $14.95

TOOLS FOR DJS

TURNTABLE TECHNIQUE: THE ARTOF THE DJ ▸ by Stephen Webber
50449482 Book/2-Record Set $34.95

TURNTABLE BASICS ▸ by Stephen Webber
50449514 Book $9.95

INSTANT SERIES

BASS ▸ by Danny Morris
50449502 Book/CD $14.95

DRUM SET ▸ by Ron Savage
50449513 Book/CD $14.95

GUITAR ▸ by Tomo Fujita
50449522 Book/CD $14.95

KEYBOARD ▸ by Paul Schmeling and Dave Limina
50449525 Book/CD $14.95

BERKLEE PRACTICE METHOD

Get Your Band Together

BASS ▸ by Rich Appleman and John Repucci
50449427 Book/CD $14.95

DRUM SET ▸ by Ron Savage and Casey Scheuerell
50449429 Book/CD $14.95

GUITAR ▸ by Larry Baione
50449426 Book/CD $14.95

KEYBOARD ▸ by Russell Hoffmann and Paul Schmeling
50449428 Book/CD $14.95

ALTO SAX ▸ by Jim Odgren and Bill Pierce
50449437 Book/CD $14.95

TENOR SAX ▸ by Jim Odgren and Bill Pierce
50449431 Book/CD $14.95

TROMBONE ▸ by Jeff Galindo
50449433 Book/CD $14.95

TRUMPET ▸ by Tiger Okoshi and Charles Lewis
50449432 Book/CD $14.95

IMPROVISATION SERIES

BLUES IMPROVISATION COMPLETE ▸ by Jeff Harrington ▸ Book/CD
50449486 Bb Instruments..$19.95
50449488 C Bass Instruments..$19.95
50449425 C Treble Instruments..$19.95
50449487 Eb Instruments..$19.95

A GUIDE TO JAZZ IMPROVISATION ▸ by John LaPorta ▸ Book/CD
50449439 C Instruments..$16.95
50449441 Bb Instruments..$16.95
50449442 Eb Instruments..$16.95
50449443 Bass Clef $16.95

MUSIC TECHNOLOGY

ARRANGING IN THE DIGITAL WORLD ▸ by Corey Allen
50449415 Book/General MIDI disk $19.95

FINALE: AN EASY GUIDE TO MUSIC NOTATION
▸ by Thomas E. Rudolph and Vincent A. Leonard, Jr.
50449501 Book/CD-ROM $59.95

MIX MASTERS: PLATINUM ENGINEERS REVEAL THEIR SECRETS TO SUCCESS ▸ by Maureen Droney
50448023 Book $24.95

PRODUCING IN THE HOME STUDIO WITH PRO TOOLS ▸ by David Franz
50449526 Book/CD-ROM $34.95

RECORDING IN THE DIGITAL WORLD
▸ by Thomas E. Rudolph and Vincent A. Leonard, Jr.
50449472 Book $29.95

MUSIC BUSINESS

HOW TO GET A JOB IN THE MUSIC & RECORDING INDUSTRY
▸ by Keith Hatschek
50449505 Book $24.95

THE MUSICIAN'S INTERNET ▸ by Peter Spellman
50449527 Book $24.95

THE SELF-PROMOTING MUSICIAN ▸ by Peter Spellman
50449423 Book $24.95

Prices subject to change without notice.
Visit your local music dealer or bookstore, or go to **www.berkleepress.com**

REFERENCE

COMPLETE GUIDE TO FILM SCORING ▸ by Richard Davis
50449417 Book $24.95

THE CONTEMPORARY SINGER ▸ by Anne Peckham
50449438 Book/CD..$24.95

ESSENTIAL EAR TRAINING ▸ by Steve Prosser
50449421 Book $14.95

MODERN JAZZ VOICINGS ▸ by Ted Pease and Ken Pullig
50449485 Book/CD..$24.95

THE NEW MUSIC THERAPIST'S HANDBOOK, SECOND EDITION
▸ by Suzanne B. Hanser
50449424 Book $29.95

POP CULTURE

INSIDE THE HITS ▸ by Wayne Wadhams
50449476 Book $29.95

MASTERS OF MUSIC: CONVERSATIONS WITH BERKLEE GREATS
▸ by Mark Small and Andrew Taylor
50449422 Book $24.95

SONGWRITING

MELODY IN SONGWRITING ▸ by Jack Perricone
50449419 Book $19.95

MUSIC NOTATION ▸ by Mark McGrain
50449399 Book $19.95

THE SONGS OF JOHN LENNON ▸ by John Stevens
50449504 Book $24.95

THE SONGWRITER'S WORKSHOP: MELODY ▸ by Jimmy Kachulis
50449518 Book/CD..$24.95

SONGWRITING: ESSENTIAL GUIDE TO LYRIC FORM AND STRUCTURE
▸ by Pat Pattison
50481582 Book $14.95

SONGWRITING: ESSENTIAL GUIDE TO RHYMING ▸ by Pat Pattison
50481583 Book $14.95

Music Business and Reference Books from Berklee Press

As Serious About Music As You Are.

COMPLETE GUIDE TO FILM SCORING
▸ by Richard Davis
Learn the art and business of writing music for films and TV. Topics include: the film-making process, preparing and recording a score, contracts and fees, publishing, royalties, and copyrights. Features interviews with 19 film-scoring professionals.
50449417 Book...$24.95

THE CONTEMPORARY SINGER ▸ by Anne Peckham
Maximize your vocal potential by learning how to use and protect your voice properly. Develop stage presence, microphone technique, stamina, range, and sound with exercises for all voice ranges and types on the accompanying CD. Includes lead sheets for such standard vocal repertoire pieces as *Yesterday, I'm Beginning to See the Light*, and *I Heard It Through the Grapevine*.
50449438 Book/CD $24.95

ESSENTIAL EAR TRAINING ▸ by Steve Prosser
Step-by-step introduction to the basics of ear training and sight singing, as taught at Berklee College of Music. Develop your inner ear and musical vocabulary, learn to hear the music you see, understand the music you hear, and notate the music you have composed or arranged. Complete course with rhythmic and melodic studies using conducting patterns.
50449421 Book...$14.95

THE NEW MUSIC THERAPIST'S HANDBOOK, SECOND EDITION ▸ by Suzanne B. Hanser
Dr. Hanser's well-respected Music Therapist's Handbook has been thoroughly updated and revised to reflect the latest developments in the field of music therapy. Features an introduction to music therapy, new clinical applications and techniques, case studies, designing, implementing, and evaluating individualized treatment programs, and guidelines for beginning music therapists.
50449424 Book...$29.95

HOW TO GET A JOB IN THE MUSIC AND RECORDING INDUSTRY
▸ by Keith Hatschek
The bible for anyone who has ever dreamed of landing a job in the music business, from producing or engineering the next Top 10 hit to running a record company. Featuring advice and secrets to educate and empower the serious music and recording industry job seeker, including: details on booming job prospects in new media, a resource directory of key publications and top industry trade organizations, interviews with pros revealing how they got their start, and networking tips.
50449505 Book...$24.95

THE SELF-PROMOTING MUSICIAN
▸ by Peter Spellman
Take charge of your career with crucial do-it-yourself strategies. If you are an independent musician, producer, studio owner, or label, you should own this book! Features tips for writing business plans, creating press kits, using the Internet for promotion, customizing demos and getting music played on college radio, along with a comprehensive musician's resource list.
50449423 Book...$24.95

THE MUSICIAN'S INTERNET ▸ by Peter Spellman
Promote your music online! Learn to reach new audiences, expand your online presence, and attract thousands of new fans. A must for any self-managed musician.
50449527 Book $24.95

For more information about Berklee Press or Berklee College of Music, contact us:
1140 Boylston Street ▸ Boston, MA 02215-3693
617-747-2146
www.berkleepress.com

Visit your local music dealer or bookstore, or go to **www.berkleepress.com**

DISTRIBUTED BY

Prices and availability subject to change without notice.